A LIFE IN FOOTBALL

A LIFE IN FOOTBALL

IAN WRIGHT

MY AUTOBIOGRAPHY

with

Lloyd Bradley

Constable • London

CONSTABLE

First published in Great Britain in 2016 by Constable

1 3 5 7 9 10 8 6 4 2

A CIP catalogue record for this book
is available from the British Library.

ISBN: 978-1-47212-358-9 (hardback)
ISBN: 978-1-47212-359-6 (trade paperback)

Typeset in Bembo by Hewer Text UK Ltd, Edinburgh
Printed and bound in Great Britain by Clays Ltd

Papers used by Constable are from well-managed
forests and other responsible sources

FSC
www.fsc.org
MIX
Paper from
responsible sources
FSC® C104740

Constable
An imprint of
Little, Brown Book Group
Carmelite House
50 Victoria Embankment
London EC4Y 0DZ

An Hachette UK Company
www.hachette.co.uk

www.littlebrown.co.uk

For my teacher, Mr Sidney Pigden.

Contents

PART THREE: LIFE GOES ON

PART FOUR: WRIGHT NOW

Introduction: Arsène Who?

The very first time I laid eyes on Arsène Wenger was on 24 September 1996 in the dressing room before the second leg of the UEFA Cup game against Borussia Mönchengladbach, the away leg. We knew he was coming to Arsenal, because by that time it was a done deal, but none of us players had met him. Then, quite late on in the trip to Germany, David Dein told us the new manager would be coming to meet us before the game.

It wasn't an announcement that had too much of an effect on us, because that dressing room was as crazy as it always was – we were shouting, laughing, messing around, doing our things . . . we were having such a good time getting ready to play, it was like a chimps' tea party in there. Then David Dein came in with Arsène Wenger and Patrick Vieira.

It would be good to say their entrance made such an impact on us it was like a scene in a Western where the gunslinger walks in to the saloon and everything stops, with the piano player's hands in mid-air, but it wasn't like that at all. It was totally low key. The three of them just seemed to slip into the room, and it was only as we began to notice them things gradually went quiet. After it had calmed down Mr Dein said something like, 'Hi boys, here's the new manager, Arsène Wenger, and our new

1

player, Patrick Vieira.' David Dein brought Arsène round to introduce him to everybody individually, and he shook us each by the hand and said, 'Good luck, good luck for the game.'

My immediate impression, before he'd even said anything, was 'How can this man be a football manager?' He didn't even look like a football man! I was seeing this very tall, very thin man with this very big, ill-fitting jacket and great big glasses. I didn't know anything about him, other than Glenn Hoddle had been saying lovely things about him and so too had George Weah. When the newspapers got hold of his name and the *Evening Standard* in London ran that 'Arsène Who?' headline across the back page, that was exactly what we were thinking at the time – who is this guy?

The speculation about who would be our next manager began as soon as Bruce Rioch was sacked, a few weeks earlier, but we, the players, don't get told what's being done while it's being done. We knew no more than the fans, which was nothing beyond the rumours that got into the papers. As an example of how much we knew about the appointment, David Dein said to me almost casually, right after the sacking, 'Don't worry, Ian, we've got the perfect man!' Of course, I was like a little kid: 'Who is it, David? Go on, go on, tell me who it is.' But he wouldn't say anything more than it was *exactly* the right man.

So when this guy showed up, I didn't really know what to think. At that time, though, we were focusing on getting ready to play, so didn't give it much more thought – he was to be our fourth manager in two years, and as a player you just get on with it and see how it works out.

Before that game, the three of them stayed in the dressing room for a while, just standing there off to the side, as we carried on from where we'd left off before they arrived and the noise level started to rise again. As it got nearer to the match, Arsène and David Dein left to take their seats in the directors' box, but Patrick stayed behind, all the time just sitting in the corner smiling.

Because he was a player, I thought about him more than I thought about the new manager, and I really wasn't any more convinced. Obviously he's gone on to become this great, unbelievable man, so big in stature, but that evening I was looking at this really tall, skinny kid, with this big round face and thinking, 'What position's he going to play? *Midfield?!* No midfielder ever looked like that.' Although behind that smile he was probably looking at us carrying on like we were, and thinking, 'What on earth have I got myself in to?'

That's how quietly it was done. That's how Arsène Wenger was introduced to Arsenal. Which is really fantastic, given this was the single most significant moment in the club's modern history, and one of the most important things to happen to English football as a whole. No fuss, no fanfare, just, 'Hi boys, here's the new manager.'

Then we soon got to find out that this sort of calm, quiet way of doing things was a real Arsène Wenger trademark, which came to signify a real alternative to everything that had gone on before. It changed the club, it changed football in this country and it changed the way I looked at things from then on.

Part One

Highbury High

Chapter One

The Man in the Overcoat

Arsène Wenger's arrival transformed Arsenal in a way that hadn't been seen since Herbert Chapman in the 1930s, but the massive irony was it might never have happened had it not been for the most shameful episode in the club's history – the Bungs Scandal, and George Graham's sacking because of it.

Looking back, the scandal was the first and most important step towards what Arsenal would become as the club moved in to the twenty-first century. What's most remarkable, though, is this wasn't something that was at all obvious when Bruce Rioch took over, and could not have been further from my mind on 21 February 1995, when it was announced to us players that George was no longer our manager.

When it happened, it happened instantly. *Bang!* And he was gone. There was this footage on the news and pictures in the newspapers of him leaving the training ground in his BMW: he was just gone. One day he was taking training, same as normal, next day he wasn't part of Arsenal Football Club any more and it literally felt like a death to me. I found out from watching those same news reports and it hit me like a hammer, '*My God! They actually sacked him!*' It was as if somebody had said to me, 'Ian, such and such is dead.'

In the time leading up to the sacking, we players didn't know any more about it than the fans did. There was no way we were going to find out anything more. Nobody from the board or David Dein or George himself was going to talk to us about it. Quite apart from not wanting to say anything until it had been sorted out one way or another, they didn't want to destabilize us or disturb the routine. Of course, we talked about it among ourselves but, really, we were scratching around for information just like everybody else.

At first we assumed it would all blow over because, back then in the game, there were brown envelopes all over the place . . . wads of cash . . . bungs . . . whatever you want to call them. Everybody knew what was happening. Tax-free payments, under-the-counter bonuses for players, finder's fees for transfers, money to just keep you sweet . . . all sorts of things.

I remember my first brown envelope was in my early days at Palace: we'd just won a game, and when I came back to the dressing room there was an envelope with my clothes with five hundred quid in it, which in the mid-1980s was a lot of money. Nobody told me what it was for, and I never asked, I just took it. It's not like I'm talking out of class because literally *everybody* has been involved at some stage – that's how it could get to a situation with FIFA, in 2015, in which £1.3 million allegedly got stuffed into Michel Platini's brown envelope.

Also, when the George Graham thing was just a rumour, we didn't take too much notice because inside the game there were always these sorts of rumours and some of the biggest names had been mentioned: Harry Redknapp; Sam Allardyce; Alex Ferguson . . . But none of that talk ever came to anything so we didn't take the stuff about George Graham too seriously.

Or at least we didn't in the beginning. Then the evidence seemed to be mounting up. The whole thing started to take on a momentum of its own, and as the figures involved began to come out – over £400,000 – the talk and the mood in the dressing room started to turn. Understandably so, because the Arsenal wage structure, ruled over by George Graham, was notorious as the lowest paying in the division for a team of that calibre.

Since he'd arrived in 1986, that group of players had won the title twice, the League Cup twice, the FA Cup and the Cup Winners' Cup. Arsenal were flying – they'd beaten everybody between 1988 and 1991 – so many of the players were internationals, yet players at other clubs were earning two or three times what we were.

Of course, we knew what other players were on, because when you go away to England camps there's so much time spent sitting around and many players couldn't wait to tell you what they were earning. 'I'm on this . . . I'm on that . . . I got a signing-on fee of this . . . the club bought my car . . . the club paid the deposit on my house . . .' Everybody knew about the Arsenal wage structure, so when you've got players like we had at Arsenal who have been winning cups, winning the league, regularly being the tightest defence in the Premiership, taking the kind of teasing they sometimes had to, of course they're going to start grumbling about it.

It was becoming a weird situation within the squad because the paper talk was steadily escalating, but George was still taking training and we still had to go out and win matches, as if everything was normal. Then it really blew up when it looked like the FA had got him bang to rights. That's when players like

Steve Bould, Lee Dixon and Nigel Winterburn – the players that had done brilliantly for him and who he had pushed really hard every day on the training ground – started to lose it. Then it was: 'Fuck him, the thieving bastard! We're here slogging our guts out for him, can't get a decent pay rise after winning the second title, and he's helped himself to *how much*?'

Of course, I joined in with that talk. And of course I knew he was scrimping and scraping with our wages – he had been for years – but that in itself wasn't the problem. While the lower pay might not have been right, at least it was something we all could have done something about – any one of that back five could have gone anywhere, like Liverpool or Manchester United, and earned proper money, but they *chose* to stay at Arsenal. Every time a new contract came up, they signed on the dotted line; the only one who ran down his contract and left was Mickey Thomas, and when he went to Liverpool he must have been on three or four times more than he had been at Arsenal.

When Arsenal came in for me, Ron Noades, the Crystal Palace chairman, offered to double my money if I stayed another season, and all George Graham was offering was £700 a week more than I was on at Palace. When I took Arsenal's offer I remember driving home crapping myself about what my wife would say because of the amount of cash I'd turned down to make the move. But it was my choice: I wanted to be at Arsenal.

We all made that choice, and for most of us it wasn't about money but about being at *the Arsenal* because we all bought into what the club was about. When I went to Highbury to sign my first contract, before I put pen to paper my agent took me out to the front of the directors' box and let me appreciate what I could become part of. I signed before the details had been filled in: I signed a blank contract and learned how much I'd be earning afterwards.

They are a solid, reliable club too, and, if you don't let them down, they won't chop and change players every couple of years, like a lot of the so-called ambitious clubs. This makes a difference when you want to settle your family in an area. Then there was the team spirit at Arsenal, which was partly down to George Graham – I loved my teammates, we all loved each other. That was half the battle in keeping us. There was such a feeling of togetherness in that dressing room that you didn't even want to be away from them for the close season, let alone leave and go to another club!

George always seemed very aware of what the club meant to us, which he wasn't above using to his advantage. After my first season, Parma came in for me and my agent, Jerome Anderson, went in to see George with me. They were talking in general terms, very agreeably, until Jerome mentioned Parma, and George said, quite quietly, 'Ian, could you excuse us, please? The conversation's over with you.'

I left, but was still outside the office door when and I heard him tear into Jerome. It was brutal! George steamed into him: 'He's playing for *the Arsenal*, and you're coming in here telling me about fucking Parma!' He ranted about all sorts of stuff. Then he finished up with, 'Fucking get out!'

On the other side of the door I just thought, 'Wow!' Parma were doing quite well at the time, but this is what Arsenal thinks of them and this is how much they want to keep me. It did make me feel like I was wanted.

In spite of all of this, the dissent had a point: we were the ones out there doing it, we were the ones getting kicked every week, being worked so hard in training. So to find out that the boss is involved in a £425,000 bung scandal was always going to be too much to take. OK, so he didn't spend it and tried to hand it back . . . but, *really*? It just wasn't right.

Other clubs in that situation may have tried to cover it up but there was never any question of Arsenal sweeping it under the carpet, or even trying to, and not simply because this was an FA investigation so it was out of their hands. It didn't matter that George Graham had been consistently winning things for Arsenal, and at that point was their most successful manager of modern times: the Arsenal are the Arsenal. They do things properly there, and this was a stain they had to do something about as quickly as possible. They took their decision and sacked him before the FA announced they were banning him for twelve months.

When he went it was business as usual for us players on a day-to-day level. Stewart Houston, who had been George's assistant, took training that day and I think he might have made a little speech about George no longer being with the club, and he'd be in charge until further notice. The idea was to make as few waves as possible within the squad, because while we weren't doing brilliantly in the league, we had a good run going in the Cup Winners' Cup.

In the dressing room there was some teasing of John Jensen – his transfer was one of those caught up in the scandal so people were telling him he got the gaffer sacked. And, naturally, there was a fair amount of 'Glad he's gone'. But while there wasn't a great deal of sympathy for George, there was quite a bit of sadness as a lot of players realized he was the one who brought them to the fore, made them part of a very successful team, and turned them into internationals, into great players.

In the end, he had to go. I can't argue with that, but really, it was horrible. Not only for the club but for me personally, to the point at which I feel uncomfortable admitting it. I love George Graham; he was the most important manager of my playing days. Steve Coppell gave me the original chance at Crystal Palace, taking me on at a time when I was ready to give up trying to be a professional footballer. Arsène Wenger took me to another level as far as my understanding of what it means to be that professional footballer, and Glenn Hoddle gave me the opportunity to represent England. If I did go into football management I would take bits from each of them. But the man who had most impact on my football career was George Graham. He was the best because of how he motivated me at a time when I needed motivating in exactly that way.

George and I had a unique relationship because in many respects we were polar opposites, and at times it could be like metal grinding against metal. If he said anything to me I'd just blast off at him – 'You sweaty this . . . you effing that . . .' – so we would have some blazing arguments in front of all the guys. Then he'd call me into his office the next day and tell me, 'Ian, you can't say stuff like that to me in front of the players.' To which I'd reply that I was really sorry and that I would apologize in front of all of the guys – which I always did. Then he'd tell me, 'But I love your passion, because it shows all of this means something to you.' He'd knock me down but he'd always bring me back up.

He always needed to show his players who was in charge. I lost count of the amount of times Kevin Campbell, when he was on the bench, would tell me after a match, 'He slaughtered you through the *whole game*. He was just about to take you off, shouting "Get his number! Get his number!" when you scored and he sat down and start cussing, "Fuck! Fuck's sake!" ' It was like he'd be looking to take me off just to get into my head or to teach me some sort of lesson, or because we'd had a row earlier and he didn't want to back down from a situation.

It was all so petty, but until Arsène Wenger came along I thought that was what football management was.

A great deal of what we'd row about would be in training as a result of George's approach to the game – that defence was everything, that if the other team couldn't score then you weren't going to lose the game. When I arrived at Arsenal, Alan Smith and Paul Merson were the two hardest-working forwards I'd ever seen, because the George Graham Philosophy was all about defending from the front. As soon as an attack broke down, he wanted his two forwards to retreat so our opponents had three banks of people to get through before they could get at David Seaman or John Lukic. Merse and Alan Smith would literally close down the whole of the opposition's back four, so our midfield and back four were able to push up and press.

George Graham got this from Liverpool. He would talk about how Ian Rush would close down defenders and try to win the ball back, and often it would never get through to the actual defence because the defence up the field was so strong. With us, when our forwards were winning the ball, and you've got players like Anders Limpar, David Rocastle and Paul Merson on the counter-attack so far up the pitch, the results could be devastating. But the first consideration was always keeping the defending as strong and as solid as it could be, so that was what

George's training sessions were about, and we'd work on defending day in and day out. Literally.

One of his favourite exercises was to put a whole team – eleven of us – against Dave Seaman, Lee Dixon, Nigel Winterburn, Tony Adams and Steve Bould, sometimes with Martin Keown in front of them. We'd have to break them down, but most of the time we couldn't do it – that's how well-drilled that defence became. Sometimes we'd do sessions that were all about keeping the ball, but again that was more about not conceding goals rather than starting off attacks.

I came to appreciate the Art of Defending, if you like, and how important it was to defend from the front to try and win the ball back high up the pitch, but it got to the point where the sessions would be so boring. Some mornings I'd be out there doing these exercises, and thinking to myself, 'What the fuck am I doing here? I've come to Arsenal to learn and go to the next level as a striker, but all I'm doing is defending. I'm supposed to be a front man!'

I wanted to work on my finishing because I knew I'd have to sharpen those skills and keep them that way now I'd made the move to Arsenal, and that is when we'd argue. Sometimes, when a game was all about defending, I'd tell him I wanted to do some finishing, and he'd stop it and just bawl at me, 'Oh for fuck's sake! Just shut up and get on with it!' Or after training, the session would end and I'd say, 'What? Is that it? I wanted to do some finishing.' He'd reply, 'Well, fuck off and do some!' So I would. I'd practise technique and shooting by myself, often all afternoon. Every now and then he'd train me on finishing or would take a few of us to do some crossing, shooting and finishing, but it was mainly on my own.

★   ★   ★

As successful as he had been, and messy as it was for Arsenal when George Graham was caught holding the smoking gun, in many ways I think it was a blessing for Arsenal in terms of their progress as a club. There were too many questions being asked about what sort of progress the team was making. There was a growing dissention as more and more of his decisions were being questioned, and there was real concern about the way Tony Adams was at the time due to his drink problems.

Most of all, though, George was starting to sign players that many people believed weren't the kind of players to take Arsenal forward to a Premier League title. I don't mean to be disrespectful, but the fans all know who I'm talking about: Chris Kiwomya, Glenn Helder, my dear friend Eddie McGoldrick, Pål Lydersen. Not just the fans, either. Inside Highbury a lot of the guys were thinking, 'How are we going to kick on with those kind of players coming in?'

I have no idea why he started making those signings. It may have been the case that we had success with players who weren't the most glamorous – Ian Selley and Stevie Morrow won the Cup Winners' Cup when it was worth winning and David Hillier's got a League Champion's medal – but they all came through the Arsenal youth system, whereas these were transfer signings. By that last season, in 1994–95, it had gone beyond the point of eyebrows being raised: people were saying he'd lost the plot.

The real sign that it had been time for George to leave Arsenal came six months after he left, and is only obvious in hindsight: George Graham never would have signed Dennis Bergkamp. Before any of us had ever heard of Arsène Wenger, before we were anything other than *boring, boring Arsenal*, there was Dennis

Bergkamp. Single-handedly, he changed the whole ethos of Arsenal Football Club to start us on the path to become the Invincibles ten years later. Yet if George Graham had stayed, Dennis Bergkamp wouldn't have come.

The reason is that, firstly, he didn't like flair players at all. I think he didn't properly understand them because he would expect to see them do their stuff every single time they went out on the pitch, like they could turn it on at will. He would give them hell, all the time – he'd give Anders Limpar shit all the time, he'd give Merse so much shit, Rocky Rocastle too. He'd slaughter them after games, at half-time, during train- ing . . . swearing at them, shouting at them. They used to hate him; they'd talk about him all the time. It was the same when he was at Millwall with Teddy Sheringham. Teddy remembers George was always getting on at him for not scoring enough goals, telling him he only wanted to score great goals. Sometimes I think he just resented flair players because they didn't do what they were told all the time. He seemed to want to crush their spirits.

Also, there was no way on earth he would have paid a club record £7 million for any footballer, let alone one who was coming off a career in Italy where everybody said he couldn't hack it. Four years previously, he had been willing to let the deal for me fall through for the sake of £250,000. The price tag was £2.5 million and Palace were sticking at that, but George wouldn't go higher than £2.25 million and he was willing to say, 'No, I don't want him', and walk away. In the end, David Dein had to pay the outstanding quarter of a million on the side, without George Graham knowing about it, otherwise the transfer wasn't going to go through. So for him to buy Dennis

Bergkamp at that price? It was never going to happen. And that's without even mentioning the wages he would have been on at Inter Milan.

So if George hadn't gone, the greatest, most significant signing Arsenal ever made would have been a non-starter. As people often say, everything happens for a reason.

On a personal level, I hated the way George Graham exited Arsenal. Hated it. Quite apart from what he did for me and my career, I genuinely think he was one of our greatest managers. It was George Graham who took Arsenal from the wilderness – we hadn't won the league for fifteen years when he arrived. He broke the stranglehold the great Liverpool side had on the title during the 1970s and 1980s, and he deserves something for that alone. He changed the way the team played and became one of our most successful managers ever, then left that back five as a legacy for the managers that came after him, Bruce Rioch and Arsène Wenger.

It shouldn't be forgotten what a huge amount of stick he took for taking that defensive line. It used to frustrate me, but what he did wouldn't have worked any other way – no team has ever won the title with a bad defence. That's something that's not appreciated too much these days, because the selling of football on television these days means it has to be exciting and free-flowing, yet that alone isn't going to win you trophies.

Take Brendan Rodgers at Liverpool recently, one of the so-called new generation of coaches, building a team playing dynamic, attacking football. In the 2013–14 season he had that team with Stirling, Sturridge and Suárez, with Steven Gerrard and Philippe Coutinho buzzing about behind them . . . I challenge you *not* to win the league with that team! Yet he didn't, because he never really replaced Jamie Carragher and he got rid of Pepe Reina and Daniel Agger, good solid players on the pitch and in the dressing room. And unlike the great Liverpool side or a George Graham side, the forwards and the midfield weren't organized to stop people getting through and they conceded too many goals. If you'd given George that side, he would have won the title with points to spare.

One of the strangest things that happened as the scandal was starting to break was he called me into his office to talk about what I was doing outside the club. It was a time when things were really happening for me commercially – I was doing adverts, I was sponsored by Nike, I was doing brilliant – and he told me, 'I don't like it, Ian, you're doing too much. I'm seeing you everywhere, you're not focusing on your football.'

I started to argue: 'Gaffer, I'm still playing, I'm still doing my job, I'm still scoring goals . . .'

But he cut me off with, 'I don't like it, Ian, I don't like it. It's not doing you any good.'

I was supplementing what Arsenal were paying me with the adverts and he didn't like that – I guess it loosened his hold on me as I was earning a lot of money elsewhere, so he tried to tell me it was going to affect my job. It was irrelevant to him that I knew I couldn't have the commercial success without continuing to perform for Arsenal. He was telling me that I shouldn't really be worried about that sort of instant gratification, that I should be concentrating on my career. This was two or three weeks before he got caught for taking a £400,000 bung!

About a month after he got sacked I went to meet him for dinner, and we were sitting down eating when he said to me,

'Ian, it's the game, it's a short time. You're only in it for a short time and you've got to do as much as you can, get as much as you can out of it.'

What?! I was eating, and I nearly spat out my food!

I steamed in to him. 'You what? No more than a few weeks ago you were telling me I was doing too much . . .'

He said, very smoothly, 'I know, I know, it's all a game, the management game.'

To me, although what he was saying didn't make sense as it was totally contradictory, it summed up how George was. But if you knew him you couldn't hold it against him.

What I do find strange is that he went to Tottenham. It was hard enough for the Arsenal fans to accept he had to leave in those circumstances, but then to manage Tottenham after that . . . That's when fans lost pretty much all respect for him. It's an irony that he might have been able to recover from the bungs scandal, but one of our greats going to Spurs is a different matter entirely!

From his own point of view he couldn't win either way. Over there, they were never going to appreciate him: he won them their first trophy in years *and* he brought Ledley King through, but those fans were never going to give him credit. And the Arsenal fans are never going to forgive him. If I could go back in time, I'd go and see him and say, 'George, man, don't do it, don't take the Spurs job. You're at Leeds, just wait until another one comes along. Take any other job.'

You don't really see many players going from Arsenal to Tottenham – it's always the other way around. I wish George had remembered that.

★   ★   ★

I'm very much in touch with George these days. We're with the same management company so I would see him every Christmas and at certain golf dos, anyway, but I see him more than that. We play golf together or go out to dinner, and now he's an older man we deal with each other as friends. We talk about golf, we talk about the old days and when we used to have those blazing arguments, we talk about the kids, we talk about my missus . . . All the kind of stuff I would never be able to talk to him about if he was my manager. These days George Graham is like an old uncle and I can tell him anything – *anything* at all.

In many ways this is still very strange and quite hard for me, because the George Graham I remember so vividly from my playing days was somebody who was like a headmaster when you were a kid – you wouldn't even look him in the eye or talk to him unless he spoke to you. Which was exactly what I needed then, that kind of authoritative figure around me, but now it's a different relationship from both sides and he always listens.

Not so long ago I was telling him that I had some massive problems with income tax owing, and he told me to make sure I saw this guy and that guy. He kept phoning me up afterwards making sure I talked to the right people and told them the right things, really trying to look after me. He'll send a message if he sees something I've said on the television that he particularly likes, or read something in one of my columns. Which is great, because when you're involved in the media like that, there are always people criticizing, and he'd advise me that as long as you're saying stuff because it's what you believe and not just trying to score points, then nothing else matters.

I really do love George Graham, and it hurts me deeply that he's been tainted the way that he has, because he's a man of dignity, elegance and class. The funny thing was that, at the time, quite a few of us thought the whole scandal almost made him human when to us so often he seemed like a machine. 'Dress right . . . say the right things . . . do the right things . . . be the right things . . . be professional . . . remember who you represent . . . We're the Arsenal . . .' These things were drummed in to us all the time. Then being caught with not just his hand but his whole arm in the till showed us there was a chink in his armour after all.

For him to have that stain on him . . . it hurts me. It hurts me as well that when people talk about the greats at Arsenal, he's not among the names. It's a hefty price to pay for somebody who took Arsenal from going nowhere to a winning side – like Merse has said, 'Winning side, winning mentality, winning medals.'

George should have a statue outside the Emirates, or it should at least be discussed. Instead, his name has just slipped out of the Arsenal pantheon, when he should be being remembered as one of the Arsenal greats.

Chapter Two

The Year of Living Dangerously

I'm sure he was a good manager at Bolton, but the real problem Bruce Rioch had as our manager was that he never made the step up from there to a club like Arsenal. It's true that during his season at Arsenal, in 1995–96, our league position improved from finishing twelfth to finishing fifth, but that was really little more than where we should have been given the team we had and what they'd already won. Also, that year we had Dennis Bergkamp and David Platt in the team, and we didn't have the distraction of George Graham's sacking.

The bottom line was Bruce Rioch never grasped that he was at the Arsenal, where they do things differently and he'd have to raise his game accordingly.

It's exactly the same for managers as it is for players; we have to think, 'I'm at a big club now, everything's got to change. I've got to raise my work rate; I've got to raise my technique; *everything*'s got to step up – my mentality, my professionalism, my fitness . . .' At Arsenal he was dealing with players who had won everything, who were established internationals, at a club that had its own traditions and ways of doing things, so he had to adapt his thinking to work within all of that. But he didn't; he didn't change that Bolton mentality.

It was obvious as soon as we started training with him. We

used to joke about putting our tin hats on while we were getting changed, because we were in the Army now – with the running and the drills it was like being in the Marines. He came from an Army background, his dad was a regimental Sergeant Major in the Scots Guards, so I guess it was all part of his make-up. Pre-season with him was little more than three or four days of hard, unadulterated running. Whole days spent running round the London Colney training ground, until people vomited, with him shouting, 'Come on, we're fit, everybody's fit! We're Army, we're Navy SEALs!'

This carried on in regular training, too. He'd have us running six or seven times around the perimeter. Then, when we thought we'd finished and we could get on with some football, he'd shout, 'Right, you're going round again, but this time nobody comes in in front of the slowest runner!' That doesn't sound like much, but the weakest runners would be thirty or forty yards behind the rest of us, really flailing because they just couldn't do it, then having to run that slow to stay back with them – after you're already done half-a-dozen circuits – was a killer.

That is a very Army boot camp type of exercise, and Rioch used to concentrate on stuff like that because he used to say it built team spirit, but he was wasting his time trying to ingrain team spirit into a group like that. If he'd known anything about us, or actually looked properly at what was in front of him, he would have known we already had team spirit. George Graham had built that, and everybody fought for everybody else on the pitch – Tony Adams wouldn't have had it any other way. Bruce Rioch should've been working on more important things because we didn't need that sort of constant motivation.

★   ★   ★

Bruce Rioch loved confrontation, but whereas George would shout and swear at us and never shy away from an argument, there was usually a humanity in the way he dealt with us. He was more than capable of showing compassion when he had to. With Bruce Rioch, however, I can't ever imagine him putting his arm around a player, it seemed like he was always trying to put us in our places by digging players out in front of the whole team.

He did it to me in the first game of the pre-season, against Boreham Wood or St Albans, tore in to me in front of everybody. I thought then, 'That's not right . . . that's not Arsenal.' We didn't get on from that point, and it didn't get any better when he stopped a training session once to tell me, in front of everybody, what I could learn from watching the runs made by John McGinley, his striker when he was at Bolton! He'd do that to others too, use Bolton players as examples of what they should be doing.

In the beginning I used to think maybe he wanted me out and to bring one of his own people in, then when he started doing it to others as well, I realized it was his way of trying to bring Arsenal down to his level rather than him making the step up.

Sometimes I used to think he was a little bit unstable. For real. There was always such an edginess to him – he had this look in his eye like he was ready to explode at any time. He had to leave Torquay United back in the 1980s because he broke some kid's jaw at the training ground – he got into it with a seventeen-year-old, Colin Anderson, lost it and kicked him in the face. We knew about that, so we're thinking, 'He can't be a reasonable man, because that's not right.' We were amazed at how it could have happened, then after a few training sessions we could see how.

Rioch used to join in the training matches and would be kicking people up in the air – players, first-teamers who had to play on Saturday, would come off the training pitch with their manager's stud marks on their ankles. I can remember us looking at each other, gobsmacked, thinking, 'Hang on a minute – *he's tackling!*' It was astonishing. I remember, particularly, he used to kick Chris Kiwomya and John Hartson all over the place. He really used to go for it!

I'd never seen that before. George Graham didn't join in games: he'd watch to see what we were doing and tell us what we should be doing. At Palace, Steve Coppell would join in, but he was always at the edge of the game, not coming up behind people, cleaning them out or leaving his foot in after a tackle. Bruce Rioch was always right in the game, which was just part of how he was.

I'm assuming that he felt, at that time of his life, that he was still fit enough to play with our first team squad. I can understand that. After you've played professional football, you can't get that out of you – you might slow down but the technique and the ability never go away, so of course you want to play.

I have a mate called Tony, who taught me to play golf, and he has a Sunday team that I go and watch. If they're a man short and somebody's got boots size seven and a half they can lend me, then I'm on! I wouldn't leave my house with my kit in the car, or anything like that, but if the chance comes up . . .

I still play five-a-side with my Albanian mates. The people on both teams love it, everybody get's a lift and for me it's brilliant to talk to your team while you're playing: 'If you drop back five yards there, then that will happen . . . if you do this, you'll force them to do that . . .' Then watch them do it and see how they love it when it comes off. There's a great YouTube clip of Robert Pirès joining in a local game when he was on holiday in Greece: he scores one, then gets an assist for the winner. He's a World Cup winner, so imagine what a buzz that was for everybody. Former footballers always want to play.

I'll play given pretty much any opportunity, but I wouldn't leave my studs in or clean players out – there's no point, you should be encouraging them. Bizarrely, though, Rioch seemed to expect it from us as well. Once, I had endured enough of it during a game and absolutely took him out with a tackle, smashed him. Nobody knew what would happen next, and the game stopped like it was frozen, but he just got up and said, 'Great tackle!' and restarted the game.

I believe that some of the way he acted on the training ground came out of frustration from how he fitted in at a club the size of Arsenal, especially only six months after the George Graham scandal. At Bolton he was in charge of everything, he ran the whole club from the top to the bottom, then at Arsenal he was a cog in a machine that involved many other people, particularly when it came to transfers.

Previously, he would have conducted all his own transfer business, but after George's sacking, the Arsenal board – David Dein specifically – would have handled all of that. That's really quite easy to understand, but what it meant for Bruce Rioch was if he fancied players, his proposals would have had to be examined and vetted by the board in all sorts of detail, then any actual dealings done through them. In reality it was not much different to what became the Director of Football situation so many clubs have adopted. Back then, though, things would have taken so long I can see why it frustrated somebody who was used to being in complete control. Indeed, there was friction between Rioch and David Dein from early on – maybe he resented Mr Dein's relationship with the players.

David Dein loves Arsenal. He has from way, way back. You could take the most diehard Arsenal fans out of the crowd on match day, and you would be hard pressed to find any of them that love the club more than David Dein. He was always very close to the players, he knew us all and was always concerned with how we were, how things were going for us, away from the club and within it. He was like a father figure to us, and everybody loved him. He had a particular match-day ritual, in which he would come to the dressing room before every game to shake hands with every one of us, make a bit of small talk and wish us good luck. He'd say something to me like, 'How you feeling? You got a goal for me today?'

We all loved it, but Bruce Rioch seemed to take an instant dislike to the fact that Mr Dein came in to what he thought was *his* dressing room and started talking to *his* players. I watched him some of those times and I could see the frustration boiling up inside him. Maybe he felt undermined, because at Bolton nobody would have dared to do it, but here it didn't mean anything other than it made the players feel happy and wanted. He should have been thankful for that.

It would have been David Dein who was chiefly responsible for bringing Bruce Rioch to Arsenal and, from what I believe his thinking to have been, it made sense. The club was recovering from the bungs scandal and Bruce Rioch offered a stability after George Graham and Stewart Houston, both discipline-focused Scots. Also, to his credit, Rioch did get us passing the ball about more than George did, and he had us building attacks from further back.

A large amount of that, however, was due to us having Dennis Bergkamp in the side, and while it was widely assumed that Rioch signed Dennis, that was never the case. David Dein signed Dennis, and Plattie too, and he should take credit for that. How is Bruce Rioch, from Bolton Wanderers, going to be in a position to sign Dennis Bergkamp before he's even started the league season at Arsenal? Sure, he's going to know who Dennis is, but he's not going to know the European market and then spend seven million of Arsenal's money on him. He's not going to be able to make contact with Dennis's people to find out if he's even interested in coming to Arsenal. Then he's not going to be able to talk to them in the way they need to be talked to, and tell them what they need to hear. David Dein is the one, he signed Dennis. *Bang*! He did it! He signed Plattie. *Bang*! He did it! Then he gave those players to Bruce Rioch.

David Dein is a visionary. He had a vision for what he wanted Arsenal to be and how they needed to get to that level – this was long before Arsène Wenger was in the frame. He knew we needed continuity, but he wanted to move on from the George Graham style of playing. Although we had been consistently winning things, the chants of 'Boring, boring Arsenal' got to him like they did to every other fan. It was as if the achievements weren't being recognized and he wanted an Arsenal side with success *and* flair.

On paper Bruce Rioch seemed like the ideal fit, and Mr Dein thought that by giving him the team we had plus Dennis Bergkamp and David Platt, he would be able to deliver that. I think he thought that players of that calibre would bring Bruce Rioch to the next level, but Rioch still had his Bolton mentality.

It meant there was a lot of dissent in the dressing room, mostly because of how Rioch treated the players. He loved Tony Adams, Lee Dixon, Nigel Winterburn . . . he never seemed to have a problem with any of those guys – why come in and mess about with a back five like that? He loved Dennis, too, but who wouldn't? Coming from Bolton Wanderers and being given Dennis Bergkamp, the greatest player he's ever going to work with, must have been like being handed the keys to a Ferrari and told it's your company car. On the other hand, if he made up his mind he didn't like you – it was bullying, plain and simple.

By the middle of the season, I couldn't see it getting any better for me. Since I started playing football and turned pro with Palace, this was the closest I ever came to not enjoying it. I know what a privilege it is to be able to play football as a professional, but this situation, at the club that I loved, was pushing me to the limit. Of course I was still giving everything on the pitch and still scoring goals, but this was the worst period of my footballing life.

I assumed Rioch was there for the long term, because this was Arsenal and they don't do stuff like get managers in and then sack them straight away. Also, that wasn't the norm in football in those days, so I was left thinking that I was going to have to leave this club in order to leave this guy. I was going to have to ask for a transfer.

It was the end of February or the beginning of March 1996, and I brought my transfer request in to him in his office.

He took it and said, 'What's this?'

I said, 'What do you mean "What's this"? It's in a brown envelope and I'm not smiling.'

He looked at it and said, 'Are you taking the fucking piss?'

I told him it was because he'd made my life a misery practically from the moment he arrived. He never even replied. He just put the letter on his desk. So I said, 'And I've sent one to David Dein.'

Then he looked at me.

'Why did you do that?' he said. 'Why did you send one to him?'

'Because Mr Dein's the Vice-Chairman of this club,' I told him. 'He's the one who signed me, and I want him to know how I feel.' I told Rioch that I was doing something that was totally going against what I really believed, because it felt like I was giving up.

He told me, 'Well, you are giving up, aren't you?'

I said, 'Giving up on what? The fact that everything was going right for me until you came and made my life a misery? Why didn't you just speak to me at the start of the season? If you had a problem with me, why didn't you sit me down and we'd sort it out, then let me get on with playing football. Now I've got to go. I've had to put a transfer request in to leave the club I love.'

When I left his office, it was then that what I had done really hit me. I was devastated because, really, I was bluffing. Now I'm thinking perhaps that's what Bruce Rioch wanted, he wanted me to leave, and I'm thinking back to something Merse had said to me: 'If it comes to a straight-up fight between Ian Wright and Bruce Rioch, there can only be one winner.' And I knew he was right, because I was still thinking this is Arsenal and Arsenal doesn't sack their managers.

As it ended up, the board turned down my request. It was all kept in-house, but it got leaked to the press, maybe by my agent at the time just to test the water, which is why it became a big deal. The board didn't even consider it, and I realize how fortunate I was – if they'd said I could leave, it would have been something I would have regretted for the rest of my life. Chelsea would have signed me. I had spoken to Glenn Hoddle, who was their manager at the time: he wanted me to come and it could have gone through very smoothly.

I just can't imagine how I would have felt if Arsène Wenger had got to Highbury and said, 'Where's Ian Wright?'

'Oh, you just missed him, he left a few months ago.'

More immediately, though, every time I left my house and I bumped into Arsenal fans, I realized what a mistake I would have been making if Arsenal had let me leave. That was the hardest part of making that transfer request: meeting the fans. I remember around the end of March, I scored a goal against Newcastle. Nigel had made an interception, took it on, pushed it across to me and I just dinked it over the goalkeeper. I remember running to the fans in the North Bank, putting my arms out and shouting, 'I love this fucking club.' Then, I think, Dennis came across and the moment was over, the spell was broken, but I remember feeling really strange inside, thinking, 'I might have to leave here, leave all of this. My God, what have I done?'

After that, given the love the board had shown me, I just got on with giving my best to Arsenal, *the club*. Bruce Rioch couldn't upset the enjoyment I had of playing and training with those top players; even if he didn't pick me I'd sit in the stands, fine, I'd just watch the game and go home. It was all about the football for me, and nobody could stop me from enjoying being part of Arsenal.

★   ★   ★

I believe it was during the Bruce Rioch season that David Dein fully came to terms with how far Arsenal could actually go. Maybe, as he saw how Dennis Bergkamp was starting to change the club, he realized the extent of his vision: it was much greater than simply building on what George Graham had started. As soon as Dennis came and we started to do our stuff on the pitch, then there were rumblings in the dressing room. It must've hit David Dein like a frying pan in the face in a cartoon: 'This isn't the manager for us. This is isn't the manager to take this team or this club forward'.

People often don't realize that while clubs sometimes sign players that shouldn't be there, it happens with managers as well. At what point Mr Dein realized he'd made this mistake I don't know, but in order to have Arsène Wenger come in during the next season, Mr Dein would have started the process months before. He would have done his homework on him to the most minuscule point. He would have known about the nutrition; he would have known about the training methods. I know the two had known each other socially for a while, but Mr Dein would have started researching him thoroughly before he even made the first approach. Then everything would have had to have been in place before he even started thinking about getting rid of Bruce Rioch.

Bruce Rioch was sacked just before the start of the 1996–97 season because he couldn't have taken the club, not just the team, to the level David Dein could now see. It wasn't because I had put in a transfer request; I didn't 'force him out', as it was said at the time, although if people want to maintain I'm responsible for his departure, they ought to be applauding me. I stand by what I said in that newspaper column the next day, that I fully supported the board's decision and that other players did too. David Dein had asked me to gauge what I thought the mood of the guys would be if they got rid of him and I said that nobody will be disappointed if that happens, everybody's being professional but nobody really likes him, he's not an Arsenal man.

To give Rioch his credit, he stuck with Dennis during that time when Dennis didn't score for his first seven games. The press was starting to get on his back, calling him a £7-million-pound flop, and the opposing fans were chanting, 'What a waste of money.' Rioch always played him and never took him off when things weren't going well.

The seventh game in that sequence brought out the worst in the media: it was a Coca-Cola Cup game away to Hartlepool on 19 September 2005, and although we won three-nil Dennis didn't score. The back pages the next day are full of pictures of Dennis looking forlorn and they were writing about how he couldn't even score against a Third Division club's second-string goalkeeper. Rioch still started him in the next game, at home to Southampton, and he scored twice to shut everybody up. Disregarding that, though, and looking at the way Bruce Rioch was and the trouble he had seen with George, then you can see what David Dein had in mind when he appointed someone with the temperament of Arsène Wenger.

When Rioch left Arsenal he addressed all of the players, but after that speech I didn't clap. I couldn't. I've never been in a situation like that before where someone was treating me like that, getting at me, picking on me, testing me all the time. It was a terrible time.

Chapter Three

Walking in a Bergkamp Wonderland

We all knew who Dennis Bergkamp was as a player, but nothing had prepared us for the impact he would make as soon as he turned up at Arsenal. This wasn't on the pitch once the league had started, but before he even kicked a ball in anger. It all began at the training ground press conferences and when we started playing pre-season friendlies.

There was a massive amount of interest from the regular English football press, because this signing – £7.5 million – was not only a British record but it was being paid by Arsenal who weren't well known for throwing money around. That was to be expected, but what took so many of us players by surprise was the level of interest from the foreign media. Suddenly, there were hordes of pressmen, not just from Europe but across the rest of the world, showing up at places like Southend, Wolverhampton and St Albans to watch Dennis Bergkamp. That was when it hit us: Arsenal have just signed a world-class player, we've moved up to another level, and we're all in the spotlight now as the eyes of the world are on us.

I believe, because of the price tag, there were a few in the English press that hoped he would fail, and when he didn't score in those first few games, they were quick to write those 'Couldn't hack it in Italy, can't hack it in the Premiership' type of stories.

But we knew here was a player of real quality who was just licking his wounds for a bit after an unhappy time at Inter Milan.

We knew from what we saw of him in training and around the club in general, plus what he was contributing to the team on the pitch, that Dennis coming to Arsenal was about much more than scoring goals. And everybody in the team knew it wouldn't be long before that happened. Dennis being at Arsenal provided an example to all of us in every respect: what he could do; who he was; how he conducted himself; and, most of all, how hard he worked.

I remember being at Palace, working hard in training, saying to myself, 'This is what the top players are doing.' When I got into the England set up and saw how the bar had been lifted I realized, 'No, *this* is what the top players are doing.' Then when Dennis came to Arsenal and I saw how he worked, in a 100 per cent, twenty-four-hour way, I knew what the top *top* players were doing. To think I was able to share a room with one of them – Dennis – for three years, it was an education like I could never believe, both in football and in life.

To a man, when Dennis came we raised our game 25 or 30 per cent. We tried harder because we saw how much work he put in and could measure that immediately against what he was achieving. To the players around him he was, quite literally, an inspiration; he inspired us in the same way Maradona inspired that Argentinian team of 1986. He arrived and all of a sudden, it was like *X-Men*! His DNA just coursed through us, turning us in to football mutants because we were hooked up to Dennis Bergkamp's DNA! It really was like watching those films when you can see inside a body and see that the DNA has shifted. That's what happened to Arsenal when Dennis joined us. *Bam*!

The DNA shifted and we began to osmose into a global entity, the beginning of the Invincibles and earning the sort of respect and recognition that we'd never had before.

Dennis was the start of what came to be called the Wenger Revolution because he pushed us into realizing there was another way to do pretty much everything. How Dennis was, both as a professional and as a man, demonstrated that in order for us to progress as a club there had to be a break from the George Graham/Bruce Rioch style of management.

Obviously, it was on the pitch that he made the biggest difference to me, once he settled into that role as a kind of second striker, in which he was a provider as much as he was an out-and-out goal scorer. Basically he made what I had to do so much easier; in fact, if such a thing was possible, playing with Dennis Bergkamp for three years made my job easy.

From the moment I came to Arsenal, I didn't have to work as hard in a game as I did at Crystal Palace. Although George wanted us to defend from the front, I wasn't expected to keep going as deep as I did previously, so it cut out a lot of those lung-bursting runs I had to make to get back into the box. Now we had a player who could pass the ball with ridiculous quality. Bruce Rioch appreciated that, and one of the very few things I ever took from him was when he told me, 'Just play within the eighteen-yard box, don't get involved with anything else. Let them do it.' Arsène Wenger told me the exact same thing: 'Don't worry too much about what is going on around you. Make your moves and the ball will find you.'

Which was true, as with a player like Dennis on the pitch, the ball always would find me – I'd make a run in the box and the ball was there. This allowed me to take my game to another level because I needed to concentrate on two things, movement and finishing technique. I didn't have to mix it up trying to get the ball in the first place. So I worked on my movement, losing my markers, making runs down the outside of defences or stretching the other team, and then Dennis would feed it through to me. It used to seem that as soon I found that yard of space the ball would arrive and, *bang*, I'd be in.

Really though, that is oversimplifying what Dennis would do for me, as he would lay the ball off in a way that dictated what you had to do next and put you at an even greater advantage. He'd play the ball so it comes to you on the side that's going to take a defender completely out of the game. For example, if I'd gained half a yard with my run, Dennis would pass it to me in such a way that the defender was always going to be second favourite in a two-horse race – he couldn't get to the ball without pushing me over, so all he could do was try and jockey me. This bought the other half of that yard of space, giving me time to shoot or lay it off. His touch was good enough to play the ball in to feet in the opposition's penalty area, too, which is brilliant for a striker but a nightmare for defenders because they're scared to go for it in case they bring you down.

The quality of his passes could change the game completely, because he wasn't passing the ball to you in the manner defenders had been prepared for, as they would have been told, 'If he's making a pass you can nip in there and nick it.' When you get players of the quality of Bergkamp or Vieira or Petit, their natural instinct is, 'I'm not just passing you a ball, I'm passing you a ball in a situation where the defender can't get to it and we can then retain it.'

Dennis would create opportunities for you that you might not even have seen yourself. He would pass it so you arrived at the ball in a certain way and your first touch would have to go in a certain direction, because he had seen how a space could open up in a certain area and he wanted to influence you towards it. So much of Dennis's passing game was about influencing what could be about to happen, rather than simply what was going on at that moment. He gave himself the time and space to work this kind of magic because his first touch was always so precise – he'd not only bring the ball under control, instantly, but he'd keep it away from anybody who might be challenging him, *and* put it in a position where he could play the pass he has already seen in his head.

Sometimes he'd play you a pass that you had no other choice but to play back to him, but really he was just buying himself a second or so, by which point somebody else would have made a run and he would know exactly what he was going to do and have the time and space to pull it off. So much of the time, when us forwards got the ball, it was 'Where's Dennis? Where's Dennis?', because we knew if we got the ball to him somebody would get it back in a way that would make something happen.

These are the things that you learn when you are playing with truly great players. You discover how much they can influence how you play your game, which means how success-ful or good you become. You learn from them how much more there is to your game, and how much more there is to the game as a whole. It opens up a different dimension of playing football and makes it accessible for everybody else on that team. Gazza was in that dimension; he was naturally able to pass the ball to you to create a situation in which the defender can't get it

– often this is something that wouldn't be immediately obvious to people watching, but if you're in that game then you *feel* how it's been taken up a level.

That's how good these players are, and I was really, really lucky that I got to play with a few of them with that kind of ability.

Dennis and I used to room together when the team stayed in hotels so we used to talk a lot, and he knew enough to know he didn't know everything. He would always listen to advice and was quick to learn how he needed to adapt to the Premiership.

When he first arrived from Inter he was doing that Italian thing of going over every time somebody kicked him, not diving, just making a meal of it, rolling around on the floor groaning. I told him he was going to have to toughen up because that sort of thing wouldn't win him any friends here, among other players, referees or the fans. I used to smash into people on the pitch, always got up as soon as I was kicked, and Dennis saw that and quickly appreciated that was how the game was played here. He started to do his bit as well, to leave his foot in. This was exactly what he needed to do, otherwise every single player in the league would be queuing up to kick the shit out him, because they'd know they could stop him doing what he was capable of by bullying him.

Before Dennis came to us that kind of targeting had happened to Anders Limpar, who played unbelievably for Arsenal when he was there during my first two years. It was bliss playing with him because he was an electrifying player – passing, shooting, left foot, right foot, pace, dribbling, crossing . . . he had every-thing. He was a different player to Dennis, but he was as technically gifted. However, much as I love him, it's fair to say he couldn't take knocks. If somebody lifted him up – somebody like Julian Dicks – then that was it, Anders would disappear for the rest of that game.

With Dennis, though, once he came to terms with what was required it wasn't a problem for him, he could take a clump and he could give one. He used to get booked quite a bit, picked up three or four red cards too, and I loved that side of him. Never mind all that Ice Man stuff, that showed how much he cared, how much he'd fight for the team and that he wasn't going to be pushed around. Sometimes there'd even be little skirmishes in training.

I also used to like it because those red-mist situations were the only time you'd think, 'Hang on, Dennis lost it a little bit there, he was out of control!' It made him more like one of us. You didn't see it that often though, because that's the kind of man he is.

When Arsène Wenger took over, it was Dennis who helped me get through a few of the changes that were made. For instance, a few of us English guys were a bit suspicious or resist-ant to two of the most significant changes he made: the food at the training ground and taking the nutrition supplements. Everything had to be fresh, I think it was mostly steamed, with no seasoning, no sugar, no salt . . . nothing. I found it very diffi-cult to eat that food as I'm not a great eater at the best of times. I'm very fussy, and with my West Indian upbringing I'm used to seasoned food. Plus I was used to having the same kind of food all the time. Now, all of sudden, it had changed. I'll admit I resented it, but that was all there was to eat at the training ground.

Then Dennis told me he followed the same diet at home, that he ate that food everywhere. I realized then, when watching his performances of the pitch, that was what I had to do too. He was totally dedicated to being the best he could be as a footballer, and he saw preparation as being absolutely vital to that, so was willing to make those sacrifices in order to arrive at a game in the best possible shape.

Up until then I was one of the players who used to sneak in salt and sugar to put on my food, and when we stayed in hotels I'd take teabags with me so I could make a cup of tea in the room. The first time I did it in front of Dennis, he looked at me sideways with an expression that wasn't so much disapproval as questioning. He raised an eyebrow as if to say, 'Are you really going to drink that?'

I'd say, 'Come on, Dennis, man, it's only a cup of tea.'

And he'd say, 'Have it, go on, if you really have to have it, it's only the team.'

So, of course, I wouldn't have it. He'd say it like he was joking, but he wasn't, and he was right, my behaviour might have affected the result, which would have impacted on the whole team. I stopped doing it because he'd taught me that, even in something as seemingly small as this, to get to his level you have to be totally dedicated.

He was the model professional. When we went away there was absolutely no messing about: he always made sure he got the right amount of sleep, so he'd put his pyjamas on, get ready for bed, talk to his wife on the phone then go to sleep. But this was more than just about his preparations, this is what sort of man he is away from football: a total family man with no distractions at all. He never got carried away with anything that was going on around him, and there must have been *a lot* going on around him. He just carried on with his life.

Not like me. When everything was going so well for me and I was doing adverts and television, and sponsored by Nike, I got a bit carried away with myself because of all the attention I was getting, the money I was being paid and having so many people all over me. I got caught up in all of that and cheated on my first wife, Debbie, which destroyed my marriage.

That was a really horrible period. I was still scoring goals, still doing my job, but off the pitch I hated myself – I knew what I was doing was so wrong but I was so caught up in that moment I didn't stop it. If there's ever been a time in my life I wish I could change, that would be it.

This was before Dennis came to Arsenal and I'm sure if I'd been around him then it would have been different. I don't know anybody who loves their wife and their family more than him. I don't think it's possible for somebody to love their missus more than he loves Henrita. I looked up to Dennis in such a way that I would have asked myself, 'Do you love your missus enough?' And even if that marriage wasn't working then I would have ended it in a proper, more dignified and amicable way. I would have done the right thing, like a man, not like the cheat that I was.

I would look at how Dennis behaved and try and replicate it, in many, many ways. I remember the first time we roomed together, he went into the bathroom and came out wearing those immaculate pyjamas. I was staggered! All the years I'd been playing and staying in hotels with teams, I'd never seen another footballer wearing pyjamas – I'd just get into bed in the vest I'd been wearing all day. But straight away I thought, 'If pyjamas are good enough for Dennis Bergkamp, they're good enough for me.' When I got home I went out and bought my first pair of pyjamas.

He laughed his head off when he saw them, because Dennis has got a great sense of humour. He used to tease me all the time about how I run because I pronate and he'd do impressions of how my feet turn inwards. He'd tease me about what I'd say in my sleep because I sleep-talk, and when I'd sleep-walk and wake up and by the door, he'd kill himself laughing as I got back in to bed.

Once, he dressed me up in Martin Keown's clothes. Martin, who is about a foot taller than me, had got changed and gone out on to the training ground and Dennis had me put his clothes on. When Martin saw me, he started saying, 'I've got a jumper like that . . . I've got trousers like that . . .' I'm sure he was just about to tell me that his fitted better than mine when he realized what had happened. Dennis had suddenly gone from being completely straight-faced to killing himself.

That was the really good thing about him when something like that was going on, he could always keep a completely straight face. He didn't often start stuff, but he'd always join in. There was a time when we were all watching a game in which Igor Stepanovs was playing for Skonto Riga, and Ray Parlour and Dennis decided to wind Martin up. Stepanovs was terrible but they sat there talking, completely seriously, about how brilliant he was. They were saying he was exactly the player our defence needed, and Martin was sitting behind them fuming. I'm sure that if it had just been Ray Parlour nobody would have taken any notice, but because Dennis was part of it, it suddenly became believable. The problem was that Arsène Wenger was listening too, and he only went and bought Stepanovs!

The last season I had at Arsenal, in 1997–98 before I was injured, was possibly the best experience any striker could ask for: playing with Dennis Bergkamp in a team managed by Arsène Wenger. Dennis had played for Johan Cryuff and Louis van Gaal in Holland, and while he must've learned and grown under them, when he came together with Arsène it was plain to see how much he was in his element. It was a match made in heaven: one was dedicated to creating the perfect environment and set of circumstances for the players to do their very best, while the other would put every effort possible into giving the best performance he could.

I feel blessed just to have been able to play alongside Dennis. Then when he said that one of the best finishers he'd ever worked with, easily, was Ian Wright . . . that is it for me. Given where I came from and how I worked my way into professional football, then worked my way up to be on a level where I could play with Dennis Bergkamp, it shows how worthwhile all the effort can be – that goodness will come to you. When I heard that Dennis had said that about me, I couldn't ask for higher praise.

Chapter Four

The Quiet Revolution

When Arsène Wenger first took charge of training at London Colney, on 1 October 1996, he had already been introduced to us and had been announced in the press, so we knew who he was. Or at least we knew who he was by name and by sight. What we didn't have the first clue about was how different our lives as professional footballers were going to become.

Now he addressed us as a group for the first time, but there was no big dramatic Churchillian speech about how we were going to do this and going to do that, just a quietly spoken, very brief talk that still got across his enthusiasm and his passion. He spoke to us about what he was going to do with fitness, how fit we needed to be, and that there would be some changes in the training methods. He said how he was going to give everybody a chance to prove themselves, and that he wanted everybody to enjoy their football. It was very concise, and then he ended it with, 'OK, let's go and train.'

That first speech is the point at which players make their first real assessment of any new coach coming in. Yes, it's going to be an instant judgement, but, really, this is where you start to size him up – how he makes that first speech. We didn't know what to make of Arsène Wenger, nobody really knew who he was, he looked more like a school teacher than a football manager and his approach to us just seemed so different.

Looking back on it, I realize that so many of the clues we needed as to what he was going to be like were there straight away: he didn't waste words, but he said what was needed to be said; and he put it across with a straightforwardness and a passion. He wasn't very talkative, he didn't talk for the sake of talking – still doesn't – he was well aware that you didn't have to shout to make yourself heard and he wanted to get out and start doing things rather than talk about them.

We didn't have to call him 'Boss' or 'Gaffer', either. In fact, we didn't have to call him anything other than Arsène. This was a bit strange for us as players so quite a few of us called him 'Boss' anyway. I did – indeed I still call him 'Boss', because that's who he is.

Of course, at that first meeting Arsène knew more about us than we did about him: Rémi Garde, who was his first signing and had already been at the club for a couple of weeks, used to talk to him on the phone every night while he was still in Japan. The story was Rémi was there to look after Patrick Vieira, as he was only nineteen and couldn't speak English, but really he was there to find out the lie of the land, who the characters were, and what went on in training and around the club. It was Arsène's way even before he got there – preparation is everything,

Arsène first team talk when were away to Blackburn Rovers a couple of weeks later was like nothing any of us had ever heard before either. Very brief, in fact so brief all he kind of said was 'What can I say to this team?' He spoke a little bit about the back four and the goalie, nothing in detail, then said, 'I don't need to tell you guys what to do . . . make sure we keep the ball; make sure we play with enthusiasm and we play with joy.' That was fine, not what we were used to but it must've done the job because I'd scored after three minutes and we went in at half time one-nil up. That was when it really got strange.

We came in buzzing because we were ahead and we were playing well. We sat down and Arsène came in and didn't say a word. For a full ten minutes. He was walking about, doing his stuff, speaking to the physio Gary Lewin, but hadn't said anything at all to us. We started looking at each other and talking quietly, practically whispering, among ourselves: 'Is he going to say anything?' 'Did you hear him say something?' 'What the hell's going on?'

Then Pat Rice started shouting at us. I think he was trying to fill the silence. Arsène just calmed him down by saying, 'Pat, don't shout at the players. You don't shout at my players. It's fine, it's fine, everything's fine.' It wasn't embarrassing for Pat or anything like that, as he said it very gently; it was more like giving him advice than contradicting him. Then he just carried on with whatever he was doing.

I have to admit, I started sniggering. I'm not particularly proud of that, but Pat was old school and was clearly getting ready to give us a bollocking, which, to be fair, we were all ready for. So when Arsène stopped him, everybody was gobsmacked! *Literally.* The whole team had one of those jaws-hitting-the-floor type of moments.

It was such a complete contrast to what George Graham had been like. With him, whether we were winning or not, he was going to start shouting and bawling. In fact, it could be worse if we were winning, just to bring us back down to earth. We'd leave the pitch, two-nil or three-nil up, be walking down the corridor feeling good and talking, 'Yeah . . . brilliant . . . fantastic . . .' then we'd get in the dressing room, the door would be shut and the first thing we'd hear is, 'Right you lot! Sit down and fucking shut up!' Sometimes George would have a go, then Stewart Houston, his assistant, would have a go, then Pat would have a go, so we would get three different bollockings in the same half time. That's really what I found so amusing, how genuinely shocking this new half-time vibe was for the whole team.

So during this game against Blackburn, we were struggling to come to terms with what was happening and, all of a sudden, no more than five minutes before we were due to go out, Arsène started talking. Calmly and concisely he ran through everything he'd seen in the first half and what he thought should happen in the second. What we should carry on doing, what we should cut out and to make sure we carried on enjoying what we doing. Then *bang*, it was time to go out. It must have worked, too, because we scored again in the second half to go on to win two-nil.

These half times really took some getting used to. Sometimes I'd be sitting there thinking, '*Please*! Somebody! Say something!' and it was even worse for the guys that been there seven or eight years, as this was a massive gear change for them. He persisted with it and it became the new normal for us. I can remember going away to England matches and the half times actually feeling weird! I'd come in, sit down and I'd immediately be in Arsène Mode, ready to relax and chill – have a little meditation for five minutes – and suddenly somebody's in your earhole, 'Aarrrgh aarrgh aarrgh . . .' I'd have to remember it was different, and think, 'OK, let me get into that mode again.'

Those England get-togethers could be very funny because the other players had heard about the half times at Arsenal and would be asking me things like 'What?! Really?! He doesn't say *anything*? What do you guys do for ten minutes?'

Once we got used to it we all got into our own routines: we'd come in and go to the toilet, go to the treatment room or whatever . . . some people just sat down, closed their eyes and let it all go on around them. You knew that, ten minutes later, Arsène would come in and start with 'OK . . .' He always started team talks off with 'OK . . .'

The reason we all found it so strange at first and the reason we reacted to it so well were, in fact, the same thing – he was treating us like adults, which, as professional footballers in the Premier League, didn't happen too often. He created a calming atmosphere that allowed us to think for ourselves instead of being yelled at by somebody else.

Looking back at it, Arsène wanted us to take responsibility for what was happening on the pitch, or at least to take a share in it rather than just being told what to do. He wanted us to sort it out ourselves because if we did that using our own intelligence and communication then it was going to have a much greater effect than just following orders. It encouraged us to react to things happening within a game while it was going on because we felt that responsibility. Now, in the calm atmosphere of that dressing room, without a manager bawling at us just because he was the manager, we started talking to each other about what had been going on. That is probably why

Arsène left that ten-minute space there, so we would start talking to each other.

As captain, Tony Adams was always very good at organization on the pitch, and at half time he would start talking first, but it was easy for anybody else who wanted to join in. I might say to Lee Dixon, 'Dicco, some of the time when I'm in there, you could whip it around to me . . .' and he'd say, 'Yeah, Wrighty, I saw that . . .' Somebody else might say they'd noticed that one of the opposing centre-halves is leaving a big space between him and the fullback and we should exploit that. All sorts of things got said, even if they were a criticism, and it was a *discussion*. It was really nice, and made sure we were thinking about stuff before Arsène told us what he'd observed during that half.

Treating his players like adults was really what was at the heart of what came to be called the Wenger Revolution; that was why, very early on, he stopped Pat Rice shouting at us. When I look back on it, it wasn't rocket science – treating adults like, well, adults – but this was definitely my first experience of it. It's why he likes young players and to bring his own players through, because they grow up in their professional lives knowing they have to approach the game with intelligence and a sense of responsibility. Responsibility for their own mistakes as well as their successes. He wanted us to be able to sort things out in a game without waiting for instructions.

Tony was the master of that. Fifteen or twenty minutes into a game, he could look around and start rearranging us: 'Right, you drop back ten . . . you stay on the right . . . you hold in the centre for five minutes . . .' Then we'd going again and, *bang!* The whole team started to apply the same intelligence, so whatever the situation required we could adapt to it or deal with it, instantly, and get back to what we did best.

Arsène looks at players' character and intelligence as much as their ability when he's looking to buy, then encourages them to bring those things into their game. It's why players like Dennis and Thierry Henry loved playing for him, and could totally flourish.

Pushing us to think and behave like adults was a big part of how he motivated that team, as he was encouraging us to motivate ourselves as much as anything. Under previous managers it had all been so edgy: we'd be wound up to get angry as a way of making us perform – 'You will fucking perform or you're fucking out of here!'; or we'd just be whipped into the ground: 'Fucking perform . . . fucking perform . . . fucking perform!'

This couldn't be further away from that. Arsène's way was to give us absolutely everything we needed to allow us to perform to the extent of our talents and abilities: 'Take the tablets, eat the right food, do it at home as well as at the training ground. Chew your food properly – chew to win. Get the right amount of sleep. Train properly so that you're so well prepared, so that you are 100 per cent ready for the game. I'm giving all of this to you, Ian, to make sure you become the best you can be . . . Perform . . . *perform!*' He made sure his players had everything, but then it was up to them.

This was so empowering for us as it put the power to do well in our hands. I felt that he loved his players so much he was willing to put that amount of faith in us to pass the power over. This is why, on television, I've talked quite harshly about some recent Arsenal performances, like the one against Olympiakos at home in September 2015. Why aren't those players performing? I know they've been let off the leash, they've been treated like adults, they've got everything they could want or need to allow them to perform . . . it's down to them and nobody else.

That is a big problem with taking Arsène's approach: it isn't difficult to take advantage of it – it's almost like having a parent you think is a bit soft and you know that if you cry hard enough you'll get a sweet. It's certainly happened in years gone by, with players that are strong characters and have taken his kindness for weakness. In my view players like Emmanuel Adebayor and William Gallas have taken liberties.

For me, Adebayor looks like the biggest example of how a player could take advantage of Arsène Wenger, which probably means he's also the biggest disappointment of the manager's time at the club. When he arrived, he had everything: he was fast, he was big, he was athletic, he was strong in the air and skilful on the ground, he was a top, top player.

He came in just as Thierry was getting ready to leave, so I can see exactly why we bought him. It looked like the perfect transition, and he did very well in that first half a season – we bought him in January 2006 – scoring four goals in ten games. Then all of a sudden he wanted the same money as Thierry. I know that with so many African players there's a lot they have to deal with, a lot of people to look after, but, to a certain degree, that's the same for everybody. For him to go off like he did and start flirting with Barcelona and Inter Milan to get the sort of money he wanted was completely out of order. It was like holding the club to blackmail at a time when they had no choice, and it destroyed any relationship he had with the fans.

I think that Arsène and Arsenal relented because of the position they found themselves in: they were about to leave

Highbury, and if they'd done that without Thierry and without Adebayor what message would that have sent to the team? They had no choice but to placate him, which was the worst thing they could have done as it told the spoilt kid that if he cried and stamped his feet hard enough, he'd get all the sweets. It let him know that he was the boss.

That was when his demise started; that was when I knew that Adebayor lost sight of what it meant to be a professional footballer, and to be privileged enough to play under Arsène Wenger. Unlike myself, or Alan Smith or Thierry, he never grasped what it meant to be a front man for Arsenal. A player of his ability could have stayed at Arsenal for his entire career, and got us through some seriously bad times – there would never have been that so-called Trophy Wilderness if he'd played and progressed at Arsenal through all those years. He would have ended up earning big money along the way, in any case. Instead, because he could, he chose to try and take advantage of the greatest manager he'll ever play for to become the epitome of the rich footballer – everything in terms of money, nothing in terms of achievement.

I believe it said a great deal about us, both as a team and as individuals, that David Dein thought we were ready for Arsène's style of management, because it could have gone so wrong if we'd rejected it or tried to take advantage. How we were likely to take to it would have been a big part of the conversations the two of them had when they were discussing the job, as it wouldn't have been obvious to a prospective foreign manager that any English team was ready for such a shift. Ruud Gullit had just started at Chelsea as player/manager, and he seemed to be doing all right. He'd been there as a player under Glenn Hoddle so it wasn't a huge jump, but up until then foreign coaches and their different methods hadn't really worked out. Before Arsène, Jozef Venglos had been at Aston Villa and Ossie Ardiles had a spell at Tottenham, both in the early 1990s: neither of them had a particularly easy ride in English football, and each only lasted about a year in those jobs.

Venglos had a doctorate in Physical Education and was the first coach to introduce post-match stretching and proper warm-down sessions; also, he paid attention to nutrition in the players' diets. Ardiles wanted to bring in a different style of play. None of their ideas were allowed to take root. Back then, the players had the power in the dressing rooms, and they weren't willing to accept too much of a change from what they were used to.

Those types of training methods and the specialized approach to players' diets had been around for a long time on the Continent – I heard that the Germans had been using vitamin supplements and creatine since 1970 – but nobody in the English league seemed to know what was going on over there. It wasn't as if clubs didn't have the resources to research this sort of stuff; it was more like they were actively rejecting any attempts at change.

The press did their bit to play up any discontent in the dressing rooms. They made it all about *Englishness*, or a particular sort of Englishness: the never-say-die bulldog spirit and let's all have a beer together afterwards. The idea was football in this country should be, 'Let's go down the pub, get some bonding going! This is about character, not fancy exercises or poncey foods! Go on, have a pint . . . have a pie!'

Of course, this sort of negative coverage had a knock-on-effect. Look who replaced those two progressive foreign coaches at Aston Villa and Tottenham: Ron Atkinson and Gerry Francis, respectively! Both so old-school 'English' they were practically clichéd. The football press have always loved Harry Redknapp as one of the Great English Managers, yet compared to what was going on at Arsenal, those guys were dinosaurs. It was as if English football was scared to move forward and look beyond what it already had.

All credit to David Dein for bringing Arsène Wenger into the club in this sort of atmosphere, then sticking with him, because the press did seem to enjoy ridiculing him and his ideas when he first arrived. While much of this was down to his not being English and his methods being so different, there was also a degree of disappointment on their part as he wasn't the super-star manager they'd been expecting.

Before Arsène was announced, the back pages were full of speculation that the next Arsenal manager would be Terry Venables or Johan Cruyff or somebody else of that stature, so you can see where their heads were: they've been hyping up Cruyff, then they get this bespectacled Frenchman they've never heard of, whose name is practically Arsenal!

Of course, they reacted – remember, quite a few of them had been claiming inside knowledge about who it would be and had got it badly wrong. So the story became about all the supposedly weird things Arsène was doing, which sort of made the point that this wasn't how things were done in England. Sure, it was unfair, but they want to sell papers so that's the kind of thing they do.

In fact, it became almost fashionable to try and take pot shots at this articulate, urbane Frenchman, but that never appeared to bother him as he'd always have some kind of dry, witty come-back. He is far too intelligent to rise to that kind of winding up, from either the media or from his fellow managers. This is why when you saw him being dragged into rows with Mourinho and Pardew and losing his rag, you knew what serious pressure he was being put under for us to win something. As a player, I never even heard him raise his voice because he knows he doesn't need to.

This attitude to Arsène in the press might have caused prob-lems for our team, if it hadn't been for the fact we could feel the effects of his changes so quickly it didn't make any sense *not* to get on board. Besides, we were no strangers to media-led hostil-ity because we'd been through all those years of being written off as 'Boring, boring Arsenal'. During that time George Graham had instilled in our team the mentality that everyone's against us, regardless of what we do or how much we win – a proper siege mentality. So all of a sudden everyone's against our new manager? We could deal with that, no problem.

Such was our team mindset that criticism may even have helped us bond with Arsène. It became a case of 'We don't give a damn what you lot think. He's *our* manager!'

Then, as we were eating the food, taking the tablets and doing the exercises – and we realized we were getting stronger and recovery on the day after a game was so much easier – we really didn't care what the press was saying.

Chapter Five

Arsène's Arsenal

Everybody talks about what a brilliant job Arsène Wenger did bringing in foreign players, and so they should. At that time, it was only he who had the contacts to find the players and the confidence and the knowledge to say. 'I'm going to bring him in . . . I'm going to put him here . . . I'm going to put him there.' Who else could have got Patrick Vieira from the reserves at AC Milan? Manu Petit from Monaco? Who else would have gone to Paris St-Germain to get this youngster out of their academy – Nicolas Anelka? Or knows he's got to get somebody to replace Ian Wright once he goes, and he's thinking Thierry Henry?

He knew he didn't need to mess around with the back four or the goalie, however, so he didn't, and what he did with the English guys that were already there is often overlooked. More than simply extending careers, Arsène gave players the freedom to express themselves and try things they probably never would have dreamed of under George Graham or Bruce Rioch. His philosophy was 'Just play', and it made what we did very, very enjoyable.

What sums it up best of all is the goal Tony Adams scored at Highbury against Everton in 1998, the game that clinched the title for us. Sure, it was an unbelievable half volley, but the most significant part of it is that Tony was up there to take it, *in open play*. He'd never had that licence before, but now he could leave his position in central defence to run up right into their half and get on the end of a beautiful chipped pass from Steve Bould – who's playing in the midfield!

The whole thing was about having that sort of freedom and the encouragement to express ourselves, then us being trusted enough to know what needed to be done. Tony and Bouldy didn't neglect their duties at the back, but when they saw the chance to go up and make something happen there was no problem with them getting on it.

Arsène Wenger was the perfect person for Tony Adams at that time because of what was going on in his life. His arrival literally coincided with Tony getting sober, and Arsène treated him unbelievably. For the rest of us, it was like we'd got our captain back – I'm sure Tony will admit it himself, but in those years from about 1992 the captain wasn't there. Then Arsène Wenger came at the end of 1996 and he was back.

When I joined Arsenal in 1991, that team had already won the league twice, and I was thinking that I was probably going to win it a couple more times before we actually did in 1998. I can't blame Tony for that, because you can't blame it on just one man, but when a leader like our captain wasn't really present – apart from in body – it has to make a difference. Sure, we won the Cup Winners Cup, the FA Cup and the League Cup, but I was expecting to win the league during that time.

Everybody's seen what Arsenal achieved from 1998 onwards. As soon as Tony was back and Arsène Wenger was manager everything about the team and the club started to escalate. Things just started to get better – that's the only way to describe it. We felt it in training and we felt it in games: we were just *better*.

When you look at Tony's personal life and what he was doing just before Arsène got there, I think this was his redemption. It would have been such a tragedy if Tony Adams didn't make it through all of that hell not to be the captain of Arsenal in some of their most successful times.

He gives the manager a lot of credit for treating him like a grown-up, and that did play such a big part in turning him round, but you have to look on the other side of it: you can't turn your back on a man like Tony Adams. You just can't do that, whatever baggage he comes with, and Arsène Wenger's not stupid, just like George Graham wasn't. Everybody who's ever managed Tony Adams knows what he's about, what makes him and drives him – he's a winner, he's a leader, he wants to win and inspire. He was captain of Arsenal – of *Arsenal* – at eighteen! What does that tell you?

And, really, you can't tell me there's been a greater captain at Arsenal than Tony Adams – and that's not just because there's a statue outside the stadium. People will often say Frank McLintock when asked to name their greatest ever Arsenal captain, or Patrick Vieira. But good as McLintock was, winning the double under Bertie Mee, you can't say he was as inspirational a leader as Tony. And while Patrick comes close – in his way he was as dynamic – you have to remember he learned it all off Tony.

I've always felt very fortunate to be involved with people who have been born to do what they have been doing, and Tony was born to be a captain and a leader. Even when he went through that period where he fell off, he's put that into motivating people; what he's done with his Sporting Chance Clinic and the amount of lives he's saved is just fantastic. These days he's married to the Teacher's whisky heiress – how ironic is that? – and lives comfortably down in the Cotswolds. He's in and out of London so I see him all the time (he and his wife are godparents to my kids) if he's not off to somewhere like Uzbekistan.

You know when you just love someone? That's Tony Adams. And it's not just me thinks that. Last year on his birthday I put up on Twitter, 'Happy birthday to a great man', and among the stuff that came back there was this woman who came on and said, 'Great man????' and she was very derogatory. I mentioned what he'd done, then I passed it over to the Arsenal Nation and she got torn to shreds. People can be so judgemental.

I'm just so pleased that I was able to last long enough at Arsenal to see him come through what he'd been going through. Everybody knows about what certain people have been through with alcoholism, and they know about the amount of people who have not made that journey successfully. Tony was never going to be one of those.

If somebody had said to me, when Tony Adams was going through his darkest times, 'Do you think he'll make it through it?' I would always have said, 'Yeah! No doubt about it.' It takes a lot of strength to get through what he got through, and he's always had that. He'll always be my captain, he's my captain for life. I still call him the skipper. I'd seen him in the bars, I'd seen what he was going through, then to be on the pitch with him when he scored that title-winning goal against Everton was truly something else.

Ray Parlour is another good example of how Arsene could get something extra or unexpected out of players. I used to tease Ray all the time about how he couldn't believe he'd made it to where he was. I used to say to him you must pinch yourself every morning and say, 'How on earth did I become a professional footballer?' We still laugh about it when I see him now! I think it surprised a lot of people that Ray was one of the players Arsène kept and I couldn't blame anybody looking in from outside for thinking that way, but he absolutely loved Ray. He completely turned him around, got him into the new way of doing things. He loved Ray's strength and saw him as the balance in that team, the workhorse who would do all the heavy lifting. Arsène turned Ray into the cornerstone of that team, and I don't think Ray gets enough credit for it – he was an Invincible, and he scored some great goals for us too.

Ray would tease Arsène, too, and most of the time the boss wouldn't know or just didn't get it, but we'd all be killing ourselves laughing. Arsène had this vibe about him that was a bit distracted and things would just happen to him or around him that he might not notice – he's one of those characters who trips up on things or bumps in to stuff. Ray used to call him Clouseau in a bad French accent like Peter Sellers. Arsène has a good sense of humour and could laugh at himself, but he was so intelligent he'd often look at things completely logically and they just wouldn't make sense to him – a bit like Mr Spock in *Star Trek*.

In my last season there, we were playing Wimbledon away, the floodlights failed and we were taken back into the dressing room. The first thing Arsène asked was whether anybody knew what was happening. Nobody did, but Ray piped up, in his best Clouseau voice, 'Ah theenk eet ees a beurmb!' Arsène didn't find it funny at all, but everybody else was cracking up.

Sometimes stuff that other people might just find funny completely perplexes him: once, he caught me on rollerblades in Highbury's marble halls. I was just doing it for a laugh, but he was absolutely dumbfounded. A man of his intelligence just couldn't compute why a professional footballer, an experienced one at that, at Arsenal, would be on rollerblades. On a marble floor!

As that first full season progressed, we knew we were part of something, and we were made to feel special. I'm sure Arsène's done that all the way through his career and still does it to this day – I'm sure it's part of the reason why his players stay so loyal to him. With the training and the tablets, we were instantly thinking, 'There's a new sheriff in town', but we were never thinking, 'This is going to be massive'.

We had no idea we were blazing such a trail until other clubs started taking serious interest. Up until then, if people from outside had seen what we were doing they would have simply laughed at us. Then, because of the way Arsenal finished, getting stronger physically and mentally as we were winning games, people started asking what the hell are they doing over there? Once we began scoring goals for fun people were like, 'Hang on, they're playing really well, they're not boring, boring Arsenal anymore.'

When I went away with England, in the early days of Arsène Wenger, other guys would ask, 'What's your new manager like?' and I'd try to explain, 'Yeah, he's fine, we do exercises in the morning and this and that, then we have a game.' Nobody was taking a great deal of notice. Then, suddenly, the Arsenal lads were being asked, 'What are they giving you?' . . . 'So what's this about the creatine, then?' I might tell them, and next thing I know they're trying it at their place! Then everybody's on it, and Arsène Wenger has dragged English football into the modern world.

What I felt about Arsène Wenger's time, once I finished at Arsenal and went to different clubs, was that I had left NASA. The supplements, the training regime, the diet, the stretching, the warming down, the preparation are commonplace among Premiership sides today, but in 1996 it was all unheard of. What he was doing, back then, was out of this world.

Again, David Dein has to take the credit here. He was the actual guvnor, the sage who knew everything, the visionary who brought Arsène Wenger to the club. When you consider everybody else that Arsenal could have had at that time, how did he pick him? Where did he come from? I don't know what he would've based it on – Arsène had played semi-professional football, he managed Monaco, he managed Grampus Eight in Japan . . . it's not much to go on, is it?

David Dein would have done his homework to the most minuscule point. That's just how he was. So he would have known about the nutrition and the training; he would have known about the youth team element and how he brings young players through; he would have known that Arsène's got the link with Clairefontaine, the French elite football academy. In spite of all that, though, I still don't know if he totally knew how great Arsène was going to be.

For David Dein to find him, to find somebody that could fall in love with a club like Arsène has, wasn't much short of a miracle. Arsène and Arsenal are very much a great marriage, not just as far as the players are concerned, but across the whole running of the club. Arsenal is now in the image of Arsène Wenger, so when people talk about replacing him . . . you're never going to be able to replace him. You're going to be able to replace *the manager*, but you're never going to be able to replace Arsène Wenger. He's the epitome of what our club is about.

It's well known that Arsène Wenger was instrumental in the building of the Emirates Stadium, but what he really doesn't get enough credit for are the years right after the move. I had a great chat with Ivan Gazidis, our chief executive, in 2015, and he explained to me that, when we were leaving Highbury to go to the Emirates, we were close to being broke. It's difficult to believe: my immediate thought was how a club like Arsenal couldn't ever be on the edge, but when you think about it properly it was there for everybody to see . . . we weren't buying players . . . we were selling our superstars . . .

It was because they didn't sell the flats in the development of the old stadium as quickly as they hoped, so things were going wrong on the financial side and those were barren years. It was something that couldn't have been anticipated, because the slump in the property market came long after the development was planned. That was why it was so important to keep Thierry after the move: he was the figurehead that we couldn't afford to replace.

Talking about that time, Ivan told me how seriously bad those years were, and said to me, 'Ian, Arsène Wenger is the only manager who could tolerate what a club of Arsenal's stature had to go through with the stadium and the next ten years, and pull it off.'

It was about more than just getting through it, though. With the resources he had to work with, he kept the club in the top four and Champions League football for every one of those years.

I know there's been a lot of fuss made by people saying and writing derogatory things about how Arsène thinks the top four is a trophy in itself, but they don't realize what an achievement it was to finance the stadium *and* stay in the top four.

Tottenham will find that out when they build their stadium, but there's the difference between them and us – we *had* to be in the top four. They could be tenth and it doesn't matter because they haven't got the same ambitions as us. Spurs may not be in the top four and it won't be news; if Arsenal don't get into the top four, that news goes around the world. Arsenal has a particularly high set of standards and the team has to maintain them, regardless.

It's easy to think Arsenal could have attracted the kind of investor needed to get them through those times – I thought that myself when Ivan told me how close the situation had been. But even if they could have, I'm not sure they would have, because the board have to remain in control of the club's future. They have to be in charge of what decisions they're going to make for the club and for the fans. They couldn't afford to pass over the sort of power anybody looking to plough money in would expect – with all due respect, that sort of thing is easier for Chelsea and Manchester City. The board weren't going to risk turning Arsenal into anything other than what Arsenal is. The fact is, Arsenal do things how Arsenal do them, and how they do them always turns out to be right. Always.

Looking in at it from the outside, though, it was frustrating, and some of the time I've slaughtered the board in the press: What's going on? How did Patrick Vieira end up at Man City and then as manager of their sister club in New York? Why isn't Dennis at our club? Why isn't Tony Adams? . . . I laid the blame of financial constraint on the board, and gave them so much stick because I thought they were not letting Arsène Wenger do what he needed to be doing.

I was critical just because I wanted us to win. I was like the fans who couldn't understand why we weren't winning. We had just come off the Invincibles and I so wanted that to be the start of us winning and doing things, because I believed that time was Arsenal's chance to become like Liverpool in the 1970s and 1980s, or Man United through the 1990s. I thought it would be Arsenal's time to dominate for four or five years, to win the league a few more times, to win the Champions League. So maybe I even foolishly slipped into the same thinking of 'Have we got another George Graham here? . . . Doesn't Arsène want to pay the money? . . . Doesn't he want to buy the players?' And people started talking about him as, 'Oh, he's stubborn . . . he's too stuck in his ways.'

Arsène Wenger was genuinely doing what he could to win the games. At no point did he do anything else or have any other agenda, and despite the financial issues, he kept Arsenal in the top four. I understand that now, and I've got no problem with it. In fact, I think it's a mark of how much he loves the club: knowing what he knew at the time, he never came out and said anything about anything. He just took it, took all the crap that was thrown at him in the press and by the fans, so the club didn't have to. It's almost like there was a Jesus Christ thing about him, where he held his arms out and said, 'OK, I'm going to take on all this abuse and protect everybody, because I'm the manager and this is what I've got to do.'

That's why I know I couldn't be a manager!

★   ★   ★

So now we're a stable club, money in the bank, self-sufficient, and for the next hundred years the future for Arsenal is bright. This could only have been achieved by people like David Dein, Ivan Gazidis and the board building a whole new stadium from the ground up, on land that used to be a rubbish dump. And, what makes this even more astonishing, is this is *in the middle of London* not out in the middle of some field near Milton Keynes, but right where the club has its home and support – in Islington.

While this was down to their business acumen, it couldn't have happened without Arsène Wenger standing in front absorbing all the criticism and just getting on with what he had to do. In return, in the long term, the club has stood by him because they realize how fortunate they are to have a manager who isn't greedy, who isn't out for himself, who recognizes how much the fans love the club and who has grown to love Arsenal as much as they do. Although, at the time of writing, I do feel his cycle at the club is coming to an end, at the moment it's impossible to imagine Arsenal with any other manager in the world. Indeed, the only other manager I could see doing the job with the same dignity and lack of self-consciousness would be Carlo Ancelotti.

That's why although I've been critical of some of the decisions he or the board have made, I've never been critical of him personally. A while ago there was a time when people were constantly accusing me of having a go at Arsène Wenger, and I'd always say to them, 'Show me the quote. Show me the quote.' I remember doing a radio show when the presenters were trying to get me to actually say, 'Yes, it is time for Arsène to leave.' I told them straight, I'm not going to do that. Even if I thought that, when he was going through his worse spells

– the Cygan Years – I was not going to say anything because I've got too much respect for him.

The worst people for this sort of behaviour are Arsenal fans now aged twenty or thirty, who came along with the Emirates or with the Invincibles, who have *continuously* criticized Arsène, and expect me to join in. They don't have the slightest inkling of what Arsenal means to me, and all I've ever said to them is 'Please! Do not bother me with that!' Thankfully there aren't that many of them, but they can make a whole lot of noise in the media.

I have always been respectful, and Arsène took that on board. One of the best conversations I've ever had with him was in Brazil, at the 2014 World Cup, and it made me feel exonerated in respect of speaking about the club. We were in the same hotel and spent a lot of time talking – it was just brilliant but one particular conversation was the best. We were sitting down, having dinner, relaxing over a glass of wine, and he said, 'Ian, there are people who talk about our club, and there are people who used to play for our club, who are very disrespectful. I have no problem with you, because I know that you speak from the heart when you are talking about Arsenal. You care about the club, so you never need to worry about that.'

Arsenal, the whole club, is in the image of Arsène Wenger in the way it's set up and the way it functions – very intelligent, very calculating, whatever happens there's no kneejerk reaction, nothing rash . . . That's exactly how he is. Look how the media has been constantly trying to gee him up, always having a little dig, but he's on a different level and he's not even bothering himself. Sometimes, I see that going on and think, 'The only thing you lot can *really* criticize him for is he's too intelligent for you.' He's just got too much.

He came through the barren years with his dignity and his pride intact – that's why Mourinho cannot deal with how Arsène Wenger is, why Ferguson couldn't. He winds them up without even saying anything. Look at Ferguson and what he did at Man United, but he would still look across to Arsène and feel aggrieved for some reason. Mourinho's won more and done more than us, but he'll still look at Arsène and feel aggrieved, because Arsène is the embodiment of his own legacy. He is football. He's what it's all about, He's why any of us do this. He's all about the game in its purest sense, and what he wants to bring out of his players is part of that game. It's not about personal stuff or individual awards: it's about his players doing the best they can.

He's not just a great man, he's a really great bloke too. He has got a sense of humour, and he's got a great way about him when he does joke. He's got a lovely smile and my wife absolutely adores him. She loves the way he is, thinks he's just a wonderful guy. There's so few flaws there that when I saw those pictures of him on the bench at Monaco, I think, smoking a cigarette, I found it so strange – Arsène Wenger smoking! It seemed so beneath him. But then I'll admit that I enjoyed thinking, 'So, there is a weakness! You're not the all-seeing all-knowing all-strong sage kinda guy! You're smoking a cigarette.'

Really, though, I feel very fortunate to have been able to play under him and one of the few things I regret is that I didn't get more time with him.

Chapter Six

To Be Prepared

It wouldn't be true to say that in the very beginning there wasn't some internal resistance to the changes Arsène Wenger brought in, because it all came in so quickly. It all happened that first day he came to the training ground. Literally. Yesterday we were doing that, today we're doing this. One day we're in the Army, running up hills, never say die; today it's jumping over little hurdles and flexibility exercises. One day it's chips and pies in the canteen; the next it's vitamin tablets and mange tout. It was all so unexpected, so of course there was going to be a reaction, but it wasn't always negative.

From that very first day, when he said, 'OK, let's go and train', things were completely different. We looked out over the training ground that day and it was like nothing we'd ever seen before. We got out there and the immediate thought was that somebody was having a laugh: it looked like a cross between an obstacle course and a playground. There were big hoops, little hurdles, rows of little hoops on the ground, lines of poles . . . We were just wandering around asking, 'What's that for?' or 'What's going on here then?' Then we got to go and train with it all, and it turned out to be brilliant!

Boro Primorac, the first team coach who had been with Arsène in Japan and came to Arsenal with him, used to take us for these sessions. We'd have the big hoops and we'd have to run through them, and we'd run through the lines of poles, zigzagging – don't touch the poles! – we'd do this backwards as well. We'd do sideways running around the obstacles, stepping through the hoops on the ground putting a foot in each, do that backwards and sideways too . . . all sorts of different things.

I remember there being a load of jumping, jumping into things, jumping through things, jumping over the hurdles, jumping on and off platforms, quickly and with loads of repetitions. Naturally, as professional footballers are a competitive bunch, we'd be seeing how high we could jump or how fast we were over bits of the course or how sharp we could be. It was brilliant! After years of slogging around the training ground, this was such good fun to do, and we started warming up with it before we did anything else.

At first I used to wonder what was the actual point in all of this, then Arsène explained to me that it was all about power and explosive movement, and we were working on the weight-bearing muscles that required. He said because of the training we would have a good base fitness, and the supplements would help with recovery, so instead of working on something as general as stamina or endurance, we'd be focusing on what he called the quick muscles. These are the fast-twitch muscles, the ones used by sprinters, high jumpers and hurdlers for explosive starts or bursts of power and speed. The jumping, I came to learn, was plyometrics, which is all about getting the maximum force out of a muscle in the shortest amount of time – explosivity.

He called me to one side one day and said he needed me to focus on where my power was, which was my hips and thighs, so he wanted me to work more on the plyometrics, the jumping, and jumps from standing starts, and twisting and moving, because that was what was best for my game.

Since then, there's been so much talk about 'quick this' and 'quick that' and most of the other clubs have adopted this type of training, but all of the plyometrics and fast-twitch muscle stuff came from Arsène Wenger first.

He turned what we were doing into science, and for us this was unbelievable. We used to have to go and see a doctor in France, Dr Bousiteau, and we had other doctors and specialists coming in to look after our well-being. Then we had to see another one, Philippe, who would shake us. He'd do it to open up our chakra and channels, which is an Eastern thing that opens up energy points in the body. He'd do all sorts of manipulation with our legs and hips – he'd hold your leg up, move it so it clicked, tell you to relax and he'd shake it out, and then you wouldn't be able to train for two days.

We did stretching to warm down after games, and we did it in the morning when we went away and stayed overnight. Arsène would take this morning stretching with the whole team, in whatever large room was available in the hotel. He'd settle himself in front of us and do the stretches with us. I was amazed at this, and although some of the others used to grumble, I used to love it. Boro or somebody else would take training on a day-to-day basis, so this was one of the few things he'd do on his own with us. I think it was a very Japanese thing for the boss to do.

Quite soon after he arrived, Arsène sent me to France to work with Tiburce Darou, who was like the Yoda for all this type of training. He worked with rugby players and tennis stars like Bjorn Borg and John McEnroe. When he passed away in 2015 Patrick Vieira, Emmanuel Petit and Robert Pirès were pallbearers at his funeral. Tiburce would train me on the beach, he worked me on the sand, he worked me in the sea, he worked me on weights, he worked me on sprinting, he did just about everything with me, and then he'd tell me what to eat! 'Eat fish! Eat this! Eat that!' When I came back to the club I was flying. Although I think it was more a case of Arsène wanting to find out how much I had left in the tank, because I was in my thirties, those sessions were still absolutely fantastic.

Arsène was very aware of how old I was – I was thirty-three when he arrived. I used to stay back when team training sessions had ended to work on my finishing, but he wasn't happy with that. He'd tell me he didn't want me to do too much afterwards.

'Remember your age,' he'd say. 'Your body and your muscles are different. You have to learn to preserve – to preserve yourself, to preserve your muscles, to preserve your energy.'

He knew how much I loved to do it, and how hard it was for me to try not to, so he explained it to me like this: 'You are now in a situation where do you need to practise whether or not you can put the ball up in this top corner or you can chip the goalkeeper? No. You can do these things, you are Ian Wright. What you need to be doing is making sure the muscles are strong enough to put you in the situation to do it.'

It doesn't come any plainer than that.

Regular training sessions would last about two hours and we'd finish with a game, eight-a-side or nine-a-side, but it was always on the clock, timed to the exact last second, so when Bora said, 'Stop!' we'd have to stop. This was one of the things that in the beginning used to make me quite angry. It didn't matter that we were playing this unbelievable game and it's two-two, he would go, 'OK, enough', so everybody would have to stop. I'd be like a little kid going, 'Come on, Gaffer, come on, Gaffer! Winning goal, winning goal!' But no! No winning goal.

This was very hard for me because I loved scoring anywhere, any time – ask anybody who was there, they'll tell you I celebrated goals in training. For years at Arsenal the training had concentrated on defence, *everything* was defence, and for me that was boring. Now, we've got this continental coach, letting us do all this brilliant, fancy training stuff, I'm going to be learning a load of new stuff, and he *stops the games*! But that was just me being selfish. When I realized what we were getting out of the whole thing, those training sessions became amazing. Even with the matches on the clock like that.

The vitamins and the creatine were the most surprising thing to us, because they were so new to English football in general that we'd never heard of this sort of stuff before. As it was explained, the creatine was for increased power and performance in high-intensity bursts, like sprints, plus it helped repair muscles. The principal vitamin supplements were B6 and B12, taken as tablets or injections, which helped break down the food we were eating into glucose, which is probably the most important source of energy for us as players. It was the sort of stuff Olympic athletes had been taking for a few years, which summed up the difference in Arsène Wenger's approach to his players – he treated us as athletes, not merely as footballers.

At the absolute beginning, in the very first few days, there was some suspicion, like, 'Woah, woah! What's going on? What's this? What's it going to do to me?' And that was an understandable reaction from a dressing room full of experienced players. From our point of view, you've got some bloke nobody's ever heard of coming in and saying, 'Right! You're going to start taking creatine, you're going to start taking B6 tablets and having

B12 injections.' Up until then we'd been largely successful so we figured our training was the best it could be.

In spite of there being some kind of fuss on the sports pages about creatine and what it could do, it didn't take long for us to work out it wasn't anything that might be illegal or harmful. The club would never have allowed anything like that, and as we got to know Arsène Wenger we knew that he wouldn't do anything that put his players in any sort of risk. Also, he's not going to cheat – he's far too honest and too respectful of the game to have put anything into us that wasn't a natural vitamin.

Understandably there was a lot of typical footballer banter like, 'What are we, monkeys in a lab?' and I remember somebody saying, 'We're supposed to be a football team, he's turning us into a science experiment!' My only real problem was with the vitamin injections, which was simply because I don't like needles and not what might have been in them.

There was some moaning about the food, too, simply because it happened without warning. I had my own issues with it, and Dicco and a couple of the others were up in arms when chips were taken off the menu in the training-ground canteen. Suddenly there's broccoli and mange tout and green beans, and white rice and pasta for carbohydrate, and white meat chicken and steak for protein, all cooked in a way that made it all seemed so bland. It was eating for fuel – like going to the petrol station and filling up your car: all we were eating for was to put in what we needed to get us through the game.

As well as getting me to follow the eating plan properly, Dennis, along with the other foreign boys, Rémi Garde and Patrick, also did the same for the rest of the team. When the creatine and the vitamin tablets and shots were brought out, they literally lined up and said, 'Fine. What do you want me to take? Thank you very much.' We knew what Dennis could do, we'd quickly found out how good Patrick was and how fit Rémi Garde was at age thirty, so we thought if they were taking this stuff and eating this food, imagine what it could do for us.

It only took a couple of months before everybody who had got into the new way of doing things was noticing what a difference it was making. We didn't need to be persuaded anymore. Eating all the new food, taking all the tablets, doing all the new training stuff, I felt fitter, sharper, faster that I'd ever been. We all were. You could see how strong and powerful we were getting – we felt like we'd been reinvented as Robocop . . . *Roboplayers*!

Pat Rice used to send us out on to the pitch telling us, 'You are fitter than them! You are stronger than them! You know you are! No one's doing what you're doing! You will get what you deserve out of this game!' You listen to that in the dressing room, you're ready to go.

There were some of the team who, first of all, said they were taking the tablets then didn't take them, and there were a few who didn't get into it at all, try as they might. But they were never really Wenger players and were moved on pretty quickly. John Hartson wanted to conform and do his stuff, but he always had trouble with his weight.

And then there was Merse. I was gutted to see Merse go, but at that time he was all over the place with his own problems so it was difficult for him.

You could see who Arsène was looking at as going to have to go, and it had as much to do with getting on board the programme as simple ability.

★   ★   ★

On the pitch, the way I noticed my fitness levels were going up wasn't really about how I felt but how I *didn't* feel. In individual games it meant we could outlast the opposition. How it used to work was that you'd quickly go to a certain plateau, energy-wise, and then after the hour that begins to drop off, for both teams. Now, around that time whoever we'd be playing would be looking at us and thinking, 'They're going to flag soon, they *cannot* keep this up.' But we could. After the hour we still felt fit and strong and they were starting to wilt. So with the defence and the midfield we had, and the forwards we had, all we had to do was go out there and compete, and take our chances, and we were going to beat teams.

It wasn't as if I was trotting around on the pitch thinking about how fit I felt, but I'd make a couple of lung-bursting runs, and recover so quickly I could go on another one immediately. And then do it again, and keep this up until the end of the game. When I got into the meat and bones of Arsène's philosophy, I would come off after some football matches and think I could play again. Right away. That's how I realized how much fitter and stronger I was getting.

Other players noticed how quickly they recovered after a match – I remember Dicco saying that it didn't matter what he was asked to eat or the stretching and exercises involved, because he felt so much better when he got out of bed the day after a game. I believe the reason why Tony and Bouldy, Dicco, Nigel and The Goalie went on for as long as they did was because they totally embraced it. They literally lived the life like Dennis did, all the way through until they retired. Because it worked, they did it until they couldn't do it anymore.

★　　★　　★

The next season, 1997–98, was our first full season with Arsène, and what we were doing really showed its worth when we did the double, although it didn't start out with us exactly of full of confidence.

This was the first time he'd taken us for pre-season training and it was a complete contrast to the days of running round London Colney we were used to. Instead of being thrashed within an inch of our lives, we did a bit of running in between the poles, running through the little hoops, passed the ball a couple of times and he'd say, 'OK. Finish!'

It was so light that all of us, or at least all the English boys, were worried that we hadn't done enough, and we didn't think we felt fit enough. I even remember playing in a training game, struggling to get my second wind and telling Arsène about it, and all he said was, 'It's fine. You'll get it, you'll get it.' Then he laughed.

You know it must have been drastic for me to have said to Lee Dixon, 'Dicco, man, I don't feel fit!', because I'm the last person who wanted to be slogging around the training ground. Tony and Lee went to see Arsène and voiced our very genuine concerns. He was, of course, very calm and said, 'No, you'll be fine. If you're eating the food, taking the tablets and doing the training, you'll be fine. Don't worry.'

I can't say we were convinced, but we remembered how we felt as we'd finished the previous season and come third, two places higher than the year before, so we trusted him. And of course he was right – as we started playing games the training and nutrition regime started to kick in, and we started getting fitter and fitter and stronger and stronger.

As a rule, there was a certain point in the season when I would start to tire and I'd notice that what I had to do called for increased effort. That year, though, I just felt great. It was the same for the rest of the boys: as the campaign went on, and other teams were starting to flag, we were flying. It was almost as if he'd been pacing us as a team – we were just totally stronger, mentally and physically, than everybody else.

Starting Boxing Day, we went eighteen games unbeaten, only drawing three of those, and we won ten games on the spin to run in and take the title with two games to spare. We surprised a lot of people. I remember Alex Ferguson saying how we had a run of tough games coming up, and saying let's see how they deal with it, but saying it rather derogatorily to the effect that he couldn't see us doing it. But we did it, twelve games won, catching up an eleven-point deficit on Manchester United and the title's wrapped up. Done.

Even our own fans must have been shocked, as after the Blackburn game at the beginning of December 1997, when we lost three-one at home, I think quite a few of them wrote us off as title contenders. It was all down to the way Arsène Wenger had prepared us starting with that pre-season; by the time the second half of the season came around, we almost felt it as if we'd been given an unfair advantage. We'd go out believing the other team didn't have a chance.

I got quite seriously injured around the halfway point of that season, so I missed much of that run-in, but such was the spirit in that team I still wanted to do all I could to contribute. I was always in and around the dressing room, I went to games, I went to away games . . . Being a part of what was going on at that time was just brilliant, really special. It was a fantastic ride.

Chapter Seven

It Was My Job to Miss

I can't remember ever not wanting to score goals, or not trying to score goals at every opportunity. When I look back at playing football as a young child, I can remember scoring goals but I can hardly remember passing to anybody. That is proper passing, deliberate let-me-play-the-ball-to-somebody-else passing, or even one-twos where I pass it and make a move. From the age of about six or seven for the next three or four years, I'm sure I never even thought about passing, all I was trying to do was score.

I'm well aware people will read that and think not much changed as I got older, and to be truthful it didn't All the way through my career, I knew I should have held the ball up better or done more to link play, but every single time I got the ball played up to me I would be thinking how could I manoeuvre the ball to beat the defender and manufacture a shot. That's the first thing that would come into my mind, and very often the only thing.

There's a great example of it on a *Barclays Premier League Legends* show, when I'm playing against Everton – the only time I was captain of Arsenal. John Jensen plays the ball into me and there are two or three Everton players around me. By the time I've got the ball and made it to the edge of the box, there are four of them, yet all I'm doing is trying to jockey them into a position to give me room to have a shot. I got one away as well.

It made me think back to when I was a child, and how all little kids want to score goals, get the glory and do a celebration – it's the whole purpose of football at that age. Unless you're stuck in goal you want to be scoring. However, I genuinely had no memory whatsoever of passing to anybody else. Even as I got a bit older. All I ever wanted to be was a striker, even before I understood what a striker was.

I got my first coaching in finishing as far back as my primary school, when I was about seven or eight and going to Turnham School in Brockley. It came from a teacher called Mr Pigden. He was the first positive male figure that I had in my life, and he mentored me more than just in football. My childhood was chaotic to say the least, and I could react to stuff that was going on around me by getting so angry it could blow up into a full-on rage. He took time with me and would sit me down and talk to me – he taught me how to read and write properly, but most importantly how to keep calm and communicate with people instead off just flying off the handle.

He used to organize the football, so we had a proper team, in which I played as centre forward because I was fast and scored goals. As soon as I got the goal in my sights, I'd blast the ball as hard as I could, trying to put a hole in the goalkeeper as well as the net. Mr Pigden would take me aside and tell me about Jimmy Greaves. It still makes me smile as I can hear him saying , 'Jimmy Greaves . . . he passes it into the net. Look where the goalie isn't, and put it there. Where's the big part of the goal, Ian? If the goalie's standing there, where's the big part of the goal?'

I'd say, 'Over there.'

He'd simply reply 'Well, put it over there! You can pass it into that part of the net. *Act* like you're going to shoot, then put it in there, give the goalkeeper no chance.'

He did so much for me as a footballer, which helped me else-where in life – he taught me about playing for the team, how I *needed* to pass the ball to other people. That was all part of him showing me how to communicate properly. Like not flying into a rage was about not losing control, and he'd relate that to a piece of advice that stayed with me my whole career: 'If you blast it you're losing control because you don't know where it's going.' All the goals I scored as a professional, I seldom blasted the ball. I'd always look for another way first.

In many ways, that summed my approach to playing football, especially after I turned professional, as for me it was always a combination of natural instinct and learning from others – listening to what Mr Pigden told me, combined with my natural impulse to score goals. Once I heard Arsène Wenger say in an interview that he didn't know where I got my ability to be a great striker from. He said, 'I don't know where he got it, but I know he has it.'

I thought, I don't know where I got it from either, in the very beginning. What I did find out, though, was that to grow from being a striker to become a good striker and then a great striker you had to keep that instinct sharpened by continually learning and working at your job. It was an approach that began when I started at Crystal Palace, and it came about pretty much by chance.

When I signed for Palace in 1985, I was twenty-one and working at Tunnel Refineries in Greenwich, where my hours were from seven in the morning never finishing before six in the evening, often not getting home until eight o'clock. All of a sudden I'm a professional footballer, training with the reserves, and it's all over by about one o'clock.

The other guys shot out of the place, they couldn't wait to leave, but I didn't have anywhere to go or anything to do. I didn't have a car at that time and I'd have to wait for a train, so I wasn't exactly looking forward to leaving. I'd think, 'Just let me stay here for a bit and kick footballs.' After getting my break with Palace, after so many years of trying, I didn't want to waste any of it – they'd signed me for three months and at the back of my mind I was assuming they'd let me go after that, so I was determined to make the most of my time as a professional foot-baller. I was getting paid for kicking footballs, so I wanted to kick as many as possible! Plus, I knew my best chance of getting kept on was to be a better player after working with the club for the three months.

I wasn't sure what the form was, so I went to Peter Prentice, the guy who scouted me, and asked him, very quietly, would I be able to use the footballs in the afternoons as I just want to do some shooting? He was a really lovely man, always cheerful, smoked roll-ups all day long.

He laughed out loud and said in this gruff voice of his: 'Of course you can use the balls! You don't need to ask me that! Go and get the balls, that's what they're there for!'

It was unbelievable. For the first time in my life I had *thirty footballs* to do what I wanted with! I'd stay there until about four o'clock, just practising stuff, trying things and seeing what I could do. As it built up I asked if I could have one of the youth team players to cross the ball for to me.

'Of course you can! Do what you want!'

The next thing I know I've got youth team players practically queuing up to work with me because *they* want to practise their game too. Soon I was doing more and more as I ran through stuff with them.

Many people would have looked at that and thought, 'That's very professional of him', but at that stage I didn't know what professionalism was as I didn't really see myself as a professional footballer. I was somebody who had signed a contract and was being paid for three months, and just didn't want to sit about at home doing nothing all afternoon. Pure and simple. But it was through those extra sessions that, slowly, I discovered what it took to be a professional and it instilled a work ethic and determination that stayed with me until I retired.

I was constantly looking to improve on what I could do and if that meant working outside the regular training times, then fair enough – really, I was discovering all of this pretty much by accident by setting myself different challenges. I had two or three hours, so I'd stick at something until I mastered it, then move on to something a bit more difficult. To me it was fun, but it was changing the way I looked at playing football.

At first I used to gather up the balls and just shoot, shoot, shoot – some days I'd be kicking footballs to the point at which my legs were aching. I'd shoot from different angles and distances, I'd chip it, curl it . . . all of that stuff. After a while I didn't just want to curl it into the goal, but the side netting, then I wanted it to clip the post on the way into the side netting. I'd spend hours trying to curl the ball into *minute* spaces. I'd focus on an area as precise as four squares of the net, that looked about as big as a postcard from where I'd be standing, and keep going for that.

Golfers often say they look for the tiniest letter on the ball and focus on that, and this was the same with the squares I was aiming at. A lot of the time the ball would go just above or below or to the side of those squares, but it would be going into the goal at a pace and a height that no goalkeeper could save. You put it in the right direction and if it goes in the top corner that's even better. However, in order to get it even near that top corner you have to practise hitting really small, concise areas.

I'd whip it in with my right foot, and when that was going well I'd start with the left and in the end I'd be making things up! I'd see if I could hit the post and make it go in, or make it come out. Then trying to do the same thing on the run, or from a through ball, or a cross with one touch to control it . . .

I'd never get bored, because simply the idea of being paid a decent wage to be doing this meant it was all brilliant. I could feel myself improving, and I wanted to get to a point that I did this stuff purely instinctively. I wanted to be able to see the area I was going for with a split-second glance, then put it there without consciously thinking about it. I knew the only thing that would get me there was practising – it's like the golfers say: 'The more I practise the luckier I get.'

The idea of staying behind to work on things quickly became a habit, which I believe was down to the fact that every time I moved up a level the game would be noticeably more difficult, and I always felt, 'Oh, maybe this time they're going to find me out!' I was terrified that the man with the clipboard would stop me and say, 'Sorry, Mr Wright, your time's up, you've got to go back to work.' I figured the best way to avoid him would be to constantly do stuff afterwards to better myself and at the same time look to the experienced players for advice.

A couple of years into my Palace career, I met Chris Waddle at a Professional Footballers' Association dinner. He was flying at Tottenham at the time, just about to go to Marseille, and he told me he'd watched me so many times. He said I had everything needed to be a striker – a right foot, a left foot, I could head, I'm brave and quick. He told me finishing was the real difference between the Second and First Divisions (this was before the Premier League got going in 1992). He said in the top flight you have to finish every chance you get because you won't get nearly so many. He said you have to go for the half chances, too, because you'll be judged on whether or not you can put them away.

From that day until the time I packed up, all I concentrated on was finishing and making sure I didn't let those half chances go by. It got to the stage where I was happier taking the half chances than even going one-on-one with a goalkeeper, because the shot is far less expected, which gives the striker a huge advantage. I ended up with a one-in-two goal record over my career – I scored, on average, every other game – and I'm so happy with that.

The first, in fact I think the *only*, time I got properly found out was when I was still at Palace and played a couple of games for England, against Russia, where I got marked out of the game. I went away from those games really thinking about what I needed to do, which was to improve my movement. As it turned out it was one of the best things that ever happened to me, because in that England squad I got the chance to watch Gary Lineker close up.

He was ahead of me by a few years, but I was as quick as him and technically, I feel, I was a better player. I'd score a more varied range of goals than him, but he had something that set him apart – it was his movement that turned him into this world-class goal scorer. He told me to make two runs, one for the defender and one for yourself, and as I watched him in training games, I said to myself I'm just going to copy him, copy his runs, copy everything he did.

Seeing how hard people like Gary worked on what they did, how they thought about it and their meticulous preparation, showed me what was needed to play at that level as opposed to, well, just play. It confirmed I was taking the right approach with my extra work. I carried on with it when I left Palace and joined Arsenal.

A big factor in my never stopping learning was that I always believed I could improve as a striker because I was never – *never, ever* – satisfied with my performance in a game, right up until I retired. It's something I used to drum into my sons Shaun and Bradley: there's no performance that couldn't be improved upon – even if you score five goals, in ninety minutes you're going to find something you could have been better at. Then, if you approach every game like that, you're only going to be better.

It's only now that I look back at my career and say, 'Yeah, I'm quite happy with that!'. While I was playing, there was nothing I was happy with. Even when I scored a hat-trick . . . or when I scored four in a game against Everton in 1991 . . . I was thinking about how I should have put away the couple of chances I missed. I came off thinking I should've scored more, and thinking how I could have been among the players that have scored six in a game but I'm not even among the players that have scored five in a game, and that hurt me. I used to believe I just had to work harder at what I did, then it would come.

I set myself objectives all the time. There was a guy called Frankie Bunn, who played for Oldham, and he scored six goals in a game. I wanted to do that too. I wanted to be the only player to score in every round of the FA Cup, and I nearly did it with Arsenal in 1993. I scored in every round, including the final, except the semi-final against Spurs. I was distraught! When I scored two against Manchester United in the final for Palace in 1990, after I'd come on late, I was desperate to score a hat-trick and become the first person to do it since Stan Mortensen in the 1950s. As a professional footballer you should always try to improve, and you need to set yourself higher and higher targets.

Never being satisfied with a performance helps keep you grounded, too, as when people are saying, 'You were *amazing!*' and you know you did play well, there's still things that make you think, 'Right, I'm going to work on this bit, because I know I should be scoring those goals.' And when you watch the video, you see you gave the ball away a couple of times, it stops you getting too cocksure. Sometimes I'd watch recordings of games we had won, and I may have scored in, but I'd have my hands over my face when I'd see myself give the ball away.

I try to tell the young players, and anybody I have to deal with, that you have to set your standards to such a height that if you score three goals, four goals even, but you give the ball away three or four times, your goals could count for nothing. If they'd given those balls away and the opposition had scored off the back of them, then it's their fault they're not winning. I tell them that they have to work harder than just scoring the goals. I wanted to play a perfect football match, then if I did that, I would want to do it again, then three times and so on . . . I knew that could never happen, but that didn't mean I shouldn't have been striving to do it.

At Arsenal, even though George Graham wasn't big on finishing practice and for him it was all about the defence, that in itself gave me an opportunity – every day in training I'm going up against Martin Keown, Tony Adams, Steve Bould, Lee Dixon and Nigel Winterburn; then, if I can get away from them, I've got to beat Dave Seaman as well.

The defending that used to happen in training and the intensity of the training games were why I was able to finish as clinically as I did on a Saturday, because those guys weren't giving me even half a chance. The calibre of the player and the calibre of goalie I was up against every day – George Graham's legendary defence – were always going to be much higher than anybody else in the league. On a Saturday I'd be playing against someone who was nowhere near as tight to me as Martin Keown was being with me in training *every* day of the week, every month of the year, or someone who wouldn't be able to read the play nearly as well as Tony Adams. It was *so-o-o-o* hard to get even half a yard on them, but if they were so much as a fraction out I would be punishing them, and I was always sure that any goal I could score in training would be a goal on Saturday.

The Goalie, Dave Seaman, could be funny, because he was somebody who didn't want to dive around on the training ground. He'd do his easy saves but sometimes he just couldn't be bothered and would let in anything that required a bit of effort. Then George Graham would start shouting, 'Dave! For fuck's sake! You're spoiling the fucking session for everyone else!' All of a sudden he'd put his goalie's head on and you literally could not score, no matter what you did – you could be a yard out and you're not getting past him. That's when I knew I was dealing with a different level at Arsenal.

They all enhanced my game and made me really aware of what Chrissie Waddle had said to me about taking the half chances. Getting anything past them really took something good, and I wish the Arsenal fans could have seen some of the goals I scored on the training ground – I used to celebrate them because they were such a pleasure to score and it was an achievement I always took seriously. Then when defenders like that stop and clap a goal you've scored in training, you know it was a pretty special goal.

Of course, not all defenders can appreciate getting beaten, like the time I was playing against Sheffield Wednesday's Des Walker, one of the best defenders England have had in decades. Des doesn't get nearly enough credit for how good he was. In fact, I always scored in the next game after playing against Des because he made me raise my game.

This time I was up against him at Highbury. It was nil-nil and the game was winding down, nothing's happening, and Des had literally marked me out of the game – even for the throw-ins he got his foot round or got his head round and got the ball away from me. I did not get a touch. Then in the ninety-second minute Stevie Morrow gets the ball on his left side, he whips it into Alan Smith who flicks it on with his head and it comes straight through to me. I go *bang*, first time, and slide it into the goal.

As soon as we go back to the centre circle to kick off the ref blows the final whistle and I go over to Des and he *refuses* to shake my hand! We're talking about my mate, from the England squad, a top friend of mine, and he would not shake my hand. That's how upset he was because he wanted to make sure I didn't get a touch, just so he could say to me, 'You didn't even get a kick this afternoon'. That's how seriously he took defending, and that's how seriously I took scoring – he was forty-five seconds away from shutting me, then I got *one* chance.

After that, Des used to say about me, 'Can't leave him alone for a second – I marked him out of the game except for one second right at the end . . .'

What I used to do at Arsenal was sit down with Dave Seaman and Bob Wilson, the goalkeeping coach and one of Arsenal's 1971 double winners. They'd be doing their session with the other goalies, but after training I'd go over and we'd talk for ages because I wanted to know what would be going on in the minds of the goalkeepers when I was facing them.

Typical conversations would go like this: I'd ask, 'If you're in such and such position in the goalmouth, and I'm coming in from the right, where's the one place you don't want me to put it?'

Dave would reply something like, 'I'll know if you're good on your left foot or your right foot, because I would have studied you before the game, so obviously I've got make sure I cover the near post because you cannot get beaten on the near post if someone's on the right. If the striker has a bad left foot, more often than not they're going to blast it with their right, and if that's the case they're going to have to be very lucky, depending on where they are, for it to fly in with the angles that I'll be cutting down. If you've got a left foot, you can do anything, curl it round me, slot it along the ground . . . Because you've got a left foot as well as a right foot, you need to get it on to your left foot. But as I'll know you've got both, you have to do it quickly. If you can do that then you're definitely going to make me make a save.'

It was like a science to them!

Dave told me that goalkeepers have to, at some stage, make a little jump, just to get themselves ready. If you take your shot early, you could catch them when they're off the ground, which is when they can't make a move. When you see the ball go in the net and it looks like the goalkeeper doesn't move, when everybody watching is asking, 'What happened to the goalkeeper?', the chances are he was off the ground when the shot was taken. It's the same with penalties: they'll do that little jump to set themselves. These are the kind of things we used to talk about. Indeed, we used to talk about far more than actually do it.

Sometimes I'd put a pole in the ground, in the goal, about eighteen inches inside the post, and just curl the ball in the gap: left foot, curl it in that side; right foot, curl it in that side. I'd come in, cut inside, *boom*! All that stuff. Dave Seaman would watch me and I'd ask, 'Goalie, what about the height?'

He'd say, 'Anything you can get, if you're whipping it in. Always aim for halfway up the side netting.'

He'd say that when the goalkeepers dive there, it will normally go over them because they can't get their bodies off the ground to that height. He'd tell me, if I was through, to choose that option rather than try and slot it alongside them, where they could get a fingertip or something on it.

Bob Wilson used to give me so much confidence because he'd watch the games and if I'd scored a good goal he'd say to me, 'Ian, that would beat any goalkeeper in the world.' Or he'd analyse my misses and say things like, 'You needed a bit more on that one, that kind of finish needs pace or the goalie's always going to get to it.'

A great piece of advice they gave me was that if you're through on goal and the goalkeeper's coming out to you, at some stage he's *got* to go down, and the closer you get the more likely that is.

Everything they'd tell me I would file away in my head, and when we played Liverpool at Anfield in August 1992 I pulled up this particular conversation. Anders had scored one for us, and Ray Parlour, who was having a great game, put me in. I was so clean through I even checked to see if I was offside. I ran through on David James and he stayed up for absolutely ages! It was like we were playing a game of chicken – he just wouldn't go down and I was thinking, 'I know Dave and Bob are right so I won't let my shot off early'. I was closing in on the goal, but he still wouldn't go down, so game of chicken, game of chicken, game of chicken, to the point where I was thinking I'm going to have to knock this round him. But then, just as I was shaping up to do that I saw his body start to collapse and it finally looked like he was starting to go down and spread himself. I just lifted the ball over him, and I was so close that it actually hit the top of his body as it was going in.

It wasn't an easy finish because the ball has to be running at a certain pace – if you try to lift it when it's running too fast it'll shoot off; it's got to be slowing down so you can get something under it. I was nervous that if I had to take another touch it would be moving too fast for a controlled finish, but I just got enough under it so it lifted off. By then it was running slower than I would have liked, which contributed to me only just getting enough lift on it. When David James came rushing out like that, and he's a big guy, suddenly there was not much of the goal left to aim at – a striker could easily have panicked and blasted it straight at him or over the bar. Sure, I had the experience not to panic, but working with the goalkeepers meant I could go, 'OK memory bank! Dave Seaman's right, Bob Wilson's right, they *have* to go down.' He did go down and we beat them 2-0.

There were some general things at the foundation of what I used to do which might seem a bit obvious, but they were basics that no striker should ever forget. Number one is aim for the biggest space there is in the goal. The whole goal can look really big, but there will always be one area around the goalkeeper that is bigger than the others. I'd look for this space and try and slot the ball there. I'd rarely try and go round the goalkeeper with a bit of skill because it takes too long and the longer you leave it, the goalkeeper's already calculating what's going on, so he's got more time to work out how to stop you. I'd usually only go round them if they came rushing out too fast and committed themselves; then it wasn't too difficult to move the ball to one side and put it in the net, no messing about.

Good strikers trust their instincts. They'll learn as they become more experienced that the first instinct you have when you're put through is normally the one you should stick with. You learn that it's usually the best idea you're going to have in that situation, and leaving it to think of something else isn't going to make anything any better for you. When a striker makes it look like what they do always happens so quickly, that's because they stick with their first instinct.

I always want to go quickly, to try to make the goalkeeper go with his stock save, where he's thinking, 'He's on the right, he's cutting in, I've got this part of the goal covered.' He's comfortable going with his stock save, but while he starts thinking the only thing I can do is chip him, I've done it already. So the striker has to get his shot away as soon as possible, but at the same time not rush it! He's got to be able to know and recognize the situation – where the space is going to be, how quickly it's going to diminish and how he can take advantage of it.

When I was playing for Palace in the 1991 Zenith Data Systems Cup Final at Wembley, against Everton, I scored twice, but my second illustrates the point I'm making here. From a long clearance, the ball's flicked on to me as I come into the box from the right, and their goalkeeper Neville Southall knows I'm right-footed, so he's covered his goal for that. As I'm running through he must be thinking I'm going to wait for it to come across to my right foot to shoot across him, but before this could happen I've just flicked it with my left foot. So he's on his way to cover what he's sure is going to happen when the ball's just rolled past him from a different angle, a split second before he's expecting it. This is why there's no such thing as a stupid striker at the top level: experience and practice will move you forward, but that's nothing without intelligence.

It's not only the finishing, either. A striker needs to do just as many calculations while he's setting himself up. He'll have to work out: how to take the defender *this* way so he can take the ball *that* way, or how you make this move to come over there. It's about *always* thinking, making these calculations so you can stay one step ahead and finally get the half a yard of space you need in the box. That's why people talk about the first touch as being so important. If you get your first touch right in the box, the people trying to stop you are still committed to moving in a different way. If your first touch is really good, you see it on their faces – it's like, 'Oh shit!' – then you've got that extra split second and *bam*!

The goals I got the most pleasure from were the ones where I gave the goalkeeper absolutely no chance, when everything he'd been taught to do or what he'd been told about you as an opposing striker had been taken away from him by your ability. He would be thinking, 'I've covered this angle, I've covered that angle, I can close him down like this . . .' but your skill or intelligence made all of that useless. There was literally nothing they could do. They can't blame a defender – when you see them shouting at them at their defence afterwards, half of the time that's because they know they can't blame anybody else so they're trying to deflect criticism. You'll never hear a goalkeeper say, 'Well, I'll just have to give that striker credit for that. It was a fantastic goal – he beat me all ends up!' Never!

With those sorts of goals there's always a moment when you see it on the goalkeeper's face, when he's realized there's no way he's going to get to it and he's resigned himself to being beaten – it's there during that goal against Everton. This is just a split second, because almost immediately you see 'Who can I blame? Who can I blame?' going through their heads, when they know they can't blame anyone, they were simply beaten by a great goal.

I wanted to give them no chance. When I was going through on goal I wanted the fans to feel, 'Oh, it's Wrighty going through, *he will score!*' That was what I wanted to be remembered for: he's going to score.

A large part of scoring those sorts of goals is trying things that nobody expects – not just the goalkeeper, nobody in the ground sees coming. You need to have a combination of imagination and audacity, because it's having the front to try just about anything that leads to the really great goals.

There was another one I scored against Neville Southall at Highbury a few years later, in 1993, when a long clearance was headed on to me at the corner of the box and I dinked it twice over the defender Matt Jackson's head, first one way then the other. Then when it came down the second time I chipped Neville from just inside the box. I don't even know what made me do it because those goals were so hard to score in training, but the way the ball came down after each time I lobbed it over Matt Jackson was so perfect I just thought, 'Why not just lift it?' As the ball flew past him, he looked stunned, because that was the last thing he was expecting.

I rate that goal as one of the greatest I ever scored. It was everything I would want to be remembered for, and I was so disappointed when, on *Match of the Day*, Alan Hansen blamed the defender! He said that goal was down to bad defending. The only thing I can say about that is he's very fortunate I didn't get a good run at him, because I would have shown him how football should be played.

I vividly remember a goal I scored against Swindon in December 1993, when, for some reason, I went for a tiny portion of the goal and hit *exactly* the area I was aiming for. We were beating them three-nil, the game was winding down, I made a move off the defender and Nigel Winterburn had passed to me. I was a full thirty yards out, I glanced up and for the smallest split second focused on the stanchion in the far corner of the goal, then took my shot. It was a chip, really, and sailed over the goalkeeper to literally hit the stanchion. I looked at Nigel in disbelief, and if anybody checks it out they'll see my goal celebration looks like I'm just walking away saying, 'What the hell just happened?' I felt as if I'd willed the ball to hit that stanchion, but it was really about *trying* to hit it in the first place.

If you don't try these things they won't happen, and although that seems obvious, too many strikers don't try stuff like that because they're afraid it won't come off. Of course, they could miss, but the approach has got to be: you're a striker, and you're there to miss. Yes, they're paying you to score, but you're actually there to miss – if you score, it's a bonus. Why do you think players can go ten or twenty games and not score, but they still get picked as a striker? There's nothing that's going to guarantee you scoring, which is why those rare people that do guarantee goals get the most money. Clubs pay strikers *hoping* they'll score. My attitude towards it was, 'It's my job to miss, as long as I don't miss too many', but that was what the extra work after training and the talking with the goalies was for.

Neville Southall could have easily have been a yard further back, jumped and reached behind him to catch it or push it over, and that's always going to be the case when you try one of those chips. Like the ridiculous chip one I scored against John Lukic, when Dennis knocked it to me and it hit me in the face, then all the time after that I've got my head down trying to get this ball under control. It's finally come under control and I remembered John was a little way off his line, so without even looking up I've gone *bam* and it's looped over him into the net. That's what you do – John Lukic could've moved back while I was controlling the ball and caught it, but he hadn't. The reason why that worked is because I wasn't afraid of 40,000 Leeds fans in there who were going to laugh at me if it didn't come off. I didn't care that the goalkeeper *might* be on his line to catch it, because if he's not, it's going to be a goal that people will remember seeing.

That's what my game was about, with the chips and the cheeky this and that, the unexpected – just try it and don't be afraid to miss. That's why, when I watch a forward now who doesn't shoot in games, I'm willing him on: 'Why doesn't he shoot? Just have a crack!' What's the worst that can happen? The ball's going to fly over the bar, somebody's going to throw it back to the goalkeeper and the game goes on. Nobody ever got remembered for not trying things. Even the misses were exciting – if the goalkeeper makes a fantastic save, you get a great '*Ooooh!*' out of the crowd. Or it might smash off the post, or might blast back off the crossbar, which is always going to give people that sharp intake of breath. That's what you want as a footballer, you want those moments of '*Phwoooar*, did you see that?' I know I love them.

It was just as important to take the misses in my stride. It was easier for me because I knew the fans thought I'd probably get the next one, but when I see a striker who's obviously desperate to score, he misses and holds his head in his hands or starts thumping the turf saying 'Oh my God!' I cringe. What he's really doing is saying to everybody – on the pitch and in the stands – 'Oh my God! I just missed!' Defenders will see him advertising 'Look how that miss affected me' and know if he gets another chance he's going to be nervous and will maybe rush it. Then he's calling the attention of the crowd to his miss. Let the fans put their hands over their faces and go 'Aaaaaaaw!', that's what they do. As a striker you don't need to.

Ages ago I saw Kerry Dixon miss a chance in the first or second minute of a game, and the crowd would have thought it was offside or something from his reaction – no reaction at all! He literally walked back and may not even have shrugged his shoulders. It resonated with me because at first I said to myself, 'He doesn't even care', but he scored later on in the game with the next real chance he had and I realized what was going on: as a forward, when you miss a chance, the last thing you want to do is think about it for even a couple of seconds . . . it's like Tiger Woods talking about the last shot – after you've walked for ten yards forget it.

After the miss, forget it, look forward to the next chance and get ready for it.

With very good goals, after the celebration I'd watch the replay on the big screen if I could, just to prolong the moment for a bit longer and to be able to stand back and appreciate what had just happened. That's when, if we were away from home, you'd hear the opposing fans applauding what you'd just done, or with those goals at Swindon and at Leeds, when the game was winding down and you're more aware of the crowd, I'd hear people shouting 'Wrighty, great goal, great goal!' When you're playing at their home ground and they have had to stop and clap you for something, it's one of those things that used to make me remember that, as footballers, we owed all of the fans. I'd think that day we'd *entertained* and given everybody in the ground something they'll remember.

The absolute best feeling, though, was after a truly memorable goal, like either of those against Everton, when you heard a murmuring going round the ground. After the initial euphoria dies down, they've just kicked off again and I would be running forward, that's when you hear it, because people have finished cheering and now they're talking about what they've just seen. People who have paid their money, they know they've just seen something pretty special, and as soon as things calm down practically everybody's talking about it. We can hear that clearly on the pitch and it's such a buzz.

That, for me, is what football is about. You can't buy that feeling.

Chapter Eight

Three Lions on the Shirt

Getting the call that told me 'You're in the England squad' was surreal. Five years previously I'd been playing Sunday morning football and going to work every day. Now I was being considered as one of the best couple of dozen English players. Yes, I was scoring goals at a regular rate for Palace, but getting asked to represent your country is the pinnacle – it's every footballer's dream. After a player gets that call, he'll be sent a letter confirming it, which is when it really hits home, because then you get to see all the other players in the squad written down. Shilton . . . Lineker . . . Barnes . . . Waddle . . . *Everybody* was there on that list, and although I knew those guys would be in the squad, I could hardly believe my name was in there too. Why I didn't keep that piece of paper is beyond me.

It was for a friendly against Hungary in September 1990 and the England camp was at Burnham Beeches in Buckinghamshire. After dinner on the first day, we had to go and get the training kit. I went straight back to my room with mine and tried it on! I remember just walking about in the room wearing it and looking in the mirror.

Of course, I didn't sleep properly that night because I couldn't wait for the next morning and going out for training. Breakfast couldn't come quick enough. The warm up couldn't come quick enough. Everything couldn't come quick enough.

Then there I was, running alongside Gary Lineker and John Barnes, watching people like that in training – I was part of the England set up! The only cloud in that sky was Steve McMahon: he was really horrible to me on that first day. I was really nervous taking part in training, because even though I had been picked for an England squad I was still not far away from feeling that I was not going to be good enough in any situation, and he went out of his way to be nasty.

On that first day, we were playing in a six-a-side game and they'd picked three teams, but what happens in those games is if you lose the ball you have to go in the middle and chase it. Of course, I lost the ball quite a few times because I was so nervous and when I did McMahon really laid into me, loudly saying things like, 'For fuck's sake, who are these players?' and, 'How can players like this get into the England squad when they can't even keep the ball?' Naturally that didn't make me perform any better, and he carried on.

Bryan Robson quietly told me to take no notice of him, and while I appreciated that support, it didn't make that game any easier. I guess McMahon just thought it was the sort of thing he could get away with because I was at Palace at the time when we weren't particularly fashionable, while he was part of that Liverpool side that was winning everything.

It was just bullying, plain and simple. I wouldn't do something like that to somebody, in fact very few players would, and it was something I never really forgot.

I don't think he did either, because a few years later when I was at the peak of my powers at Arsenal and he with Manchester

City playing against us at Highbury, he had this look about him that made me think if he gets an opportunity he's going to try and do me.

Sure enough, we went in hard for a challenge, but I'm not trying to do him because all I'm thinking about is how I've got to watch myself. My foot went over, skimmed up his leg and gone bang into his groin. One of my studs has slit his penis all the way down!

After the game when he was in the treatment room with the doctor, getting himself stitched up, he called me in and said, 'Jesus Christ, Wrighty! Look what you've fucking done!'

Of course I was telling him how sorry I was, but all the time I thinking, 'Good!'

I didn't do it on purpose – there are other ways of getting your own back – but I won't pretend I wasn't glad it happened. I ran into him years later, and he told me that for a while every time he got aroused or got any type of sensation it would start hurting and he'd think of me. Even then I thought, 'Serves you right for being such a wanker when I was in the England squad.'

I didn't play in that game against Hungary. My debut came against Cameroon in February the next year, another friendly at Wembley. Just getting into the squad had been almost over-whelming, but getting to play for the first time was far greater than that.

I didn't actually cry at any point, but I remember tears well-ing up on a couple of occasions. I had to work to hold it together at the training ground, when they were calling out the numbers of who was going to start the next day: '. . . number eight Paul Gascoigne . . . number nine Ian Wright . . . number ten Gary

Lineker . . . number eleven John Barnes . . .' Everybody clapped every name that was read out, it was *unbelievable*.

At that point, after all the rejections when I was younger, when I was playing for Crystal Palace I used to think, 'These kind of things don't happen to me.' Now, I wasn't thinking anything like that, I wasn't even thinking about all the hard work that had got me to the point at which I was representing England – I was so overcome, none of that dawned on me. At that moment when my name was read out, I was just *there* and still couldn't quite believe it. It was such a strange feeling. I was very, very emotional when I went back to my room.

There was still more to come, and going to Wembley Stadium that evening was something else entirely. We went down to the dressing rooms where the kit was all set out for the next day and I saw my football boots by my kit – this was before shirts had players' names on them so it was my boots I identified. That was when it really sank in: I was on the brink of playing for England and would be on the pitch with some of the country's greatest and most iconic players.

That's when I got *really* emotional. I could feel myself welling up so I took my shirt down and I brought it into the toilets, sat down in a cubicle, shut the door and started crying. It was all too much to take.

The match itself was played on a freezing cold night – I'm sure it was written about at the time as the coldest night on record for an England international at Wembley. The Cameroon side weren't really up for it, so the reports the next day were all about how boring and uninspiring the game was, how the spectators couldn't wait to go home . . . that sort of stuff.

Not for me. I flitted around, making runs, trying to create chances and it was simply beautiful. I never ran out of breath, I could have played for ever. I would have scored on my debut, too, if Gary Lineker hadn't taken one off my toe! It was my shot, it was going in, but he got a touch on it before it crossed the line, then he kind of smiled at me, pointed to his boot and then to himself, telling me, 'That's mine!' In fact, I think he actually said it.

I didn't mind because it was Gary Lineker and I was so happy just to be there. I thought to myself, 'It doesn't matter, I'll have plenty of chances to score more goals for England.' To this day, though, I never miss an opportunity to give Gary a hard time about it.

All of it, from start to finish, was brilliant. I'd just played my first game for England, it was one of those experiences that was, literally, a once-in-a-lifetime so I just didn't want it to end. Even when I was going home in the car they provide for you, it was as if I didn't want to get there.

Being with an international squad and playing in the team is a real step up from even the top of the Premiership. Often, I think too many people outside the game – and quite a few in it – don't fully appreciate what a jump it is. Everybody there is first class, so the sides you'll be playing against will have very few weak points.

When I joined up with England back then was the only time I've really questioned my ability on the pitch, because as a striker with Crystal Palace I could usually find a way through most teams' defences. Now, at this level, I was always up against players who, at the very least, were as good as me. In training, I would play against people like Des Walker, Terry Butcher and Paul Parker *in the same team*; if I ever got a bit of joy out of that sort of defence I used to think, 'Wow! Does that mean I'm world class, as I'm going round these guys?'

When you get into competitive games at that level you really feel how good the opposition is, just because there seems to be so little on for you – it's such a step up it's easy to feel you might be out of your depth. Like when I was up against Fabio Cannavaro in Rome in 1997, when England played Italy in a World Cup qualifier. I'd played a couple of friendlies against him, but this was on another level and I honestly believe it was the greatest ninety minutes I ever played for England.

He could jump higher than me, he was quicker than me, he could read the game better – he would read the midfielder on the ball, so he knew what my options would be from the pass he figured was going to come through: 'Well, he can't run there, because he hasn't got enough time . . . he can only go in front of me and I'll cover that.'

That calibre of defender covers the bases in their minds as quick as a forward checks out his options. It was like playing a chess match against Garry Kasparov. He always seemed to be one move ahead of me, like he knew everything I was going to do so would be making his move practically before I made mine. And this is even though I had players like David Beckham and Teddy Sheringham behind me who could lay the ball in to me in places where even Fabio Cannavaro couldn't nick it. When the ball came through to me he was so close I hardly had a chance to do anything with it.

This was at a time when everybody was saying that I couldn't play up front on his own – they'd say I couldn't hold the ball up well enough, but that night I kept at it. I concentrated on my movement, stayed as mobile as possible and ended up tormenting their back four. I ran them ragged and constantly closed them down. Then right at the death I ran at Cannavaro, roasted him, went round the goalkeeper and hit the post!

I've never been pleased with games that finish nil-nil, because it means I didn't score, but if I'd only got one cap for England as long as it was for that game I'd be happy. Much later, I was doing punditry for a World Cup with Cannavaro and he was saying how hard it had been playing against me. '*Veloce, veloce!*' he was saying, '*Fast, fast!*' He was talking about how quick and sharp my movement was. Coming from him, the only defender ever to be voted FIFA World Player of the Year and a Ballon d'Or winner, that is all the praise I could ever ask for.

Because the quality is so high at international level, being in a squad is the greatest place to learn more about your own game and how to improve it. I was always watching Gary Lineker and the runs he made, but it was his preparation to making his move that was totally different to mine. It seemed like as the ball was getting to the right midfielder he was already away, he was gone, so I asked him what it was he looked for that set him off.

He told me it was a case of looking to see how much time the midfielder had, then how deep the defender who wants to stop you is. Gary said as soon as you see the build-up play start in defence you should be looking for this, so at the moment the ball goes across to the midfielder and he puts his head down to control it, that's when you should be doing your stuff. You should be making your move then, so as soon as his head's up he sees you running this way or coming that way and knows what to do immediately.

Once I understood this, I watched him do it on so many occasions. I figured, 'I can do that too', so started introducing it into how I made my runs. That, and other little things I learned from watching Gary, did a massive amount to hone my game, just to make me sharper. I have to give him credit for so much, it pretty much makes up for that goal he nicked off me in my first game.

Even on a more general level being with England improved me, because the training was amazing, the pre-match preparation was amazing – remember, this was way before Arsène Wenger. After I'd been to a training camp for the first time, I went back to Palace and my whole ethos about preparation started changing as I now knew what I had to do to be among the best.

Even as much as Steve McMahon gave me a hard time, he made me realize that I had to be more vigilant with the ball. I couldn't give the ball away if I was really going to make an impact. For sure, he could have had a bit more decorum about how he chose to tell me, but it stuck with me – I remember nagging my boys Shaun and Bradley about it, how if you want to play at a high level don't give the ball away.

I really can't understand, these days, how players don't want to go to England camps or get-togethers, or their clubs don't want them to go, because it can only improve a player's game and his attitude. When people say my England career was a dead loss, in respect of doing anything or winning anything, I just remember how much I learned about my own game through training with and closely observing Gary Lineker. Or just being around such a high-quality situation and experienced players relatively early in my professional career. And let's face it, the only thing that England have won since 1966 is the Tournoi de France in 1997 and I was part of the squad for that. I scored in it as well!

★   ★   ★

Off the pitch, too, becoming an established international puts you at a different level in all sorts of areas, particularly the recognition you get as you go about your business. England players were famous on a national level and that was a huge step up from club level.

I was still at Crystal Palace when I got my first call-ups, where I was well known locally, but now it just blew up! I didn't realize exactly how much until people started stopping their cars in the street to ask for an autograph because I was an England footballer. I'd almost instantly become so well known. Then when the Nike 'Can You Kick It?' campaign I was involved in started up, which was making Nike really cool, things just got ridiculous. People would come and block the pavement, then a big crowd would start forming. I really couldn't walk down the street. That was all because I played for England, not just Crystal Palace.

It affects what you earn, too, as any contract a player signs for a club will have a clause in it that gives him a bump in salary if he gets called up for a national squad. That will be followed by another raise when he plays his first game or makes his first start. It's because the recognition factor from the public and among the football establishment means your potential transfer fee goes up – you're an international now – you're therefore a much bigger asset to the club. You know it, they know it, other clubs know it, your agent knows it . . . so it's reflected in all your future financial dealings.

On a wide commercial level, it was unbelievable. When you're an England player rather than a club player, it means that advertisers feel safe using your name and face everywhere in the country. Like Gazza or Gary Lineker, everybody knows you, it's not just your club's fans or even simply football fans. All of a sudden you're nationwide, as you're in the England team, you're playing at Wembley and everyone in the country will be watching the game, so everybody knows you.

Back then, that was what you needed to make the big step forward commercially – there was hardly any football on television, so national level was the only real chance to get your face seen. Now, in respect of eyes on television seeing you, the Premier League is so vast and such a massive business, you don't need that stepping stone of playing for England to get yourself out there.

Once I was involved in England, I started getting offers from all sorts of blue-chip brands that wouldn't have looked at me twice otherwise – Nescafé and brands like that. It took things to another level. It didn't just affect the future contracts either, but existing commercial contracts were all incentivized. On my Nike contract, for instance, I got a bonus if I got called up for England, another one if I played, and another for every goal I scored.

Even without all that, I loved just being part of the England thing. There was a kind of camaraderie among England players you could see when you played league matches and they would greet each other in a certain way. You kind of knew they were part of something a little bit extra, something exclusive, and it was great to be in that club. That's the same even now, when I'm working for television: I go to these great stadiums and see ex-international players and I'm so happy that they know me on the same level as they know each other. They know me as one of them.

I particularly loved it when we all used to go out together on official outings, like when Graham Taylor would take us all out to the theatre, or whatever. I loved getting off the coach in the West End wearing the England gear. Everybody was so nice to you and treated you so well. It was always special because you were with the best.

However much I loved all of that, it was really just a bonus. What I wanted from an England career was to be able to perform on the European and world stage, and in that respect it's safe to say things didn't work out brilliantly. It was frustrating more than anything, as playing in friendlies and qualifiers is one thing, but as a player all you're thinking about is being at the finals.

You've got to be at the party, it's as simple as that, and to have missed out so many times is very, very hard to take.

It started in 1990, in Palace's first season back in the old First Division, when I'd been doing OK but broke each leg in the second part of that season. Coming back as a sub in the FA Cup Final, I scored twice, but because I'd spent four months more or less continually on crutches, and was only used from the bench in that game and the same in the replay, Bobby Robson didn't think I was fit enough to take to Italia 90. Apparently, if I'd started either of those games he was going to take me.

Graham Taylor didn't pick me for the Euros in Sweden in 1992; in 1994 we didn't qualify for the USA World Cup; Terry Venables left me out of the Euro 96 squad; and for the World Cup in France in 1998, when I was absolutely on top of my game at Arsenal, I got injured.

Sometimes, when I sit down and think about it, it's difficult to accept because it wasn't for the lack of trying or commitment on my part. I know I was somebody who worked hard to try to get to a big tournament. I couldn't have done any more to get there, so either through form, injury or managerial decisions it was out of my hands.

People are always saying to me how I should have got more caps – I got thirty-three – and I would have loved to have got to fifty caps, if for no other reason than to say I represented my country fifty times. I honestly believe that what I did between 1992 and 1998 was enough to prove I was at that level. Between 1990 and 1997 I didn't score less than twenty-three goals in a season and scored more than thirty for five seasons, yet I only ever started three England games in a row twice.

It's well known I had a problem with Graham Taylor. He was the manager, however, and I respected him as that, although away from the coaching the way he treated some of the players wasn't pleasant at all. He was all over people like Gazza, Alan Shearer and David Platt, but there was an aloofness about him with someone like myself on the fringes of the squad.

He'd either barely talk to us or sometimes his explanations of things were so long and so patronizing they either ended up confusing us or we'd just stop listening. Then on some occasions I'd go to the squad and he wouldn't even say hello: he'd just walk past smiling vaguely because I was in the vicinity. Too often I'd be in the squad but I might as well have not been there, as I didn't feel like part of it.

He could be offhand with others, and most people moaned about how much he talked. I know that Gary Lineker didn't get on with him and that he kind of ended Gary's England career with a shrug – *phhhht!* – by taking him off against Sweden in the Euros. After the international career he'd had, it should never have been allowed to finish like that.

I knew I was good enough to warrant a place in his squads,

but Graham Taylor and I had a few run-ins because I might have been laughing at the wrong point, or didn't pay complete attention to one of his tedious explanations. He was the perfect Yes Man for the FA, and expected his players to be Yes Men to him, which I didn't know how to do. It didn't mean I was being disrespectful, but I don't think he understood individuals.

The final straw came in June 1991 when he picked me as part of the squad for a tour of Australasia. I only got on in one of the games and didn't score in that. Then against Malaysia, I was on the bench and Gary Lineker had scored four. I was standing up, and Paul Parker looked over at me and said, 'What you standing up for? Sit down?'

I said, 'I'm not sitting down. I'm not used to sitting on a bench!'

Graham Taylor and Lawrie McMenemy were looking down at me exactly as I said it, and I didn't play for England again for eighteen months.

I believed his leaving me out of the Euros in Sweden was really harsh, and I let him know exactly that when he told me of his decision. I was at Arsenal by then, having just finished my first season there. I won the Golden Boot and at no stage did I think I wouldn't be going to the tournament.

I was at that training camp at Burnham Beeches just before the squad set off, when they whittled down the squad from twenty-eight to twenty-three. I was called into Graham Taylor's office and he straight out said, 'I'm not taking you.'

No reason. That was it.

Of course I blasted off at him. '*Not taking me?!* Why the fuck not? I've gone to Arsenal now, you hadn't picked me for eighteen months leading up to that, then as soon as I get there you pick me. Everybody said I wasn't going to do anything there because I wouldn't get in the team, but I've won the Golden Boot and you're sitting there telling me you're not taking me to the Euros? What the fuck's it all about? If I can't go after I've proved to everyone that I can be the best striker in this country, *then what*?' As I said, I blasted into him.

He couldn't say anything off the back of that because there was no excuse for me not to go, so I just got up and said, 'This is fucking shit! What do you know, anyway? Just fuck off!' And I left.

Straight away I phoned George Graham to tell him I'd been left out and all he said was, 'No problem, don't worry about it. Get yourself some rest.'

Arsenal offered me an improved contract just after that, to show their appreciation. I thought that was a real nice thing to do – with the England business I might have been a bit down over the summer, but that picked me up. I will admit there was a point at which I was sat at home watching us play poorly and thinking, 'Serves him right!'

It was because I was establishing myself at Arsenal that I got back into the England set-up. While there wasn't too much fuss made about me not going to the Euros in 1992, once I started scoring at the rate I was at Arsenal it could have been embarrassing for Taylor to continue leaving me out of his squad. As it turned out I didn't need to say anything as the back pages were doing it for me: 'Why aren't they picking Ian Wright?' headlines were popping up all the time. I played intermittently for him, but any contribution I had to make never really got going, as my scoring record was nothing like it was for Arsenal.

In spite of all the problems I had with him, I won't blame Graham Taylor for how my international career panned out during that time. Not totally. I thought the way he treated me was unnecessary, but as regards my form there are huge differences with getting on for England and at club level. As a striker, because the games are so few and far between you have to start scoring goals immediately – like on your debut. It doesn't matter how much you run around or how good your touch is because it's not like league football when you'll get another chance to score next week, your next opportunity might be three months away.

Then during that time, especially if you haven't scored in two or three games, the press are hounding you, and then they're hounding the manager for the next person to come in. That's what happened to me.

I didn't score in my first few games and Alan Shearer came in and scored on his debut – it put Gary nicking that goal off me in my first game into a whole new light. Bringing Alan Shearer in was a decision Graham Taylor made that was justified: he saw him as the future of England as he was only twenty-two.

Graham Taylor and I do punditry together quite often now, and we've had long conversations about those days, including his leaving me out of the Euro 92 squad. Back then I was a young man and totally passionate representing my country, but I've mellowed quite a lot now and understand that throughout all of his time as England manager he was only doing what he thought was best for the England team. Although I won't pretend I didn't think that at times he was being very unfair – he should have picked me for Sweden – I am quite embarrassed about that outburst.

★   ★   ★

When Taylor got sacked after England didn't qualify for the 1994 World Cup, Terry Venables came in and he will probably go down as a Great England Manager because of his handling of Alan Shearer. After scoring two in 1992, his debut year, Al didn't score for England for twenty-one months. In fact, he only scored five goals in his first twenty-three England games, but Terry Venables said to him, 'I don't care what happens, I don't care if you don't score up until then, you will be starting up front in the first game of Euro 96.' When you hear that, it's all about faith.

Al had gone to Blackburn by then and was scoring goals left, right and centre, and his strike rate was amazing, but for an England manager to have that kind of faith in you, it's a dream. I think most of my managers have had faith in me at club level, but *this was for England*. Could you imagine how Alan must've felt? He can just carry on doing his stuff knowing that when the competition starts he's the number nine, so he's got nothing to worry about and can concentrate on honing his game leading up to it. Meanwhile myself and I guess several other players, all we can think about is 'Please God let me get picked! At the very least get in the squad!' You can't relax. Venables picking Alan was justified, however, because he finished the tournament with the Golden Boot.

I was always looking forward to being in the squad under Terry Venables, because everybody spoke about how great a coach he was. Then one of the first things he did when he took over was leave me out of the squad! I got into it in the end because somebody got injured. This was naturally quite a big deal and my dear friend, the sports photographer Dickie Pelham, called me up to do a thumbs-up 'I'm back in the squad'-type photo.

I was on the bench for Terry's first match, against Denmark in March 1994. I arrived at Wembley wearing this new Versace suit I'd got, a double-breasted suit that fastened with a kind of wingtip collar, so I wasn't wearing a shirt with a tie. The first thing Terry said to me was, 'What? No Peckham Rye?'

I replied, 'No, with this suit you don't need one.'

He looked at me with something between pity and contempt and said, 'You need one with England.'

From the way he said it, I knew my days with him would be numbered.

We never really conversed too much after that. I played a few games for him, often coming off the bench, then after the Romania game in October, in which I seemed to spend all my time chasing Dan Petrescu back, he phoned me to tell me he was getting ready to do the next squad and he wasn't picking me. He said, 'I'm going to be having a look at some people, so I'm going to leave you out of this one, but I know what you're capable of.'

I said, 'No problem, as long as the door's not shut.'

He assured me with, 'No, no, no! The door's not shut on anyone.'

But it was one of those things. He just didn't fancy me for whatever reason – maybe my age as I was about to hit thirty – and I didn't play for him again.

It still burns that I didn't get into the squad for Euro 96. Maybe Terry had it in his mind that Alan Shearer was enough. What it showed me, though, was that even though the six goals Al scored were brilliant, and he scored in that semi-final, the team still needed something else, and Terry didn't have it. He didn't have it off the bench late in the semi-final against

Germany, and when the one chance appeared it was a tired Gazza trying to get on the end of it. That's when I should have been there to come off the bench, for the last fifteen or twenty minutes of extra time, and I would have scored the Golden Goal. The England fans would have loved it and we would have gone on to win that competition!

It's a pipe dream I just can't give up, because I honestly believe it was my destiny to score that goal – that it was written in the stars somewhere. *It was my goal!* Terry and I used to do a television show together and he was always teasing me about how I never failed to bring that up, every time I saw him. But it's something I can't let go of because I know it's what I was born to do.

To make matters worse, years later he came out and admitted to me he thought leaving me out of the Euro 96 squad was a mistake. But what could I do about it then?

I got on really well with Glenn Hoddle as an England coach, and not just because he brought me back into the squad but because of the way he was. All he ever wanted out of the players at an England training camp was the absolute best they could do – it was, he would say, no more than their country deserves. Every time we trained he would absolutely go ballistic if players weren't putting everything they had to give into it.

He demanded the best from the so-called best – when he'd get the hump he'd say, 'Look, you're the best I can find at the moment, and you can't even do this session!'

It was clever, because without totally humiliating anybody he was letting them know there would always be others out there, and what would happen in a match if they couldn't handle the

It really is the greatest job in the world!
© Getty Images

(top) I'm on the second row, fourth from the right.
© Author's collection

(above left) You can't go training every day!
© Author's collection

(above right) It's a tough old life!
© Author's collection

(right) What!?! You've never had a budgie?
© Author's collection

My first time abroad on a Crystal Palace trip to Qatar – when I was picked to go I didn't even have a passport! © Author's collection

With goalkeeper George Wood on a Crystal Palace trip to Qatar. © Author's collection

(left to right) Me, Andy Gray and Tony Finnigan in our Palace days – two of the sharpest, coolest brothers I've had the privilege to hang with. © Author's collection

With Jim Cannon on a Palace trip away – usually he was making my life a misery! © Author's collection

With Crystal Palace kit man, Morris Drewitt. © Author's collection

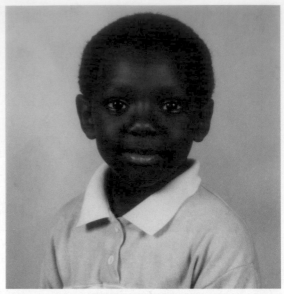

With Shaun *(left)*, just after I adopted him, and his cousin Dean. © Author's collection

Shaun has always been a little charmer. © Author's collection

(left) Even at eight years old Shaun had ridiculous skills! © Author's collection

(right) My brother Morris, always happy to be in the background. © Author's collection

Bradley's christening. © Author's collection

Gary Lineker, Rocky Rocastle, David Seaman, Alan Smith and me in 1990 or 1991, judging by The Goalie's barnet.
© Bob Thomas/Getty Images

(above) My second goal for Palace in the 1990 FA Cup Final.
© PA/PA Archive/Press Association Images

(left) On my England debut, against Cameroon in 1991 – it was said to be the coldest night ever at an international at Wembley.
© David Bagnall/REX/Shutterstock

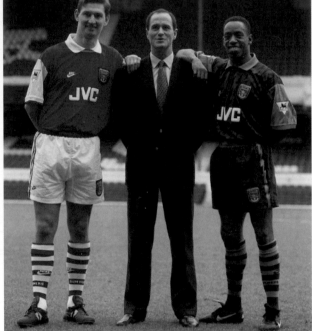

(above left) Looks like the Sunday morning football worked out OK.
© Author's collection

(above right) He always spoke quietly, but you'd be daft not to listen.
© Colorsport/Stuart MacFarlane

(left) The Skipper and the Gaffer, two Arsenal legends.
© Steve Morton/EMPICS Sport

Taking the League Cup through Islington in 1993, with David Dein and George Graham.
© Colorsport/REX/Shutterstock

I've just become Arsenal's highest goal scorer ever – of course I'm going to go nuts!
© Colorsport/REX/Shutterstock

Being applauded onto the pitch before the game – after breaking the record.
© Colorsport/REX/Shutterstock

Two boys from Brockley celebrate scoring against Southampton in 1991 – probably my proudest ever football memory. © Colorsport/REX/Shutterstock

training. He was a smart man, because it would give the players the hump in a way that meant they'd would try harder. It was all he wanted from us, a higher work rate.

A lot of people didn't like him, though, partly because he was brilliant as a player and still had all the technique – that never leaves you. There was one quite famous time when he wanted the ball put in a certain place and David Beckham just couldn't do it properly, so Glenn stepped up and did it perfectly. He wasn't trying to show anybody up. Quite simply, he believed that if he could do it and we were supposed to be the best of the best, then we should be able to do it too.

I didn't have a problem with that: we *were* supposed to be the best our country had to offer, so even if we couldn't do some of the stuff he could then at least we should be knocking ourselves out through trying.

Glenn was also clever enough to know how to play the FA's game. He wasn't one of the FA's stooges, but he knew how to fit in OK so they weren't on his back all the time. Or not until the end, anyway. For so many of us that was a like a breath of fresh air. Graham Taylor was just the right man at the right time for the FA and, with all due respect, Roy Hodgson was too, but Terry Venables was never really an FA person so you got the impression he was always under scrutiny. I don't think anybody knew what they were getting with Glenn. He obviously wasn't an outsider like a Brian Clough or a Harry Redknapp, but at the same time you couldn't look at him and say, 'Yeah, he's an FA man,'

He could take a joke, too. There was always a lot of laughter around his training camps because he knew it was good for the group morale. I used to take the mickey out of him, because

I'm a good mimic and I'd do him in the meetings before he got there. I'd stand in front of the board he'd prepared and do my impression but saying all sorts of ridiculous things, and have the boys in stitches. I'd get to my seat before he came in, but everybody would obviously be trying their hardest to keep down the laughter. He'd look round the room, roll his eyes and say, 'Is Wrighty taking the piss again?'

There was usually a very good atmosphere around his camps because he never took an aloof attitude, and he didn't want to turn little rows or disagreements into a *thing*. He didn't make anything personal, as all he cared about was the England team, so he didn't mind the fact that you might not approve of what he was doing. His attitude was 'OK, fuck you if you dislike me. All I want is the best out of you and that's what I'm trying to get. That's your problem, it ain't my problem. Now, can we get on with what we're here for?' I was all for that as a way to deal with us players.

When Glenn first came in, he spoke to me about being in the squad, and, to be perfectly honest, at that point I wasn't at my prime any more but he still gave me the opportunity to prove that I could do it on that stage. I knew who his main guys were. The difference between him and Taylor or Venables was he knew that I knew I still had something to offer at that level at some point. He was aware of my age – I was coming up to thirty-four at this point – and knew if I couldn't last ninety minutes at that level I could always come off the bench and give him a goal. He was always on at me, saying, 'Keep the ball, Ian, your movement will cause anybody problems.'

He always made me feel I was as important a part of the squad as Shearer or Sheringham or whoever he's going to start with

– and I started a few games as well. He gave me that break, and it made me feel great as it gave me back the belief that I could do it at international level.

I loved playing for Glenn Hoddle. The Tournoi was brilliant, and then there was that game in Rome, my best ever game in an England shirt. It was a game that was foreign to me because I was going to be playing up front on my own, but he kept telling me, 'You can do it! You can do it!'

Afterwards he told me I'd be going to the World Cup in France, but I got the injury against Morocco in the last warm-up game!

I believe Glenn was the best manager England have had in recent years. If he'd had the team that Terry Venables had at Euro 96, we would have won the World Cup in France.

In the end, the way my England career panned out, if it hadn't been for Glenn Hoddle I wouldn't have had any sort of England recognition. From the outside it may have seemed a little disappointing and I wish I had got more caps, but to get international recognition is the pinnacle, and I think I did enough to prove I was good enough to be there. I scored a goal against Poland when we needed to get back in the game; and those two games I played against Fabio Cannavaro and got the better of the best defender in the world . . .

What I took from it improved me as a player in many different ways; and, of course, it gave me the indescribable pride of going out on the pitch wearing that shirt.

Chapter Nine

One–Seven–Nine

When I look at Arsenal and how magnificent our club is, I feel proud to know that, whatever else happens to me or them, I'll always be able to hear Martin Tyler's commentary saying 'He's done it, he is now the record goal scorer in this great club's history!'

That is still a fantastic personal moment, and one I would never in a million years have dreamed of when I signed for the club. Back then, I didn't even know what the goal-scoring record at Arsenal was, I wasn't interested because it didn't seem relevant at that point. Immediately, I just wanted to score goals and help the team win the league again, and if I could win the Golden Boot as the league's top scorer while I did that, I would take that too.

It really wouldn't occur to any footballer when they start at a club like Arsenal they could possibly write a page in their history. They just wouldn't be thinking that long-term about something so specific. And most strikers are even worse as their concerns are so selfish: win the league and get recognition as somebody defenders fear.

It was only after I'd been at Arsenal a few years that I became properly aware of the record, because chasing a fifty-year-old record was never something George Graham was going to let me worry about. All he ever did was berate me: not making enough runs; not holding the ball up well enough; getting suspended; getting booked . . . It was when I got to 150 goals and passed John Radford to go to second on the list, it got through to me I was closing in on the record. That was in September 1996 as part of a hat-trick against Sheffield Wednesday. Then, during the next season, as I got closer and closer to the magic 179 and there was more and more about it in the press, I really started to get it, what it meant to be Arsenal's all-time record goal scorer.

When I stood on the verge, it seemed like it would never happen. I don't like to think that closing in on the record affected how I played, but it seemed I was stuck on 177 for ever! I had scored two against Coventry in the middle of August 1997, taking me up there to one behind Cliff Bastin's record of 178. Then we won the next two games, against Southampton and Leicester, but I couldn't score – Dennis got five in those two games!

After those games, when it seemed so much attention was on me and the record, I can remember thinking the one great advantage of how it was turning out was it looked as if I was going to do it at home, in front of our fans. The next game was against Spurs and I so much wanted to break the record as we beat them. That would have been perfect, for them to have to congratulate me and their fans to have to applaud – or some of them, at least! Our fans would have absolutely loved seeing Spurs forced to play that part in Arsenal's history.

But it wasn't to be. That was a nil-nil draw. I missed two good chances, in fact I'm pretty sure I hit the woodwork with one of them. After that, as if all that waiting wasn't enough, the next week there was no Premiership because of an international break.

When I went out against Bolton Wanderers at Highbury on 13 September 1997, it was the fourth game in a row I'd worn that '179 Just done it' vest under my shirt, but I knew this would be the day I'd get to show it off! The sun was shining, it was a packed house, the crowd were really up for it . . . and then Bolton scored!

It was the first goal we'd conceded at home that season and that definitely wasn't in anybody's script – Arsenal fans' or players'. It shook us out of any complacency, though, and we definitely upped our game. About five or six minutes later, Dennis threaded one of those perfect through balls to me. I just needed the finest touch to guide it on to the right, then blasted it past the keeper inside the far post. The crowd exploded, and I was so caught up in the moment I took my shirt off to show the vest then, although I'd only equalled the record at 178.

The record breaker came literally a few minutes later, and it would be great for the story be able to tell you it was one of the best goals I've ever scored, a fantastic shot or a cheeky chip, after a brilliant first touch or run. The truth is it was such a simple tap in, there was absolutely no way I could not have scored that goal.

Dennis had carried the ball into the Bolton area, while I'd peeled off and made a run to the right and nearly got tangled up with a couple of their defenders. Dennis had a shot that was parried away by the goalie, straight into a ruck of players in the box. The ball ran loose and Patrick got to it first, pushing it towards me as I'd continued my run. I was about a yard off the goal line with the ball in front of me, and this is for my hundredth Premiership goal as well as to become Arsenal's all-time leading goal scorer!

As I said, there was absolutely no way I could not have scored that goal, and the noise the crowd made as I tapped it in was unbelievable. It was total euphoria. One-seven-nine. Now I could show off the vest, so I pulled my shirt over my head and started running round the pitch. I got to about the halfway line and got buried by our players. Manu Petit got there first and even The Goalie came up to join in. It was fantastic. The whole stadium was singing 'Ian Wright Wright Wright!', the words were coming up on the big screen in time with the chant, and the Bolton players were applauding.

One of the truly great moments in my career, because I'd worked hard for it, given everything to that team and achieved that sort of reward. Everybody connected with the club was showing their appreciation.

I scored another goal in the second half, which was beautiful because the hat-trick meant I got to keep the match ball. Perfect.

After I'd celebrated the record-breaking goal with the team, I started just walking around the pitch in front of the East Stand by myself. The crowd was still going wild, and I got a bit emotional. I saluted up to the directors' box, because my older brother Morris was up there and I wanted to acknowledge him as he gave me my determination and drive to become a footballer.

When we were kids he used to tease me all the time about my footballing skills, teased me to death about how I'd never make it, or how I couldn't head or how I couldn't do this and that. My drive came from a determination to prove him wrong, and now I wanted to salute him to say, 'Look where you teased me to! Number one Arsenal goal scorer!' He loved that I thought about it like that.

My mum was up there too, which was a weird one. I'm pretty certain it was the only time she came to watch me at Arsenal – and I don't think she ever came to watch me at Crystal Palace. She was never supportive and I found it strange that she was there at all.

In that same rush of emotion, I thought of David Rocastle. This was four years before his passing and he was playing for Chelsea at that time. We grew up together in Brockley, south-east London, and I remembered when he was about sixteen, just getting into Arsenal, and we used to talk about football. I was a couple of years older but I was still a long way from making it. He'd tell me how he was getting on, and he would also always tell me to keep going. He'd say, 'You know you're good enough – don't stop.' Those were the first conversations I'd ever had about Arsenal, so now to be their record goal scorer brought all of that back to me.

That afternoon was a real mix of emotions for me. When I came off – I was subbed after my third goal – I was drained. More mentally than physically. I did an interview afterwards and was saying things like, 'Yeah, I just want to get on with it, all I want to do is score goals and score as many goals as I can for as long as I can.' Real 'footballer' stuff.

I wish I'd said more about what that moment meant to me, but I think I was so overwhelmed by everything that had happened I couldn't have been expected to come out with too much more.

★   ★   ★

It wasn't until a few years after that, when Thierry started closing in on my eventual total, that I fully came to terms with what I achieved. My record of 185 stood for eight years, and then when it went, it went to the man I consider to be the greatest player who's ever been at the club. Dennis was the greatest *signing*, but Thierry is the greatest ever Arsenal *player*.

As his total was building, people were constantly asking how I felt about my record being about to go, and wanting me to say how gutted I must be. But they simply didn't understand. Thierry is one of the best strikers that's ever played football. He's a World Cup winner, he's won the Euros, he's won the Champions League, he's won the title in England and in Spain . . . *That* is the calibre of player it took to come and topple me.

Also, I got to Arsenal when I was twenty-eight, while Thierry arrived when he was twenty-two, just about to turn twenty-three, so of course, with the ability he's got, he should break that record. I got to the pinnacle of being Arsenal's record goal scorer, broke Cliff Bastin's record even though I had played over a hundred games fewer, stayed there for that length of time, and nobody can take that away from me. It certainly doesn't diminish my achievement because I'm second to Thierry Henry.

It all sits very easily with me for a number of reasons. Firstly, because of the team Thierry played in. I'm not going to be disrespectful to players like Ian Selley and David Hillier, who was very underrated, Stevie Morrow and John Jensen, who all won the Cup Winners' Cup, but we're not talking about super-creative genius-type midfield players. It was only in the very latter stages of my time at Arsenal that I got to play in front of

Manu Petit, Patrick Vieira, Marc Overmars and Dennis Bergkamp. If I'd had four years with that level of player behind me, it would have been a different matter. Like now, looking at somebody like Mesut Özil, I see the amount of chances he creates and know if I was out there with him I'd break Thierry's record by thirty or forty goals. If I was playing with Mesut and I wasn't scoring at least one goal a game, I'd be very disappointed.

Secondly, I honestly think the record I broke and the record I set weren't nearly enough goals to be top of the list at a club of Arsenal's stature – maybe with fewer suspensions and less time missed through injury I would have put it out there. But what it said to me was there was a long time at Arsenal when the strikers were nowhere near prolific enough. I wanted to get to 200 goals for the club, and because of my age I knew I wasn't going to have much time – I blame myself for not getting there because of the games I sat out through suspension, when I should have been out there scoring goals.

I know for a fact that if I'd had another two years I would have set a record nobody would have got near. When Thierry broke my record and I made a presentation to him on the pitch, literally handing the record over, I said to him as I gave him the trophy, 'You don't want to be doing this one day, go on and put it out of sight.' His final figure of 228 goals is where it ought to be, and my 185 is a decent enough second or third.

Chapter Ten

Time to Go

I believe that through the training regime, the weights and the diet, Arsène Wenger extended my playing days by two years. The downside of that, however, was those two years weren't at Arsenal.

I'd always had it in my mind that I was going to retire in the year 2000, and I never really considered it would be anywhere other than at Arsenal. I just kind of assumed that I would be at the club, but the reality was that was never going to be.

I was nearly thirty-three when Arsène arrived, and everybody knows how he feels about older players. This was going to be a particularly touchy time, too, because he was still getting his feet under the table, and wanted to build his team his way, which meant looking beyond the next two seasons. For him, it was about that all-important progression from the team he inherited into the club's next phase.

This was a delicate operation, and a transition I simply wasn't going to be part of. He had Nicolas Anelka there now, and nobody knew how that was going to pan out; we still had Marc Overmars; he'd just bought Freddie Ljungberg; then he had Ray Parlour balancing it up from the other side. There was no space for me, not even in and around the bench.

At the time, in 1998, people were saying I'd left because of money, but that's what people always say – 'Oh, he's leaving, it's because they won't pay him any more money!' That's just narrow-minded. Although the truth was I did get more money when I went to West Ham, quite a lot more, that time would not have been the right time to leave Arsenal because of the wages – Arsène was in the process of re-doing all the contracts, and pretty radically too.

I started to read the writing on the wall when Nicolas arrived, quite soon after Arsène, and I saw him play. He was just magnificent. I'd never seen anything like it. He was like a young Brazilian Ronaldo – he'd get the ball, take everybody on and score. He could do everything: his touch was amazing; he was so fast; his physique was fantastic; he could finish . . . everything was brilliant. And he was only eighteen.

Just watching him made me feel thirty-two and I was definitely starting to think, 'You know something? I can see the exit door!' Although it didn't happen for over a year after that, it was obvious it was coming.

I could see the progression from me to Nicolas happening, and happening quite quickly, but I wasn't panicked or anything. The turnover of players was natural, especially with a relatively new manager, and I figured there'd be more coming in. I just got on with it, worked harder and harder in training and on my sharpness, worked hard on my muscles, because I didn't think I was going anywhere and therefore I had to compete. It was the 1998 Cup Final when I got wind that things had come to a head, as Nicolas started that game. I was on the bench but didn't even get on as a substitute.

It's interesting that the other big theory going around about why I left Arsenal was because, apparently, I was fuming about not starting or even getting on during that Cup Final. That's not true either and, once again, it seems so small-minded. I knew beforehand I wasn't going to start, the boss told me that Nicolas was, and I took it on the chin because I would like to think I'm professional about that sort of thing. I was desperate to get on, though, and did a lot of warming up, so it came as quite a disappointment when I wasn't used. But again, it didn't really bother me.

My abiding memory from that day was, after the lap of honour, me and Lee Dixon took the FA Cup and we went and sat in the centre circle at Wembley Stadium, looking all around us and taking it all in. The Arsenal fans were still there and that moment was just priceless. We were saying to each other how there's not many people that can do this, how this was really special stuff. That was how I finished that Cup Final. It was just so cool.

It wasn't my choice that I left Arsenal when I did. I believed I could still contribute, if not as a starter then coming off the bench, and I could still score goals. However, as much as I would have loved to have stayed, and David Dein would have loved me to stay, I had simply run out of time. Arsène Wenger said to me, 'I wish it could be different', but what I could see was he didn't want anybody to be around the place just to be around the place.

I found out I wasn't going to be at the club any more in France right after the 1998 World Cup. It seemed as if everybody in English football had been out there for the tournament and my agent and I were called to a meeting in a hotel room. Although I had an idea that things were changing for me at

Arsenal, I wasn't expecting what happened next. In the room were David Dein and Arsène Wenger, and Arsène told me, with no preamble, 'We have accepted an offer for you from West Ham.' He went on to sweeten the pill a bit by saying, 'I would love you to stay, as much as I know you would love to stay, and I know you've still got a lot to offer somebody. At the moment, however, we don't have the space for you.'

It was that clinical. I do think now, as he's got older, he wouldn't be quite so brutal about it, but back then that was it.

Technically, I didn't have to leave because I still had another year on my contract, but the way I read the conversation was I didn't have any choice in the matter. If I had wanted to stay it would have been against his wishes and there is no way that could have worked out well. What he was really saying was that in an ideal world it would be great if I could stay but this was the real world. The bottom line was he was giving me four or five reasons why it would be great for me to go and only one reason for me to stay – because you're a legend at the club.

Within fifteen or twenty minutes of walking into that room my Arsenal career was over. It was absolutely horrible. I looked at David Dein, who was in tears, and I started welling up, then I started seeing all these flashes of my time at the club running through my head. This was a really weird one: it was like how they say people who are about to die get their lives flashed before them. Suddenly I saw us win the Premier League, I saw me getting the Golden Boot, I saw goals I'd scored in important games, I saw myself celebrating breaking the record in front of the fans . . . And then it was done, literally. I left that room and I'd left Arsenal.

We went straight into another room in the same hotel and there was Peter Storrie, West Ham's Director of Football, and some other club officials waiting for us. Before I really knew what was going on we were negotiating my contract with them.

I didn't have time to properly think about anything, I was probably in a mild state of shock! I didn't even leave the building, to walk about a bit and reflect on the fact that I was no longer going to be an Arsenal player. I honestly don't know how it would have worked out if I had had more time. I don't know if I would have just dug my heels in and said, 'No, no, I don't want to leave! I'm not going to leave. I'm just going to see my contract out.' Would I have had a real problem letting go if I'd had even ten minutes to think about it?

I know that staying wouldn't have been a good idea, so I'm glad I didn't. I'm pretty sure that the idea for me to go in one room and sever the ties, and then straight into another and be faced with 'Here, sign this!', with no time to think about it, was all part of the plan to make it happen with as little fuss as possible. Whatever the reason, it worked because it left me no time at all to mourn my Arsenal career before I was officially a West Ham player.

When I play that scene back, the manoeuvring comes over as very cold, very calculated, very business-led, which it was, and it made me realize exactly how much of a business the Premier League is. Players might feel a certain way about clubs they play for, but ultimately, that is going to count for very, very little. It really doesn't matter what you do for a club or how much you love them. I signed two contracts at Arsenal without even looking at the figures because I wanted to play for the club. It was never about dollars and cents.

I gave my ankle to that club. Today it's fused and I walk with a limp because of the painkilling injections I took before the 1993 FA Cup Final. I'd broken my toe, my arch had collapsed and my ankle was gone from the wear and tear of the season. I shouldn't have played; indeed, Gary Lewin didn't want me to. I was on crutches as I travelled to Wembley, but when we got there George Graham told me to leave them on the coach and walk to the dressing room like nothing was wrong. I did and my ankle was absolutely killing me by the time we got to sit down.

I took the injections and had to wait for them to set in before I could come out and warm up. That's why I was late out to warm up, both then and for the replay. Those six injections allowed me to play and, ultimately, ruined my ankle, but I scored in both games and we ended up winning the FA Cup. To me it was worth it, and I'd do it again for Arsenal, but at the end of the day football moves on. Arsenal move on.

I came to understand that for it to end that abruptly wasn't anything personal, and there are a lot of players who've been treated far worse than that. Arsène just isn't sentimental when it comes to football and Arsenal – the way he thinks and the way he speaks about it all is as close to a computer as a human being could be, in respect to having feelings! I completely accepted that – it was just football.

In that hotel room in France David Dein, who was like a father figure to me at the club, may have been in tears when they're telling me it's all over, but as soon as he came out he stopped crying and got on with it. He brought other players in and moved on, because that's what happens.

★   ★   ★

I came back to London pretty soon after that. I didn't start calling up the guys and saying 'Guess what, I don't play for Arsenal any more' because it was announced straight away. In France I always had a lot of people around me, and the first real chance I had to get it straight in my head was on the plane going home.

I wanted to stay as positive as possible, and I was quite excited about going to West Ham. During my early days wanting to be a footballer I'd had so many rejections that they were always at the back of my mind, so it was nice to have somebody take me so quickly. I thought I might not have much time, but I still had some work to do.

The only real worries were about having to go into a new dressing room with new people – at my age! Plus, I signed for twice the wages I was on at Arsenal, and although I was never motivated by money it was a show of appreciation I really valued. However, even after doubling my money, there were still players at West Ham on more than me, which shows you Arsenal were still lagging behind. My main concern was wondering if I still had the power to go to a new club and perform at the level I wanted to.

Underneath it all, though, I was really sad. Just before pre-season started, it hit me really hard that I wouldn't be going back to Arsenal anymore. I was lying in the bath at home and suddenly tears were flooding down my face because I was thinking about what I would miss on a purely personal level. It was as simple as that. Because I'd be going somewhere else, I wouldn't be with Tony, Dicco and The Goalie and all those guys anymore. I'd been part of that clique for ages, we'd just been the Champions, all together, and it was over. Quite simply, I was going to miss my mates.

At that moment I understood how David Rocastle had felt when George Graham let him go to Leeds. He'd been at Arsenal since he was fifteen and made over 200 appearances for the first team. To be told it's all over at the club was devastating. I met him in the car park right after he'd been told. He was in tears and pretty soon I was too – Tony Adams had to come over and talk to me, telling me how these things happen in football. In that moment in my bathroom I knew exactly what David had been feeling when he had to leave the football club when he didn't want to, and how much he was going to miss us.

Lee Dixon's testimonial gave me the chance to say goodbye to the fans, though. It was over a year later. Although I had been back with West Ham during the previous season, this was different. The reception the Arsenal fans gave me and the love they showed me that night left me in no doubt of what they thought of me. It was against Real Madrid, and although I don't usually like playing in testimonials, this was Dicco's, one of my best mates, plus it was a chance to go back to Highbury, wear an Arsenal shirt again and to salute the Arsenal fans.

I came on with about twenty minutes to go and it was as if the whole crowd had been holding their breath waiting for that moment. When I was warming up and stripped off ready to come on, the entire stadium was chanting 'Ian Wright Wright Wright . . . Ian Wright Wright Wright . . .' for what seemed like ages. Then the ovation I got when I actually stepped on to the pitch, in Arsenal kit, was absolutely overwhelming. If there had been a roof it would have come off! It was such a reception that Dicco said to me, 'Thank you for letting me play in your testimonial, Wrighty!'

Because it was a friendly there was no real intensity to the match – that's why I don't really like these games because I find it hard to dial back – but I made some runs and made some moves and I had three good chances but didn't put any of them away. Now that was really funny because literally the *whole* ground started singing 'You couldn't score in a brothel!' I even think a few of the players joined in!

I couldn't stop laughing and ended up really enjoying myself because this is the only time you get to play in a football match in front of a big proper crowd and be an idiot. You can do what you like, try what you like, mess up, the fans can sing exactly what they like and you all have a really good laugh together. It was great.

It was fantastic off the pitch too. It wasn't one of those games when everybody is focused on the game itself. In fact, it seemed like everyone around the club, behind the scenes, was focused on me. It was all so relaxed I could wander about before the game and talk to people, who were saying how sorry they were I wasn't there any more, how the whole club missed me.

It was wrenching, really emotional, and although that's when I was at my saddest about leaving the club, I felt so lucky to have had that chance to say goodbye to the fans and everybody else under those circumstances.

Watching the team kick on after I left was an absolute pleasure. Mostly! When I came back with West Ham on Boxing Day 1998, I realized how hard it was to play that Arsenal team and come away with anything. They were strong and solid at the back, quick and vibrant through the midfield, pacey and punchy up front . . . they were brilliant. We only lost one-nil, but they were organized in a way that made it so tough to play against. There were a few times that afternoon when I watched something they did and thought, 'Blimey! I used to play for them!'

Oh, they were brilliant! Nicolas was in it now, kicking on and doing what we all expected him to do – I was a bit disappointed with seeing him go in summer 1999, but he went to Real Madrid for £23.5 million so that wasn't too bad. Then Thierry came in right afterwards and what was so pleasing about it was that there was an obvious progression. Every season since I left, they got better and better and better until the Invincibles in 2003–04.

In the years that followed, there was never any jealousy or bitterness that this team was hitting those extraordinary heights without me – I might have watched them and been bitter if the transfer request I'd put in to Bruce Rioch had been accepted. If I'd gone at that point, I never would have won the double, I never would have played under Arsène Wenger, I never would have become Arsenal's top goal scorer for a length of time. I didn't quite get into the Champions League era, but I won a European medal for the Cup Winners' Cup, when it was still worth something. When I left I'd done everything I'd wanted to do while I was there. Then when I saw what they were doing with Invincibles, I was very proud to think I used to be at that club and that they still thought very highly of me.

Also, I was grounded enough to know that Arsène was right, there was no room for me in that team. Watching it afterwards, it's jaw-dropping stuff – when they were beating teams, in the space of ten or fifteen minutes the score would go from nil-nil to five-nil. It was fantasy football they were playing, the kind of football that even if I was younger I wonder whether I would have been able to play.

I find it really flattering that people put me in their greatest ever Arsenal teams, but, *really*, when you look at the Invincibles, who would you drop to put me in? Would I have played up top? . . . Then where's Thierry going to fit? Would you put me as a second striker? . . . Then where's Dennis? . . . Where's Freddie going to play? . . . Push somebody out to the wing and you've got to drop Robert Pirès . . . I could easily have accepted being a squad player. I would never be able to start, yet there was Sylvan Wiltord on the bench, who scored some really important goals . . . Where are you going to put me?

Of course, I would have loved to put myself in that team, and watching them on a weekly basis I would sit there thinking, '*Oh my goodness*, how many goals could I score in this team!?' There's not an Arsenal player or former player alive who wouldn't have wanted to play in that team, and if anybody from any other team – player, supporter or official – says they didn't admire the Invincibles, they're either jealous or lying or both!

What there was with me was a degree of frustration that I came just too late, because arriving at Arsenal at twenty-eight years old I literally couldn't have done any more than I did. But then if I'd had another three years and arrived at Arsenal when I was twenty-four or twenty-five, it might have turned out completely different, and none of what eventually happened would have happened.

My real pipe dream is to have got to Arsenal as a younger man, but with Arsène Wenger there, so I could grow into my top end with Thierry and Nicolas and all of them – to have had seven years under Arsène from the age of about twenty-two. I don't care what anybody says, if I was young enough to have been in the team with Patrick, Thierry, Dennis, Robert Pirès and all the players they had got, we would have won the Champions League.

Chapter Eleven

Briefly Blowing Bubbles

As soon as the 1998 pre-season came around, naturally I felt odd as I was starting at West Ham. On a purely practical level, I was feeling almost cheated because I wasn't going to get the chance to use Arsenal's new training ground at London Colney.

The old facilities had burned down a couple of years before, so we had no changing rooms or gym and we'd been training at Sopwell House, one of those manor house-type hotels just outside St Albans. I'd spent ages training at this hotel, which was perfectly adequate as a spa, but not really designed for Premiership footballers, plus everybody at the club was talking about how brilliant this state-of-the-art complex was going to be, real twenty-first-century stuff. Arsène had practically designed it himself, and as we knew how he'd revolutionized everything else, this was undoubtedly going to be fantastic.

Now I'd never get the chance to use it – I felt I'd definitely missed out on that one. But really, pre-season was when it fully hit me I wasn't going to meet up with the Arsenal boys anymore, because I was no longer an Arsenal player.

I didn't have a problem playing for West Ham, they were a London club, my brother Morris loved West Ham, and they played a brand of football that was always pretty good – the so-called West Ham way, which Sam Allardyce used to poo-poo, but I understood what they were about.

The first football kit I ever had when I was a kid was a West ham kit, because of my brother. He had number ten, I had number eight, which is where the love of number eight came from. Really, my earliest affinity had been with West Ham, so it wasn't like it can be when players join a new club and trot out 'I've always supported whoever . . .' I genuinely had loved West Ham since I'd been a little kid.

The first thing to make an impact was exactly how advanced we had been at Arsenal – I don't want to sound disrespectful to Harry Redknapp but the diet, the supplements and the approach to training there were like stepping back in time. They were so far behind when it came to fuelling the body and preparing to play it was a shock to me – two teams playing in the same league, yet one was from a different planet. Like so many other clubs in the Premiership, they were dinosaurs.

At least Harry seemed to want to learn and he would quiz me on a daily basis. It was all 'What did Wenger do here? What were you taking there? Why did you do that? What did you go to France for? Why this? . . . What's that? . . .' He jumped all over me with the questions.

It wasn't all positive, though, because there was such a back-wardness in some of the senior staff's approach to preparation. I knew that at my age I would have to keep up with so much of what I'd been doing at Arsenal if I was going to carry on performing at the level I wanted to be at – or, more to the point, the level *West Ham* wanted me to be at.

I told them I needed to go and train with the specialists we used to get sent to by Arsenal, and they just poured scorn on me. When I asked, Frank Lampard Senior started telling me 'Big time! Big shot!' But they would have been the ones who benefitted.

Then I'm saying to them I need to get these certain tablets, and they wouldn't get them for me. Just for the sake of my own preparation I would go and see Gary Lewin and get tablets from Arsenal! I tried to keep things going like that because where I'd come from was so far ahead of what was going on at West Ham and I couldn't afford to let them hold me back.

Of course, when I arrived there were a few West Ham fans saying they didn't want me there, I was Arsenal scum and so on. I think I got a few letters, which showed how determined those people were, because this was before social media so they had to go to the trouble of actually putting pen to paper. Although it sounds horrible, it's not such a big deal, you get that sort of thing all the time when players change clubs – I got it from Arsenal fans when I came from Crystal Palace. Most of us take no notice of it.

What I didn't get, I'm proud to say, is any abuse from Arsenal fans, which was a change from when I left Palace and some idiots spray-painted 'Judas' on the wall outside my mum's house.

My first game for West Ham was away to Sheffield Wednesday on 15 August 1998. Some 6,000 fans came up and I scored the winner – that changed any minds about whether I should be there or not. Next came a home game with Wimbledon, which we lost three-four, but I scored twice, and by now they were welcoming me with open arms – it was the same at Arsenal after I scored on my debut and got a hat-trick in my first league game. I do what I do – I score goals.

The West Ham fans were brilliant towards me. They knew who I was, knew I was a Londoner, knew what I was about and just wanted to be sure that I hadn't just come over there for a stroll-about. They knew that my affinity and my love for Arsenal would never go away, either, but it didn't seem to bother them because they knew I was giving my new club my everything and really enjoying my time there.

Where it got tricky was coming back to Highbury as a West Ham player. It was a really horrible week leading up to that game, and I'm sure if social media had been around it would have been even worse, because everybody would have said their bit. As it was, it was just the papers and the sports radio shows but they made such a big deal of it that, as the game got closer, it felt like being caught cheating on the wife! Such was the emotion I felt going back to Arsenal and having to play against them, I really felt I was being unfaithful. Then to make matters worse, Harry made me captain for the day.

It was a very confusing afternoon, very emotional. Because of how close season transfers happen it was the first time I'd come back to Highbury, so I hadn't been able to say goodbye to the people who work there that I'd known for seven years. Meeting all the people there, the commissionaires out front, the ladies who did the catering, the guys who made Highbury run on a match day . . . it was very moving, and made worse because I was a West Ham player – their captain, no less – so I had to be with them, rather than wandering around greeting old friends.

It wasn't the first time I'd been in the away dressing room because I'd played there with Palace, but after all that time going down to the end of the corridor to the home dressing room, it was strange to turn into the away one now. I couldn't show my feelings in the dressing room, although the West Ham players understood what I was going through – a few of them had been through the same thing themselves.

Funnily, the whole vibe around the ground was so exciting that *they* were looking forward to the reception I was going to get when the teams came out, because they'd got a taste when we all went out for the warm up.

It didn't disappoint! When I led the team out of the tunnel on to the pitch, the reception I got was *unbelievable*! The Arsenal fans were absolutely loving me, the entire stadium was singing the songs about Ian Wright's a Gooner, will always be a Gooner, chanting my name. It was so emotionally charged I felt that at any stage I could have broken down. I know I had a job to do for my new club, but I swear that if I'd have scored in that game, I probably would have cried!

Before we kicked off I do remember thinking, 'Oh my God, if we win this game it'll be like insider trading or bet fixing or something!'

As it was, I didn't have to worry. While I gave the best that I could give, we – West Ham – lost one-nil to a Nicolas Anelka goal. And so ended what I believe to be the worst game I've ever played in my entire life.

When you first get involved with Harry Redknapp, he makes you feel you're the greatest thing in the whole wide world. Sometimes you can't believe the welcome you get. Every time you see him he's hailing you like you're his long lost brother, he talks to you like he couldn't be more pleased to see you. When he's talking *about* you, introducing you to the media or anybody else, it's all, 'I can't believe Arsenal let him go . . . He's one of the greatest finishers in Premier League history . . . still as sharp as ever . . . and we've got him . . .'

Three or four weeks later, normal life takes over and he'll blank you in the corridor, or never quite find the time to meet with you to talk something over, that sort of stuff. I liked my time with the West Ham team because it was a dressing room with an unbelievable bunch of characters in it, who kept things going for themselves. It was a nice place to be, but he was such a confusing manager to be under. One minute he'd be making you feel wonderful, then after that he'd make you feel like shit and not give you so much as a clue why. Then if you did something that apparently gave him a reason to freeze you out, that was your lot.

After I started that season at West Ham, I was doing OK and I'd scored half a dozen goals in the first couple of months. I got in a couple of bust-ups with the authorities – especially when I made a mess of the referee's dressing room after being sent off – but that was nothing new, I'd been blasting off since I was a very young kid, and although my self-control was much better I still lost it from time to time. However, I became disappointed with Harry pretty quickly.

I'd been injured in a training game, and then when I scored a goal against Newcastle in October 1998 I did a knee slide and felt as if something had gone. It didn't make any real difference, so I carried on playing and training, but I was always aware it was there. A couple of months later we were training before we had an FA Cup third round game against Swansea when something clicked in that knee and it stiffened up.

I said to Harry that I could feel something was seriously wrong with my knee and I didn't think I'd be able to play. He was immediately convinced I just didn't fancy it for whatever reason – too cold, it was the Cup, didn't want to play against Swansea because they were a lower league side . . . He got the right hump! He was mouthing off at me, really having a go, giving me all the nonsense about how I was having a cigar, how I was taking the piss. I had a bit of a go back because I wanted to make the point that I genuinely had done my knee, but that was literally it. After that I don't think he really spoke to me for the rest of my time at the club.

I played some more games for West Ham, then got injured once more and came back again, and I scored three more goals. But both Harry and I knew it was finished. At the start of the next season, 1999–2000, I got a call to go in and see him, and he said, 'Yeah, Nottingham Forest want you on loan and you can go.'

That was it. I can't even remember him looking up at me properly. And that was the end of me at West Ham.

I didn't see him for ages after that, quite a long time after I retired, and of course once more he's greeting me like I'm his best mate, but I don't find I've got that much to say to him.

The greatest thing about going to Nottingham Forest, who had just been relegated from the Premier League to what was then called Division One, was that the preparation was way more advanced than at West Ham.

This was because David Platt had not long taken over as manager. He already had his Italian mentality from playing and coaching down there – he'd really embraced the culture and learned the language – plus he'd played under Arsène at Arsenal which had rubbed off on him, so he was far more progressive in his methods. The food and the diet was something he was trying to bring in and while he didn't take it to the scientific level that Arsenal did, he was definitely on the right track. It was ironic really that I had to go from a top-flight club to the lower league to get the high level of preparation I knew was needed.

I loved it at Nottingham Forest – the people at the club were amazing; the city itself was amazing, everybody was so welcoming; the fans were amazing; and I always got on well with Plattie. He had a lot of young and aspiring players and I was going in there as an experienced old pro, which was fantastic as I was able to work with them and inspire them a bit. I loved that, and I loved the fact that I could still play well and score goals at a reasonable level. Just like at Arsenal and West Ham, I scored on my debut at Forest, but missed a penalty as well that was quite disappointing. I even got sent off in one game with them, which was really embarrassing because Brian Clough was in the stands at that game and he was such a hero of mine I desperately wanted to impress him. I was hoping to meet him after the game, but he left at the final whistle.

I was only at Forest for a few weeks, not quite two months, but I was still a West Ham player and they wanted to let me go on a free transfer to Celtic. Plattie wanted me to stay at Forest, and with hindsight perhaps I should have, but the opportunity to play for Celtic was too good to turn down. John Barnes and Kenny Dalglish were there, as head coach and director of football respectively, so I thought staying on loan would be something I would later regret.

I went to Celtic on a short-term deal, I think it was supposed to be until the end of the season. Henrik Larsson had badly broken his leg and was due to be out for a while, so John wanted somebody to fill the gap. I loved Celtic when I was a kid, Kenny Dalglish and Danny McGrain were two of my favourite footballers, and this was a chance for me to finish playing at what, in my mind, was one of Europe's biggest clubs. I loved being at Celtic, and for the most part the fans were amazing. But I couldn't play well there and although I got four goals in eight games – yes, I scored on my debut! – things turned out very badly.

It was Barnsie's first managerial post, and he'd had one of the best starts any manager's had to their career – he won seven of his first eight league games – and everything was fine. Then he lost a few games and the fans turned pretty quickly. I think they had expected Kenny Dalglish to be the first-team coach, or at least more involved, but he clearly had faith in John who he'd signed to Liverpool from Watford in 1987.

This was the end of October 1999 and coincided with me going up there. I got sucked into it almost immediately. A certain section of the Celtic supporters who had been getting nasty about John were saying his appointment was a case of jobs for the boys from his mate Kenny. Then they never gave up on how John had brought his mate up from London – me – just to nick their money. I'll stress it really wasn't all of the fans, but the minority were relentless and were making a whole heap of noise.

Then there was the religious aspect of football up there. I've never been in the middle of anything like it. I thought I knew what the rivalry between Rangers and Celtic would involve, what the intensity would be like, but I was naive because I was looking at it from a purely football point of view. This wasn't football . . . listening to songs being sung from the start to the finish of the game saying 'Fuck the Pope and the IRA', or you're in your car and people start banging on the roof shouting 'No retreat! No surrender!' At first, I didn't even know what they were talking about.

There was a vile atmosphere, fuelled by hatred, especially at the Auld Firm derby. Fans love to talk about it like it's this unbelievable thing! It's not an unbelievable thing: it's a nasty, tense, unsporting environment of super-intense religious bigotry that's nothing to do with sport. I had people say to me, 'Oh, you can't handle the atmosphere of an Auld Firm derby!' Of course I can't! I can handle the atmosphere of footballing rivalry, but this transcended football.

And I'm not just talking about Celtic against Rangers, either. We would turn up at Hearts or Hibernian or Motherwell or wherever, and it would be the same crap. It was despicable. You can't just come into that and start playing your best, but I never gave anything less than the most I could.

The press up there seemed to be very pro-Rangers, too, so journalists had so much fun ridiculing me and my so-called lack of form there. They'd follow me all over the place and try anything to get some story, and they'd write about how I was a big-time Charlie just looking for a final pay day . . . all that sort of thing. It was so petty. They even resorted to ridiculing the TV adverts I'd made! When the end finally came, they jumped all over it, writing how Scotland had chewed up Ian Wright and John Barnes and spat them out. How can I put this? Absolute rubbish!

The end at Celtic was awful, one of my absolute worse foot-balling experiences. On 8 February 2000, we're at home in the third round of the Scottish Cup to Inverness Caledonian Thistle, who were a division below us, and I was on the bench. It was a game we should have won, but at half time we were two-one down, it was not going at all well and the fans were getting on the team's back.

This is the only time I've ever seen anything like this happen – Mark Viduka came in at half time, took his boots off, said 'Fuck this bollocks' and refused to go out for the second half. He refused to play for the club he was contracted to! John Barnes was stunned and called him a *complete* disgrace; Eric Black, who was the assistant manager, was equally shocked and called him a *fucking* disgrace. But he just got up and walked into the shower.

I had to go on, but after a scene like that in the dressing room the whole team was unsettled, I couldn't do anything and we ended up losing three-one after Regi Blinker gave away a penalty.

It was like that result was a disaster – it was the game that prompted that famous *Sun* newspaper headline 'Super Caley Go Ballistic Celtic Are Atrocious'. When we left the stadium Celtic fans were literally all over the place, booing, shouting and spitting. I came out with Regi and we had to have a police escort to our cars, which were covered in spit. Then as I drove out of the car park they were banging and kicking my car, like the whole thing had been my fault.

It didn't end there, either. The kitman Johnny Clark, who had been one of the Lisbon Lions, told me that messages had come through from fans threatening me because I was laughing when I came out to my car! That really freaked me out and I told John to let them know that there was no way I was laugh-ing, especially not at them – if I was smiling it was at sheer disbelief at the situation in that car park.

We came out just behind Mark Viduka, and they gave him a hero's reception, cheering him all the way, yet a couple of hours ago we had seen him refuse to play for the club they love. It was such a ridiculous state of affairs. It was the irony of it all that made me smile as a reflex more than anything else.

It was at that point I had to hold my hands up and think, 'Let them say what they want to say, because they can't hurt me any more. I've only got a few more weeks here.'

Four months previously, I'd been so keen to come there, now I couldn't wait to get out. I didn't have to wait long. John Barnes was sacked a couple of days after that game against Callie and I was let go a few days later.

After that I was without a club, and seeing as I didn't fulfil my original dream, which was to retire at Arsenal, I thought it would be a good idea to retire at Millwall, the first football team I fell in love with.

I got in touch with them and asked what would the chances be? I told them I only had two or three months left, I didn't want any money for it, and I didn't expect to start any games. Just sit me on the bench and if you need me for ten or fifteen minutes to get a goal, I'll come on, I just want to finish my career at Millwall. Of course, they said no. I was told it was Theo Paphitis, who was then the chairman there, had the final say, but I just said, 'Fine!' It was an off-the-wall idea anyway, and I didn't have to wonder what to do for too long because Stan Ternent, the manager at Burnley, gave me a call.

I knew Stan from back in my Crystal Palace days when he was Steve Coppell's assistant – in my most successful period at the club, coaches Ian Evans and Alan Smith were fantastic to me when I got in to the first team, but Stan Ternent was awesome. He was this confident, funny, good-looking north-ern bloke who had a real swagger about him who absolutely adored me and I adored him.

Burnley were well up in Division Two, pushing for promo-tion, and he said to me, 'Ian, I've got a good bunch of lads here, I think the way you are that if you come into this dress-ing room you might just be the little boost we need to just push us into the play-offs, or maybe even into going up automatically.'

It helped that Mitchell Thomas, the former Spurs player and my best friend in football, was already there. As soon as Stan asked, I agreed.

It was fantastic from the moment I arrived. Of course, the conditions, the ground and even the town itself were like going from colour to black and white compared with London and Arsenal, but the people were brilliant and everybody around the club was too. In the dressing room it was typical old-school, with lads like Ronnie Jepson, Paul Cook, Chris Brass, Micky Mellon, Paul Crichton the goalkeeper . . .wonderful people . . . and, of course, Mitchell Thomas.

I'd spent the vast majority of my professional career at the top level – England, Arsenal, Palace in the First Division – being treated so well, then all of a sudden to come out to this was actually refreshing and I knew I was only there for a few months. These were players that were not going to reach to the heights that I had, but they were hard-working, brilliant, unbelievable professionals who gave everything . . . They were real! I had nothing but respect for them. We finished up getting promotion to Division One because they were good enough and they were totally prepared to put in the effort that was needed.

I had to tell Stan not to start me, as I found that very hard because I couldn't get to the pace, so he ended up using me for the last quarter of an hour or so. That worked much better. I scored a few goals for them, including a couple of important ones that helped them on the way to going up, but I didn't score on my debut!

Stan let me do what I liked in terms of training, and I knew what I needed to do in order to be able to sit on the bench there, but as regards to what I ate it was a totally different matter. As you'd expect, Burnley was still very old-school about nutrition, and I was actually quite grateful for that. I felt at that stage and at my age I'd kind of had enough of all that stuff and just wanted to relax a bit in the last few weeks of my career.

I'll admit it – I did take advantage of my situation at Burnley and I was like a spoilt kid! The boys in the team knew that I was just taking the piss, but not disrespecting them, and because we were winning and I was doing what I'd been brought there for, it was all cool.

I'd have a laugh with Stan too. Once I went to his house and he had these boxes of chocolate truffles put out. I bit into six or seven of them – I'm not sure I really liked them – replaced them in their lovely individual containers, and then put them back in the boxes. Later, he called a family meeting about the truffles with his wife and sons Chris and Danny, who were all fantastic people. He went mad: 'Who's done this to my truffles?!'

They told him, 'Ian! It was Ian did it when he was here the other night!'

At training, I told the lads what I had done, just before he came in screaming 'Wrighty, you fucking bastard!'

I had so much fun at Burnley!

The crowds down in that league were something else too. Apart from maybe an FA Cup game against a top team, this was the level of football they were going to watch for the majority of their lives, yet they would still turn out to watch every other week and they would still love their team. That made me think about how much I loved the game.

The abuse from the crowds down there was a definite step up from the Premiership, in terms of intensity and invention. Yes, it could be intimidating at times and a lot of the abuse I got was racial – when I was warming up at Blackpool was particularly horrible. I'd half forgotten that football fans could be like that, and really it wasn't too important, it was just what they did. Our fans abused other teams and they loved us; other fans abused us but loved their teams. It was passionate – I don't think racial abuse should ever be called 'enjoyable' but the whole charged atmosphere in that league, at every game, was genuinely refreshing.

As I knew I only had a couple of months of it, my attitude was to suck it up and appreciate how fortunate and how happy I was that I didn't take the level I'd played at for granted. That I worked hard to make sure I had stayed at that high level. Now I was at Burnley, doing an old mate a favour, and in my head I was in a really wonderful place.

I remember thinking that I had done everything I wanted to do in football and now I'm here at Burnley for Stan Ternent, and I'm going to run up and down this line warming up because he wants me to and he might need me to go on and do something for him. Any amount of abuse from those fans couldn't hurt me. I was about to finish the season getting promotion. And then I was going to stop. It was perfect. In those last few weeks nothing could have spoiled what I felt.

Stan said to me, at the end of that season, 'Ian, just give me one more season! Please!'

I had to tell him, 'Stan, I can't do it, mate. I literally cannot do it. I've had enough. I can't play any more football.'

I'd always planned to retire in 2000, whatever club I was at, because I was thirty-six years old and had had fifteen years as a professional. Ever since I'd left West Ham I knew I was in the last furlong. I'd just won promotion with Burnley, so I was going out on the up, I'd got ovations at some grounds because they knew I was retiring, and I felt like I'd truly done my bit.

I'd played for four clubs in the one season, which must be some sort of record and wouldn't be allowed today, and the interesting thing about that was I'd done my declining years all inside the same twelve months! I didn't feel like I was one of those players who moves down the divisions over the years and people start saying, 'Look at him, he's just not good enough any more, he's fading down.' In the end I really didn't fade down – I started that season at a Premier League club, then ended the season at a club that was about to move into Division One – not too much of a drop. True, there were my adventures at Forest and Celtic in between, but because it ended up like it did, rather than any sort of demise it seemed to me a case of, 'Yeah, this is it, the curtain's coming down and I'm going out on a high.'

I never ever felt like I'd gone on too long because during the previous season at West Ham I was still playing for England

– Glenn Hoddle called me up when I was thirty-four – and Stan had offered me that extra year in Division One. Physically, I know I could have done that last year. My ankle was aching and I would take longer to recover, but I knew I still had it in me to do one more season starting from the bench. Easily.

But I knew it was time. Mentally, my career as a professional footballer was over. I was satisfied with my lot, too. I was so fortunate to know I had played football at the top level for so long, won what I had won, represented my country, scored the goals that I had and left a lot of memories for people. I probably felt this more acutely because it took me so long to get started as a professional.

Now this stage of my journey was coming to an end, and I was completely content with that.

Part Two

An Incredible Journey

Chapter Twelve

School Daze

I liked *going* to school, actually being there, the banter, being with friends, rolling with the crowd, playing football in the playground . . . stuff like that, although I wasn't what you might call fully committed to the academic side of things. There were some classes that I just got and when I contributed to them I was pretty good; others that I really didn't engage with – I was OK in English, for example, yet in maths I was pretty slow. I wasn't particularly terrible at anything, not that great at very much either. In the main, it didn't really happen for me at school.

At that age, like so many other kids, I don't think I realized the importance of working hard to get the most out of it, so I was good at the subjects that came naturally, not so much if something required effort. For example, I was brilliant in French because I've always been a good mimic, so I could do the accent. I got 87 per cent in a French exam once and I can clearly remember the teacher, Mr Bishop, naming the top kids in the class. He read out the numbers three and two, saying how well they'd done, then said, 'And in first place, Ian Wright!' The whole class were like *What?!* For me to come top in anything would have been unheard of before that!

We used to have to do this little French cartoon character called 'Pmf' – you pronounced it *poomf* – and I just got it! I got it! He used to say words in the accent, and I could repeat them back. I could do the months – *janvier, fevrier, mars, avril* . . . and the counting – *un, deux, trois* . . .

At Arsenal, I used to talk a bit of French with Patrick and the others: *Comment ça va, Patrick? Ça va bien?* I can still speak a bit of French, and if somebody tells me the words I can say them properly. The same with Italian. Because I go there quite a lot, I can mimic the accent and people think I'm much better at it than I actually am.

Sometimes at school, though, I could get it terribly wrong. Once, in the first year, I had been talking in class too much and I got sent to the Unit, which was the classroom where the disruptive kids were sent for periods of time. There were all different ages in the Unit, because kids from every school year could be sent there, so for me, as an eleven-year-old, the lessons could be quite grown-up. This time they were having a discussion about Jesus, and wondering whether Jesus was a homosexual because he only had men around him and no women. I didn't know what homosexual meant, but I kind of absorbed what was being said.

A couple of days later, I was back in the regular class and we were doing religious studies. I was not really taking much notice, then all of a sudden I thought I knew what they were talking about – Jesus. Because of what I heard in the Unit, I felt I could contribute in a pretty grown-up way. I put my hand up and asked, 'Sir, was Jesus a homosexual?'

That's when I learned another new word – 'Blasphemy!'

He literally dived from behind his desk to get to me. He grabbed me, totally aggressively, and dragged me out of the class up to the headmaster, shouting 'Blasphemy! Blasphemy!' For me, it was one of the most confusing things, because I thought I was actually contributing to the class and he turfed me out.

It was things like that, when set against being good at French, that contributed to me not really making the effort in school. Good or bad things just seemed to happen, so I thought whatever I did wouldn't make any difference.

I did learn a few life lessons at school, one of which was about being brave. A few of us came late to Mr Giuseppe's class: me, Nathaniel Small, Anthony Small (who weren't related), Chris Dyer and a couple of others. I think we'd been smoking, which of course he knew about, and he told us we could have detention or we could get the cane.

To a man, or maybe that should be 'boy', we said we'd have a detention, except Nathaniel Small who said, 'I'll have the cane, please sir.'

Everybody was stunned but Mr Giuseppe let him off: the rest of us had to do detention while he got nothing.

Obviously the teacher was testing us, offering the choice between ten or fifteen seconds of quite excruciating pain or an hour of sitting in a classroom after school when you could or *should* be doing better things, and he was going to reward the bravery. Really I think it was about not being scared to take the uncomfortable option.

It wasn't as if Nathaniel was some sort of nutter. He was just a really funny, really cool guy, For him, at age eleven or twelve, to make that decision to take the pain rather than be kept in, I thought it was fantastic. I should have taken the cane too, but I wasn't brave enough, and since then I've wanted to get into a position where I could test myself again because I still wonder if I would show courage.

I do quite a bit of work with our armed forces, and I go to the Military Awards where I meet people who have literally put their lives on the line and lost a limb for other people. Those are truly heroic acts. Would I be one of those people? I'm not sure, but I know my friend Nathaniel Small would be.

I know I probably should have done better at school. Teachers, particularly Mr Curzon at Samuel Pepys Comprehensive in Brockley, were always saying, 'One day you'll regret not paying attention at school.' And they were right.

I regretted it as soon as I left school because it looked like I was going to be doing manual labour for the rest of my life. What the teachers were really saying was if you work hard now it'll be much easier later. Even though I went on to play professional football at the highest level, not paying attention at school is my biggest regret.

After I finished playing I'm sure I would have made an easier transition into television if I'd been better educated, and I really believe I would have been more confident in general. I've drummed it into my kids, and the kids I meet when I do things at schools: pay attention to your teachers.

The truth was, I did just enough to be able to go to school to do sports. I played cricket and basketball as well, but really it was all about football for me. At Turnham, my primary school, I played my first organized games – or as organized as any little kids can be – and started as a striker, simply because I could run the fastest.

When I was about six, that's when I met Mr Pigden, who not only gave me my first football coaching but was a fantastic teacher and became a real mentor to me. I can honestly say that if he hadn't worked to put me on the straight and narrow, I wouldn't be the person I turned out to be.

The same happened when I went to secondary school. Mr McCarthy, another brilliant teacher, helped me with my football and mentored me through adolescence. These guys were like surrogate fathers to me.

Ernie Hutchins, who I played Sunday football with at Ten-em-Be, was another big influence; then Steve Coppell and Ron Noades between them at Palace; David Dein at Arsenal; and Dennis, who although younger than me was so much more sorted. I am certain that because my dad left before I was two, I was always looking for a father figure and these guys filled that gap for me. Once again, they made me realize just how much I'd been missing that sort of positive male influence.

Outside of school I used to play football all the time, in the flats, at Honor Oak sports ground, anywhere ... When we didn't have school, we'd have these epic games of football that went on all day, starting about nine in the morning with kids turning up. We'd be saying, 'OK, we'll have him, you can have the next one comes along.' At their height there could be thirty kids on each side and we'd have to move the jackets and bags that were the goalposts further back to make the pitch bigger.

Those games were mayhem: the fat kid would be in goal; there were always arguments about whether the ball went over the post or in the goal; the best player was the fastest runner and everybody on both teams used to chase the ball! It looked like a swarm of bees because there would be this moving wedge shape behind the fastest runners.

Everybody wanted to score goals – that's probably where I got my greed for goals from – so if you got the ball you'd try to keep it for as long as you could, running away from the pack and trying to get to the opposition's goal. Sometimes you'd be so caught up you'd be going in the wrong direction!

About five o'clock, kids would go in for their tea and the game would wind down by about half past six. Then you'd get up and do it all again the next day. Those games were amazing, and we'd never get tired.

All that little kid football was hilarious. At Samuel Pepys, there was this tiny kid who used to play in goal, which was unusual in itself, but he was so small he couldn't take the goal kicks, so Mr Pigden used to get the biggest guy out of all of us, Michael Herald, to take the goal kicks. Mr Pigden used to teach him how to toe-poke it from the edge of the six-yard box, sometimes he'd catch it right and it would literally fly, other times it would just dribble to the edge of the area and there'd be a mad scramble to get to it. This is how football should be played when you're a kid, a bit mad, but you enjoyed yourself so much. It was brilliant!

Often me and my mate Conrad Marquis would get left on our own on the estate because everybody except us had bikes. They'd go riding all over the place – they'd leave in the morning, not come back until the evening and tell us they'd ridden all the way to east London. So the two of us would play this game called 'goalie-to-goalie' in the communal areas of the flats. There were these concrete poles for people to hang washing lines in between, and they made *excellent* goal posts.

I would be up one end and Conrad would be at the other. One player would take a shot, and the other then had to get to the ball, bring it down and shoot from wherever the ball was. No dribbling or moving it towards the other goal, so if the player was far away and didn't get back to his goal in time, the other one could have a quick shot and maybe score. It was a great game for just the two of us, and we could play goalie-to goalie the whole day. Literally.

Another football game we used to play at school was called 'boots', and to me it seemed like prison football! I don't know why – at that point I hadn't been to prison. It was played in this long stretch of the playground that was like a corridor with a fence on one side, and you had to move the ball around quickly.

People would blast it at you and if it touched you and went in the air and over the fence, you would seriously get the shit kicked out of you until you could jump over the fence to get it. Those were the rules: it happened to whoever had the last touch before it went over the fence. You had to run for your life to try and get over the fence before you got caught. Sometimes I'd be playing out there but wouldn't want to get near the ball.

Apart from when I've played in finals, the only times I've had butterflies playing football is when I was playing boots. It was kind of a good laugh, though, and definitely taught you to keep the ball low.

As a kid, I'd play football anywhere, all the time. Although I loved playing, this was as much about not wanting to go home. I'd stay out all day, I'd go round other people's houses, hang about at school . . . *anything* so I didn't have to go home.

The only word to describe my home life is 'horrible'.

Life at home wasn't always bad. I was born in Woolwich, south-east London, in 1963. Things were more or less OK until we moved to Turnham, on the Honor Oak Estate in Brockley, when I was about six or seven.

In the beginning there was just my mother, me and my older brother Morris in Turnham. My dad had moved out when I was about eighteen months old. I didn't really miss him because I didn't really know him. I still don't know him, even though I used to see him from time to time. Around the time of the move, my stepdad moved in. He was a really big-built, rough-speaking, hard-gambling, raving, weed-smoking man, and I was frightened of him. Right from the start he made it obvious he had no time for me, although he wasn't so bad to Morris.

Then my oldest brother Nicky, who had stayed in Jamaica when my mum came over, arrived in London to live with us. He was fine, but he was like a stranger to me as he was ten or eleven, almost twice as old as me, and Jamaican, so I didn't have any real kind of bond with him. Even now we don't have much of a connection, although I looked after him as much as I could later on.

The biggest problem for me when Nicky came across was the sleeping arrangements. Morris and I used to sleep in the same double bed, but then Nicky was put in it as well and I was moved into the middle. It was awful! If I touched one of them, he'd give me a dig; if I touched the other, he'd give me a dig; so I'd have to sleep practically rigid with my arms stiff by my sides. Sometimes I would go into my mum's room and try and sleep in her bed or on the floor in there. She'd just shout at me to get out and go back to our room, so I'd end up sleeping on the floor in there.

When my sister was born to my stepdad, things really started to go the wrong way. She was horrible. From when she was very young she'd get me into trouble all the time because her dad obviously favoured her over the rest of us. Dionne and I would be in a room, and if I had something she wanted, she'd start screaming. He'd come in and instantly, without even trying to find out what had gone on, shout me down or give me a clip. Then she'd start yelling, he'd shout even more and I'd start crying. At one stage, I got hit or I cried every single day. Dionne never really changed either. She's still vindictive and selfish, only out for what she can get, and I have very little to do with her to this day.

My stepdad was just a nasty bully, who sit around smoking weed all day long and was abusive to all of us except his daughter. He knew Morris and I loved football but he wouldn't let us watch *Match of the Day*. We slept in the same room as the television, so we'd be in bed and he'd make us turn towards the wall so we could hear it but not see it. That was horrible for us little kids.

I was talking to Morris about it not so long ago, and he said that when he sees me on *Match of the Day*, he thinks back to how hard I used to cry when I wasn't allowed to watch it.

My stepdad had this really aggressive look he did to intimidate us kids. After he'd chastised us he'd start staring at me in this way. He'd keep it up for so long that I'd get really scared and look away, then when I looked back he would still be staring. It wasn't a nice time.

He was abusive to my mum, too. He used to rough her up, which was horrible, obviously, but worse because my mum is very small. He's around six foot two and my mum's five four, and he was really rough to her. I hated him for that. It used to scare me, and when he started on my mum Morris would cover my ears or take me out of the room to try and shield me from it. We saw my stepdad recently, and he was now looking very frail and weak but I felt nothing . . . I have no feelings for him at all, just like I have no feelings for my sister.

During all of this. my mum started drinking those purple cans of Tennent's Super – a very strong lager. She'd get drunk and she'd be horrible and abusive to us. The first time I heard the word 'termination' was when she used to shout it at me, telling me that's what she should have had. I didn't even know what it meant, but I could tell she was being really unpleasant.

I don't know what she used to say to Morris, but she used to tell me that he was her good son, that he was her favourite. My mum could be so nasty to me. When I was still very young, one of my mates, Errol, was at our place and said to her, 'Why are you being so horrible to him? One day he could be the one looking after you.'

If a young kid comes out and says something like that, you know how bad it must have been. But my mate was right: I was the one who ended up making sure she never had to do anything again.

She didn't take any interest in what I did at school, and she never encouraged me in football. In fact, it was quite the opposite – she'd dismiss my interest in football, telling me I was wasting my time, that I was never going to make it. Her favourite saying was 'Many are called, few are chosen', which, after I was a success, she claimed she was using to encourage me, but that wasn't true. It was to tell me I had no chance. When I was going to my trials at Brighton & Hove Albion, my mum would see me off by coming out on to the balcony and shouting that phrase at me as I left the block. That wasn't encouragement.

For a long time, I didn't realize that my early years were different to anybody else's. Yes, I was unhappy at home but I just thought that was the way it was. Then I realized what was different. I noticed it when I saw other kids with bikes and we weren't allowed bikes because my mum couldn't afford it. First of all, I thought, 'Fair enough', but then I saw it in a way that a little kid could understand: so-and-so's mum had two jobs, and their dad had a job, so they had bikes! When we were very young my mum worked, but once she started drinking she couldn't. While my mum drank my stepdad did nothing but smoke weed and gamble. I started to resent them because it seemed like they weren't making the same effort other kids' parents were.

Morris always did his best for me. He looked after me as much as he could, even though he didn't really want me being around him too much. He didn't want me to embarrass him – I was his kid brother after all. I idolized him. *He* was the one that made me. He was a natural footballer – he could kick with either foot, he could head, he could do anything – and he used to tease me all the time about not being any good.

I just wanted his acceptance. I just wanted him to say, 'Yeah, you're good', so I used to try harder and harder. He'd never say it, even though I could see he was proud of me when he used to take me to football tournaments and I'd score five goals and be Player of the Tournament. Or when we went to visit our cousins in Hatfield and they used to call me Little Pele. What was so important to me, though, was that he used to take me to all these things when I'm sure he wanted to be doing something else.

But he teased me forever! The first time I played on the same team as him was down at Ladywell playing fields against a school called Fairlawn, and we beat them four-two. I think I scored, but he scored an unbelievable goal in that game. After all the goals I scored throughout my career, when he watched them on *Match of the Day* or Sky, he'd always say, 'It was good, but it wasn't as good as my goal against Fairlawn!' That was until I scored that goal against Everton!

Good as Morris was to me, from time to time he used to remind me that he was my older brother, like when we'd play football on the estate. I wanted to play football all the time, but my trainers would get smashed up, so sometimes I'd have to stay in the flat as I didn't have any trainers to wear. When we used to get new trainers, Morris would have two pairs because his old ones were still wearable – they would never get as smashed up as mine. He'd let me wear his old ones to play in so I wouldn't get in trouble for scuffing up the new ones. If I was giving it too much or getting leery or scoring against his team, which was starting to happen more and more as I was getting better and better, he'd say, 'Get upstairs and take my shoes off. Watch from the balcony!'

He'd do that to me just to put me in my place, and I'd have to stay up there for twenty minutes before he'd let me wear his shoes again. He'd never leave me up there for too long, but while I was playing sometimes I'd try not to do too much to make him upset with me!

At home, Morris was really good to me and I'll look after him until the day he dies.

Now I understand my mum a lot more. She was very young when she came across from Jamaica and I'm sure this wasn't the life she saw for herself, as all of a sudden she's bringing up four kids practically by herself. She must've been overwhelmed and started to feel sorry for herself.

It couldn't have been easy for her, but at the same time there was not a nice atmosphere around the home and I know it affected me. When I was playing I went to counselling for anger issues, and so much of what was wrong was put down to my childhood and how my mum treated me. It was why I used to act up at school too.

I don't know how I feel, really, because I love my mum and I wouldn't let anything happen to her, but I can't forget what it was like when I was a kid and now I suppose I'm hardened to certain situations . . . but you need affection. My defensiveness is something that my wife has helped me get past. Sometimes people just need a hug!

Football took me out of that home environment. I'd found something I was good at and other kids seemed to respect me for, but I wasn't properly hooked on it until I went to watch Millwall play. Every other weekend, I used to get sent to stay at my Aunt Sally's in Deptford, I suppose to give my mum a bit of a break. I started going around with my mate Patrick Dyas, and we started to go to Millwall.

The first thing I thought was how big the pitch was. I couldn't believe it, it felt like it went on for ever! I thought, 'How are they going to run across that?' I can't imagine what it would have been like if I'd seen Wembley. There was the noise, the speed and size of the players, the sounds from the tackles and the shots, the crowd swaying and shifting . . . for me it was the most exciting place I could have been and there, at the centre of it, was football. That was it, I was hooked.

The Den could be a confusing place. The crowd used to pass us over their heads to put us down the front because we were so small, and they'd be really concerned that we were OK. Then they'd spend the whole game hurling out really horrible racial abuse at players and talking among themselves about 'black' this and 'nigger' that. Then they'd look down to make sure we could see and we weren't getting crushed!

I'm not sure I knew what racism was at that point, but I must have subconsciously realized it made no sense.

It was there, at the Den, that my real deep love affair with football really kicked in. Forget wanting a bike, forget *anything* else. All I wanted to do was get to Aunt Sally's so I could go to Millwall.

Chapter Thirteen

Teenage Kicks

I left school when I was fourteen, about to turn fifteen, and to call it 'leaving' would be exaggerating. It was nowhere near as formal as that – I just stopped going. I didn't do the mocks because I hadn't done any revision; and if I hadn't done the mocks then they wouldn't let me do the actual exams, so by then I saw it as all pretty pointless and I simply didn't turn up any more. I'd bunked off a lot in the months beforehand, so I doubt if any of the teachers even noticed I wasn't there anymore. What sealed the fact that I had really left was when I got a job.

At the time I was going out with a girl called Andrea, who lived next door to a guy who was a plasterer and had said he needed a labourer.

I said, 'I'll do it.'

He told me, 'Fine, come on Monday and I'll pay you fifty pounds a week.'

That was it. I got there at eight o'clock and at ten past eight three yards of ballast turned up – that's three cubic yards of small stones to be mixed into sand and cement to make concrete. It was dumped by the road, and I had to bring it all in with a wheelbarrow, then mix it with the cement for this guy. I wasn't yet fifteen, and this was my first day at work! I used to come home utterly exhausted, but this was it, I'd made my choice.

This is why I was never scared to work hard later in life, because I knew what *real* hard work was. I must have tapped into some sort of work ethic that hadn't developed when I was at school – and didn't exist in my home life either.

I knew I had to have a job because I didn't want to run with those guys that steal Mars bars and steal people's bikes and just wander around all day long getting into mischief. That wasn't me – I was always too frightened of the consequences to go through with any sort of stealing.

When I was much younger, for a dare I had to nick a Mars bar from the sweetshop down the bottom of St Norbert Road in Brockley. I tried to steal it but I was physically shaking I was so frightened, and as I was coming out the hand came on to my shoulder. The shopkeeper sat me in a room at the back of the shop and just left me there. I was terrified, I was tiny and I was bawling my eyes out.

After a while he just let me go, but that cold fear of what might have happened to me after I got caught has always been somewhere in the back of my mind keeping me on the straight and narrow, which often wasn't as clear-cut as it might sound.

Petty crime was all around me – this isn't a particular reflection on where I grew up: it's pretty much all around every working-class teenager growing up in London and the pressures can be intense.

When I was fourteen I left home, it just got too much to cope with, being in the same flat as my stepdad and stepsister, and I went to live with a mate of mine and his mum on the North Peckham estate. He was a lovely guy but he was a serious crook even at that age. He was in and out of Stamford House, a kids' prison in Hammersmith. One day he came home with fifteen hundred pounds! He was thirteen and it was like we were millionaires – we went shopping for bomber jackets, jeans, pointed shoes . . . then, in all our nice new gear, we went down Lewisham Way Boys' Club, acting like big shots.

Hanging out with him and his guys, they wanted me to do some stealing as some kind of initiation. I wasn't at all keen but I didn't know how to say 'No' so we got on a number 12 bus to go miles away from Brockley, to Harlesden in north-west London. There was a C&A store on one side of the road and another big shop on the other. He told me to go into C&A and nick one of those jackets that had a suede front and woollen sleeves. He was going into the other shop and he'd meet me back there in fifteen minutes.

I went in and just hung about crapping myself. Obviously, I didn't nick anything. I don't know how long I was in the shop for but when I came out he wasn't there. I waited around for ages but he didn't turn up, and because he had all the money I was left in Harlesden without a penny in my pocket. Or the first clue as to how I was going to get home.

I set off walking the bus route because I couldn't think of any other way to approach it. Pretty soon I realized I would still be walking a couple of days later, so I stopped this old Indian lady and told her I was lost, I couldn't find my big brother and I had no money to get on the bus by myself . . . I didn't really need to lay it on because I really didn't know what to do! She gave me five pence, and that was enough money for a child fare back to Peckham – I must have been an adult fare by then, but I was so small nobody was going to question it.

When I got to his flat, everybody started cheering and jumping up and down. People were saying, 'Oh God! We thought you'd be in a police station.' Even he had been crapping himself, and told me he was sure I'd been arrested. Those greetings really rammed home what the consequences of that afternoon could have been. If I didn't know it before, at that point I was certain: I'm not a thief!

When I was eighteen I had another revelation, if you could call it that, about a life of crime. Me, Conrad and another friend called Clive got totally hammered on Tennent's Super lager and smoked some weed. I should have known better because they were exactly the things that helped make living with my mum and stepdad so miserable, which might be why I didn't like drinking that much as a teenager, but all the same it's what kids do!

The three of us were out of it and we went to see *Scarface*. I don't know if it was because of the state I was in, but it left a profound impression on me and all I could think about was how it ended for Tony Montana. I came away from that thinking, 'Hang on a minute, that guy is the *baddest* guy I've ever seen as a character in fiction and he still didn't make it. What chance have I got if I was to go down that road?' Rat-arsed as I was, the thing I took from that film was no matter how bad you are, you're going down at some stage.

Much as anybody does their best not to look for trouble, sometimes trouble simply finds them, I was always wary of the company I kept but on some occasions you can't do too much about it. Once I was walking down Brockley Road, below Brockley Cross, and opposite the Breakspear Arms I came across two guys I knew from around the Honor Oak Estate.

We're walking along chatting, just 'What's happening . . . how you doing?' sort of stuff, and we come past a jeweller's.

They tell me, 'Hang on a minute', and go inside. Standing on the pavement I see them snatch two trays of rings out of the window. They pile out of the door past me shouting '*Run! Run!*' So I do.

We ran and ran and ran, blasted up Tressillian Road, around the back, and got to Hilly Fields park, where they said, 'Listen, we got to split, we got to go!' And they disappeared, just like that. From there I zoomed over to Nunhead and just laid low for a bit, hanging about, until I figured I could go back to Brockley.

Once I'd calmed down and the adrenaline stopped, I thought about what had just happened. I was walking down from the house of my girlfriend at the time, on my way home; I know these guys so I crossed the road to walk along with them; five minutes later I'm running for my life. And I mean my life because if I get captured with them then it's all over for me – I'm in serious trouble if I'm caught. I was no part of any of it, yet if we're caught I'm in it just the same as them. This was not long before I went to the Crystal Palace trial, so if that had gone the other way then no Palace, no Arsenal . . . nothing.

Even when you're keeping yourself totally to yourself you can still get into trouble: I ended up doing time in Chelmsford prison, not because I stole anything or because I done anything to anyone, but, ironically enough, for trying to do the right thing. For attempting to be an upstanding citizen.

I was nineteen or twenty and I'd had a couple of cars, but I'd never had a licence or any tax or insurance or anything, and I kept getting caught for driving them. PC Mott, who was on the beat on the estate, knew the cars, knew I had no papers and kept stopping me, which meant I'd regularly get charged and fined. Of course, I wasn't paying these fines and they were mounting up – my attitude when I was caught was, 'OK, they'll fine me, but I'll get by.'

When I got a decent job and some money in my pocket, I reckoned I owed about four or five hundred pounds in fines and I thought I'd pay them off. I actually walked in to Camberwell Green Magistrates Court, introduced myself to a woman in there and said something like, 'I've come to settle up'.

She said, 'OK, could you wait here, please?'

She couldn't believe her luck – I'd been collecting these fines for two or three years, so there had been at least one warrant for my arrest, which I assume they couldn't be bothered to carry out because PC Mott knew where to find me, and now I'd just walked in and held my wrists out for them! All of a sudden there were two policemen behind me and that was it. I was banged up in Chelmsford nick for eighteen days for non-payment of fines.

On the positive side, that was *the* eye-opener for me: not that anything particularly terrible happened to me, but it was just so bleak in there, like the end of the road. I said to myself, 'I will never come back to this place or anywhere like it. Never ever.'

That was when I decided there would be no more skating on thin ice, I was going to work. If it's manual labour, building sites, scaffolding, whatever, that's what I'm going to do to earn a living. I am not going to do this again. I do not want to be part of this world.

When I did the prison TV show, *Football Behind Bars*, they took me back into the cell I was in on the night before my release, on C Wing in HMP Chelmsford. It did bring back some memories, and helped me take the show even more seriously as I knew first-hand how important it was to show those young guys that there is an alternative.

If you saw me as a teenager you might have thought I was pretty flash. I've always worn those big caps pulled down to one side – newsboy's caps I think they're called – and back then I had a leather one which was definitely the top end of things. Plus, I knew I was good at football which probably gave me a bit of an air.

Really, though, I was giving off a lot more than was actually there: I acted like I was cool and confident; I acted like I had girls; I acted like I was running with the right kind of guys . . . there was a load of acting going on. Which I don't believe is too different from any teenager trying to get by as they find out what life is all about for them personally.

I wouldn't say it was a fraudulent life I was leading, but it was a balancing act because I was skating between two worlds – the cool guys who would wear the Gazelle trainers and the Lois jeans; and the regular guys who went to school or work or whatever, just hung out and played football. The cool guys were glamorous, but most of the time we knew they were going to do something dodgy. I was too scared of being with them because I was afraid of the repercussions from my mum, because she might have had her problems but most of the time she was still the strict West Indian mother with me and Morris – she'd still cook and keep house too. So while I was *around* those guys I was always far enough removed not to have to prove I was one of them. I was quite happy staying on the edge of that sort of thing.

I spent a lot of time in and around North Peckham, which although it was still an estate it was very different to Brockley, it was bigger, with more people, it seemed more at the centre of thing, more sophisticated than where I'd come from, and once there it seemed like my teenage years came on in a rush. I was learning to drive cars, smoke weed, being with the soul heads at the soul clubs, being with girls, listening to guys older than me sleeping with girls in the next rooms, meeting real-life bad men . . . stuff like that.

I never really got into drink to any extent because of my bad experiences with it at home: my brother Morris can drink all night, and is a good drunk, a happy drunk; but my mum and my brother Nicky are bad drunks, very abusive, and that put me off getting into the whole drinking thing to the extent that some kids do. The first time I had a lager and lime, however, I thought it was the coolest thing ever! In fact, when I got into that bit of life around North Peckham, I was thinking, 'This is all pretty good.'

I came out of it all right – in the end – and I don't think I would change very much if I could go back. It's only nowadays that I get scared when I think back to how close I came to so much that could have gone the wrong way. Unless you lived a real middle-class life, most people of my age who have grown up in London flirted with the bad side of things at some point – you had to understand the street, but that didn't mean you had to live it.

It was funny because we all knew who the bad men were, with their nice clothes and sweetboy shoes and stuff, and would sometimes be envious because they always had the nicest looking girls around them – girls of our age that were hanging out with older guys. The worst thing you could do was to go and try and talk to one of these women because it was so obvious she was looking at you with complete contempt, just because you were a well-brought-up boy!

When I was going to the clubs I was still going over to girls and asking them politely, 'Please may I have this dance?' *Ridiculous!* Other blokes would just go over grab their arms and start doing their stuff! And they always seemed to get further than me with them. Looking back at myself I think, 'Wow! So naive.' I can remember wishing I was little bit badder just to get the girls. Later I realized that it's good to be polite and, having taken that approach throughout my life, I know you can't actually go wrong with it.

One irony is that if I go back there and pop into a club or a pub, the same men and women are there with all their badness and everything – the same people I used to be afraid to even look at – but now some of them are desperate to be seen with me.

Another thing I came to realize, when I did get to talk properly with a few of these guys, is that they're not really bad men: it was just where they were and all they were trying to do was get by. Not all of them, of course, but for quite a few of them it was *what* they were, not *who* they were. They were the ones who were genuinely pleased for me and would say things like 'Well done, man, you done well – you got out, you didn't fall by the wayside.' That's all anybody really wanted, to get out and get a better life. There's no romance in poverty and having so little control over your life.

These bad guys who I was so scared of when I was younger were just playing a role, trying to get what control they could over their lives. There was a time where if you stepped on someone's shoes or if you looked at someone too long, something's going to kick off and you'll either get slapped or stabbed. Now, these same people come over and say how proud of you they are, because deep down they're decent people.

I thought back to the advice I used to get off these guys before I got signed – to look after myself so I would be at the top of my game – and instead of thinking I got good advice off bad people, I realized they weren't really bad people. It's just that once they came out of their front door, that's how they had to act to get on. They had to keep up the pose.

I had a good mate whose mum used to get really dressed up and go out about eleven o'clock at night and say she was going to work, then come back about five in the morning. Years later, I realized she was on the game – a prostitute – but we took it for what it was: to me she was just my mate's mum, a very kind woman who was doing what she had to do to get by.

I always appeared very confident, but was never too confident underneath – there's a few people who know me now that would say nothing's changed – and this showed up most with girls. The rejection from various football trials stung me so I was always scared of getting knocked back, and as I was pretty shy anyway I didn't need much more of an excuse not to ask girls out.

I was very young when I got involved with my first girlfriend, Andrea, who lived next door to my first boss, but she was seeing somebody else at the same time, which I didn't realize. That was a bit of a nightmare, and didn't do anything for my confidence.

Being around girls was an eye-opening time for me. I didn't really know how to behave, but because I had all the front, people never would have believed that. I didn't asked many girls out. I used to fancy a girl called Hyacinth who was from Lewisham, and I'd see her in Lewisham Way Boys' Club. I used to dance with her but I would never say anything to her! All my mates were egging me on to ask her out and I finally got the courage to speak to her.

I went to meet her a couple of times, but it didn't last because I think she wanted an older guy than me, somebody more experienced. I wasn't making the moves because I didn't know how to make the moves. I didn't lose my virginity until I was eighteen or nineteen, but I don't think anybody realized that.

Then there was Jacqueline Graham, who, when I was younger, was the most beautiful girl I'd ever seen. She was always in and around the older guys, who all wanted to dance with her. I always thought she had something for me but I just felt that I wasn't slick enough for her. I danced with her a few times, which was brilliant, and everybody was saying, 'Ian, just ask her out, man! Ask her out!'

So I did it, I asked her. She obviously didn't want to go out with me, but she was clearly embarrassed and couldn't bring herself to say no, so she'd say 'Let me think about it.' She kept on with 'I'm still thinking' . . . 'I'll tell you tomorrow' . . . 'I'll tell you next week' . . . She dragged it out for weeks and weeks and weeks, to the point where she was avoiding me, her mates were telling her 'Just tell him!' and in the end she had to say it. 'No!'

I was devastated! *Devastated!*

As we got older and I still used to see her about, we spoke about it and it was fine. She ended up with a dear friend of mine called Norman, and she's got a son called Ashley Cole. No, not that one.

At the time, though, I was completely heartbroken and couldn't bring myself to ask another girl out. I was so glad I met Sharon not long after and was happy to settle down without having to worry about asking girls out again.

It wasn't long after I left school that I left football. I'd missed the boat when it came to getting taken up by a professional club: lads I knew who were pretty good had been picked up by different London clubs and I'd had nothing. Then without the organization of school football I couldn't see how I was going to get any further – ironically, by the time I got that sort of structure again, at Ten-em-Bee, I really had written off any ideas of going professional. I now believe that by stopping playing I was protecting myself against the rejection that had been happening every time it looked like I might take a step forward.

The first time was when I was still a kid at school. Henry Laville, Steven Pitman, Keith McPherson and myself were by far the best players in my year at Samuel Pepys, but when the letter arrived inviting kids to the Blackheath district trials my name wasn't on it. Of course I was massively disappointed, couldn't work out why I hadn't been picked, and figured I'd just have to live with it.

My teacher Mr McCarthy had other ideas. He said I was easily good enough for the district team and said I should go anyway. He sent me down there with the others, telling me to inform the teacher in charge of the trials, Mr McArdle, that he said I should go and if he wanted he could phone my school and check. That was a frightening trip for me because I was scared of Mr McCardle, and I thought Mr McCarthy was just forcing me on him.

When I got there, I repeated, in parrot fashion while looking down at the ground, exactly what my teacher had said. I saw him roll his eyes, but he must've made the call because I had the trial and got in the team.

That was the kind of support I got from Mr McCarthy, and it's only once I got older I realized the only reason he sent me was because he really thought I was good enough. For a long time, even though I got through, I didn't believe I was good enough and thought I was only there because he had forced me on the man.

Playing for district got me to the London trials over in Raynes Park near Wimbledon, which was the first time I met Andy Gray, who would become a good friend at Crystal Palace. I went with the same three guys that I went to district with. I was put on the left wing and I set up a goal for somebody. The other three all got in, as did Andy Gray, but I didn't.

I felt terrible when the names of those who got in were read out and mine wasn't called. All the kids who didn't get in felt like that because it's all so public. Years later, when I did *Football Behind Bars* and I had to read out the names of those who had the opportunity to get into my football academy, I couldn't speak for a while because it took me right back to when I was a kid not hearing my name on the list.

The journey back to Brockley on the bus was horrible. Because Henry, Keith and Steve got in and stayed there, I had to come back by myself and I was crying all the way.

It was from London games and trials that young players tended to get scouted. Henry signed with Charlton and Keith went to

West Ham. Although I didn't get in, I still got invited to trials for Millwall at Crofton Park Leisure Centre when I was fourteen – Keith 'Rhino' Stevens was part of that group of triallists too.

The trial lasted a few weeks, and I was sure I had done enough to get in, but at the end of it they just told me to leave my address and they *might* be in touch. Even at that age I could understand they had no intention of getting in touch and it really wasn't the nicest way to let me know.

That was it for me in terms of professional clubs for nearly five years. I played Sunday football first with St Paul's – Danny Wallace, who went on to play for Southampton and Man United, was in that team – and then Ten-em-Bee, and just got on with working for a living. Tony Davis, who became manager at Ten-em-Bee, contacted various London clubs about me but none were interested, until Brighton & Hove Albion offered me a chance.

That was a weird one. I went there to train and play training games with them for six weeks and scored goals everywhere there – I scored goals against the first team when we had to play them. Chris Ramsey was in that first team and he did a brilliant thing for me in the game when us triallists got the chance to show what we could do. He was the defender who'd be marking me but he wanted to help a brother out.

As we set up he said to me, 'I'll let you go past me a few times, but after that, that's it.'

He literally did that – I got past him maybe half a dozen times before he said, 'Right, that's your lot.'

And it was! After that I didn't get a sniff.

I used to travel up and down from London on the train with Chris, Perry Digweed and Dean Wilkins, who all used to tell me on a regular basis they'll definitely sign you, but in the end I was there for the six weeks and they signed Steven Penney, a Northern Irish fella, instead. At one point they said they were definitely going to sign me and I honestly thought I was in, but then they didn't, and that was it for me.

I honestly thought it was because I just wasn't good enough. Obviously I was disappointed, but I wasn't bitter about it, I didn't blame my size or my race, I just believed I wasn't good enough, even though I often knew I was doing more on the pitch than guys who were getting picked. I might have been tearing it up on Sunday morning, but I couldn't make that next step up to playing professional. It all added up: the rejection at London trials, Millwall and now Brighton, with other clubs not even offering me the chance . . .

Because there were so many youngsters looking for a break, it was all too easy for clubs to reject kids out of hand with a sort of flippancy – 'Nah, leave him, there'll be another along in a minute.' It was easier than choosing to invest in a player with potential and I'm sure loads that could have developed into something special have slipped through the net because of what was, essentially, laziness.

All of that shook my confidence and made me doubt myself and my abilities for years to come. More immediately, though, I just didn't want to go back to Brockley again with my tail between my legs, although most people down there were hugely supportive. There was a strong sense of community so if somebody succeeded – Rocky Rocastle, Paul Elliott, me eventually – the whole area got a boost because everybody either knew them or knew somebody who did. When you didn't have much in comparison to elsewhere in London, somebody breaking out and doing something showed what we could be capable of. But then it worked the other way, too: people were devastated when I came back from the trial at Brighton and hadn't got in, because they really thought I was going to make it. I think many were as disappointed as I was.

I was still a teenager and it did really hurt, so as protection against it happening again I stopped trying to go any further in football. I convinced myself I didn't want to. I was in a relationship with Sharon, who already had Shaun, and Bradley had been born in March 1985, and I thought I'll just stick with Ten-em-Bee and concentrate on my family responsibilities.

Once I got the trial at Palace, however, it all clicked back in.

Chapter Fourteen

Easy Like Sunday Morning

I came up through Sunday morning football. I went straight from my local Sunday team, Ten-em-Bee, to a two-week trial at Crystal Palace, then a three-month contract followed by a long-term deal. I don't really like to push it because it feels like I'm making too much of myself, but *nobody* else did what I did – I can't think of one professional footballer, from back then right through to now, who went straight from Sunday mornings to as high as the second division of English football with nothing in between. It's a massive jump.

There are a few guys the media has made a fuss about recently as having been playing *amateur* football a year or two before they exploded into the Premiership, but they were playing for the non-league clubs, Saturday afternoons, which is a completely different matter. Coming up through the top of those ranks and tearing up trees in non-league football isn't that far removed from what is on offer in the Football League or the Championship, so it shouldn't be a huge surprise when somebody makes that step.

Take Jamie Vardy. He was on fire at Leicester in 2015–16 when he broke Ruud van Nistelrooy's record of scoring in consecutive games, and people would say to me, 'Yeah . . . you and Jamie Vardy, you're the same . . .'

I had to say '*No!*', a bit like that character in *The Fast Show*, because I couldn't emphasize enough how I came from Sunday football and it was completely different set of circumstances. Jamie Vardy had been on Sheffield Wednesday's books, was outstanding at every level of non-league football, and scored loads and loads of goals on a regular basis for Stockbridge Park Steels, Halifax and Fleetwood Town. He was a prominent player, probably the best in non-league football at that time, so of course somebody was going to sign him. The only surprise was the amount of money Leicester paid for him – £1 million – because nobody had spent that much on a non-league player before.

Without taking anything away from him, I blazed a trail that was unique to me. I had played three or four games for Greenwich Borough at the end of a season but that was all. They wanted to sign me, as did Dulwich Hamlet, but I never had a contract with either and I was a Ten-em-Bee, Sunday-morning player when I was approached by Crystal Palace.

I'm proud of the way I came through, to get into the Second Division, rise to the First with Palace, then the Premiership and eventually to win the title with Arsenal. I make sure people know about it to let players know what is possible. Also, if I hadn't come straight from Sunday football, if I'd gone the non-league route, it might have worked out totally different because one of my defining traits as a footballer was my rawness. This came from Sunday football, pure and simple, and I didn't lose it because there was nothing else in between that and me turning professional.

One of the greatest things about Sunday-morning football was that you learned to deal with just about anything that could happen on the pitch, and playing for Ten-em-Bee, an all-black team in one of the south-east London Sunday leagues, that was exactly what it was – just about anything!

My Sunday-morning education meant that when I did turn professional, there wasn't a great deal that opponents could give out that was going to intimidate me. When you skinned a defender on a Sunday morning and he gave you a look, there was a good chance you'd see him waiting for you in the car park afterwards.

When I got signed to Palace, the verbals – and they were terrible down there in the old Second Division – meant nothing to me. Just after I started with them we went up to play Birmingham City, where they called me a black Brixton slag, asking me how did I get up here? Did I steal a car? This is just the players, not even the crowd. We battered them six-one, and their two centre halves were so petrified of me running at them all they could do was try to intimidate me. They started going on about how they're going to do this to me and do that to me, saying things like, 'You tee him up and I'll come in and finish him off . . .'

The last thing I was going to be was afraid of these two, because I'd learned very early on in the professional world that they were just talking, they were not going to do anything. I was never scared of characters like that.

In Sunday football, if somebody meant something, they didn't tell you what they were going to do before they did it. When I was playing for Ten-em-Bee you'd see people just walk off the pitch to go to their cars to get their baton or piece of pipe or whatever, and then they would come back to genuinely try and do you. *That* was frightening – in fact it was frightening to the point it could get addictive. You had to stay on edge all the time while you were playing, so it just became part of your game and you couldn't function at your best otherwise. I don't think that ever left me.

Then the only thing that could be worse than the players on a Sunday morning were some of the crowds, which is why the most abusive crowds anywhere in league football held no fear for me. When Ten-em-Bee played in deepest Deptford, real Millwall territory, we'd have to get everybody we knew to come down because we knew it was going to kick off afterwards.

Then when we played on the Ferrier Estate, over near Sutcliffe Park in Kidbrooke, everybody on the estate turned out to that game because they knew we were an all-black team. They would come down, totally surround the pitch, so all through the game anybody running down the wing would have spectators kicking them. Then at the final whistle we would literally have to fight our way to the car park, kit still on of course. It was like that film *The Warriors*: we'd have to fight our way out of there to get home. Crowds at Football League grounds – even the worst, most racist crowds – were never going to get anywhere near what it was like playing on the Ferrier Estate.

It wasn't all bad in those leagues, though, as the thing about Sunday-morning football is literally anybody can join in – some teams have no real ambition to play football, it's just something to do; others, like Ten-em-Bee, wanted to be the best they could.

They were a fantastic team. There were a few players who played semi-professional for Saturday teams and others that were easily good enough to have made it, so they took it very seriously. So seriously in fact, that when I joined, along with my mate Conrad, we thought they were a bunch of older guys moaning all the time! It seemed somebody was always on our case about going training or enforcement of attitude or preparation or something. We were sixteen or seventeen and took the approach, 'Give us a break, for heaven's sake, it's just Sunday morning football, what's the big deal?'

But really, once I got into it, the influence of guys like Steve Elka, Anthony Winifred, Tony Davis and Errol Palmer started to shape me, not just a footballer, but in life too.

Ten-em-Bee came about at exactly the right time in my life, as just after I left school I went for a year or more without playing football because I'd started working and in the beginning it was usually exhausting. Also, I thought I'd missed that boat and, without really realizing it, I think I'd started looking at football as something I did when I was a kid, but now I'm a working man – at all of age fifteen! – I've got to concentrate on work. Really, though, football, at whatever level and in spite of the rejections at trials, was the one constant in a life that wasn't what anybody could call 'stable'. It didn't occur to me how much I'd been missing it until I joined Ten-em-Bee.

I was living at my cousin Aiden's in Crofton Park, and we had another cousin, Shirley, who lived in Sydenham next door to Errol Palmer, Ten-em-Bee's manager at the time. Through Shirley, Aiden knew Errol and told him his cousin Ian is a brilliant footballer, and whatever players they've got Ian is better than all of them. I doubt Errol believed him, but he played up front and he wanted to stop playing, so he said, 'Bring him.'

I wasn't looking for a football team, but Aiden got me to go and play and that was it, I was in. I got my mate Conrad to come to the team with me, because we'd played football together for ages – he was the midfielder who would set me up as the striker.

There were a lot of all-black teams like Ten-em-Bee in London at the time, in the late 1970s and 1980s, not as any kind of statement, but simply because the nature of Sunday football means groups of friends tend to form teams. What was unusual was the one white guy we had in the team – a crazy white guy who we called Johnny X. He played on the left wing, yet with every other black team I knew, if they had a white guy he was the goalie.

It was a good situation for me. I had grown up without a father figure to relate to, and the teachers I looked up to at school were white, so spending time around older black guys who obviously had it together and had created their own regimented and disciplined environment made a huge impact on me. Plus, they could *really* play football, and their on-the-pitch mentoring of me took up from where my teachers Mr Pigden and Mr McCarthy left off.

There was one guy, Anthony Winifred, who we called Freddie, who was a plasterer by trade and a top, top midfielder. He wasn't particularly quick, but he was a brilliant passer of the ball. Constantly, he would walk past me during games and say, 'Composure . . . composure . . .' That's all he used to say, unless I scored, then he'd say, 'That's good . . . always composure.' If it was a really good goal, he'd throw in the name of a great player who he thought had composure! Freddie was a massive Spurs fan, but he was still really excited for me when I made it first at Palace, then at Arsenal — all the guys were really proud of me, as were a lot of other people from around Brockley, Honor Oak and Crofton Park.

During the five or six years I was with Ten-em-Bee I scored goals and the team did well. We'd win some sort of trophy every season, our division or a cup or something. This was when my name started to get known, locally, and because so many people thought I had a chance to really kick on they would look out for me. I used to go to parties and sound systems, and I'd be smoking weed or drinking rum and black or whatever it was, and the older guys would be saying, 'Look at you! . . . What you doing here? Three, four o'clock in the morning. What do you think? Do you think this is what profes-sional footballers would do? Smoking weed . . . dancing with girls . . . acting like you're a big man? You've got a chance. If you do not do the very best you can and work as hard as you can to be a professional footballer, you're going to regret it when you're an old man.' Sometimes guys would come up to me and say, 'Haven't you got a game tomorrow? You shouldn't be here!'

At the time I didn't really get it — it was like being back at school. To me, I was playing Sunday-morning football and I was doing everything I could for that — scoring goals and we were winning. I wasn't thinking about being a professional footballer, and by the time I got to Ten-em-Bee I thought my chance had gone. So if I could go out raving and still tear it up on a Sunday morning, why not?

I didn't really understand what they were saying. I later real-ized it wasn't just about trying to be a professional: they were telling me to always do the absolute best I could and not waste my talent for football, whatever the outcome. When they'd tell me, 'Look at you, wasting yourself!' it was about having pride in myself for myself, and not settling for second best. That was why the guys that played for the team took it seriously.

I did give up going out to parties, but that was only because I was fed up with being lectured. I don't think I fully took on board what they were trying to do until I got to Palace, and then it never left me. When I'd played a particularly good game or achieved something with them or with Arsenal, I'd think back to what people said to me.

Every year, in the early 1980s, Ten-em-Bee played in a competition called the Supermalt Tournament, over in Raynes Park. It was sponsored by the Caribbean nutrition drink called Supermalt, and was for black teams from all over London. It was a really big event, loads of London's black professional players used to come down and watch – I remember Ricky Hill being there every year, and Paul Elliott coming down because his brothers played for one of the teams.

It always was a great weekend, everybody knew each other, even if it was just from last year's competition, so it was a fantastic atmosphere as the players were just so relaxed – yes, of course we all wanted to win, the games would always be really intense, but the whole event was just a brilliant celebration of London's black footballers.

It meant a great deal to the players and the people who would come and watch. I still get people coming up to me telling me their dad or their uncle played against me in the Supermalt. We had a reputation down there because we had a really cool kit: it was white and shiny, sort of satiny – this is the early 1980s!

– with a red and a blue stripe through it, like Crystal Palace. They used to call us the Pretty Kit Team!

I was seventeen when I played in my first one, and I was the little guy up front who scored a few goals, but didn't think too much of it because the standard was so high there – if you got respect in the Supermalt, you were really good. We always used to do all right, but I found out other teams were coming to watch our games when they weren't playing, and that's where I started to become prominent.

I wasn't really too aware that so many people knew about me until it got me out of a very tight situation one night. I used to go to Saxon sound system's dances – they were the big local sound system from Lewisham. I went to this big sound clash they were playing in Brixton wearing this nice gold chain my cousin Georgia had given me.

I don't know why I wore this chain to a big dance where I didn't really know anybody, and sure enough these guys stopped me and one of them took hold of it. He was pulling it really tight to burst it off and all of I sudden I heard this big deep voice say, 'No, no no no! Leave 'im!'

It was this guy Clemmie, an older Jamaican guy that I'd seen at the Supermalt. It seems he used to watch all of our games when his team, Ujama, wasn't playing. He just told them, 'Mi football frien' dis. Mi likkle football frien'. Leave him alone!'

These guys just melted away, and that's when I realized that people knew about me outside my area or circle of friends. I'd only ever said a couple of words to Clemmie at the tournament, but, as I found out, he used to love me as a player. That was one of the most brilliant things about the Supermalt: when you played in it you really felt like you were part of something.

We used to do all right in it, but the level of play was incredible. I saw players in the Supermalt – goalkeepers, centre halves, midfielders, forwards – who were unbelievable. There was one guy in particular called Winnie, that's all I knew him as, and I don't think in my time playing Sunday football, and my first few years playing professional football, I saw anybody as good as him.

He had a left foot that was so good, when I watched Liam Brady I didn't even think he had anything on Winnie – when I went to Crystal Palace he was head and shoulders above any midfielder there. Winnie was phenomenal. I used to think it was a crime he wasn't a professional footballer, but then I'd look around a bit more and see fifteen or maybe twenty players that should have been professional but hadn't been picked up.

So much of that was because scouts from the league clubs didn't know something like the Supermalt even existed, and I'm not sure they would have come down if they had. Back then, in so many clubs, black players hadn't reached the level of acceptance they have today, largely we were still seen as black players rather than players who happen to be black. This played into people's judgements, so it was highly unlikely clubs would go looking for black players.

Then, because of what was perceived to be the attitude at league clubs, less black youngsters put themselves forward because it was easy to believe they wouldn't get very far, or that it would be an unsympathetic environment.

There were also internal pressures to add to this, as so many Caribbean or African parents hadn't come to the UK to have their sons play football! They were all about hard work or education or learning a trade, and rather than encourage a lad with talent, they tended to see football as play, as a distraction. Often it was, 'Don't waste your time messing about with football . . . Get a job.'

Because of the drinking, my mum's lack of encouragement was extreme, but so many of the guys *knew* they were good, but didn't make any effort to go further because they were growing up being continually told it's not a good idea.

Also, by then there were different tiers of scouting, and Sunday football had practically fallen off clubs' radars – the old guy with his dog who would watch Sunday games and come over and say, 'I'm affiliated with West Ham, and I've been watching you . . .' didn't really exist anymore. The thinking back then was if you were any good they would have scouted you at the district or the London trials or you would have moved on to non-league. So that was what they were looking at – these days they're not really looking at teenagers any more because clubs are snapping kids up when they're eight or nine, so they assume that anybody worth looking at is already signed.

I get very frustrated by this, both then and now, simply because of the opportunities for players that are being closed off. You only needed to watch a handful of games at the Supermalt to know what a range of talent was on offer, so that really was the clubs' loss. With the scouting thing, it upsets me because every player develops, or blossoms, at a different rate so it's ridiculous to write older kids off – I didn't get my break until I was almost twenty-two.

One of the reasons I make sure people know that I came straight from Sunday football is because there are players out there who are being missed – people used to say things like, 'Don't worry, you never know when a scout's watching.' Now, you know one thing for sure, those scouts are not watching Sunday morning football.

Towards the end of the 1984–85 season, for reasons I don't think I ever knew, Ten-em-Bee were without a pitch to play their home games on, so we had to play on Greenwich Borough's. Their manager Mickey Wakefield saw me play and asked me if I wanted to play the last three games of the season for them. They were semi-pro, and he said he'd pay me £30 a game. Tony Davis, who was Ten-em-Bee's manager at the time, didn't mind, so I agreed. I'd given up all thought of becoming a professional by then, and although thirty quid a game was definitely not a fortune, I could hardly believe somebody was going to pay me for playing football.

It turned out quite embarrassing, because not only did I feel like I was getting away with something, I didn't know how things worked. I played the first game for them, then didn't know what to do: does he come and give me the money? Do I go and ask for it? He didn't give me anything and I was too embarrassed to ask. I didn't know what to think. The second game came around and after that he didn't give me anything either. I was so confused. Then after the third game, he came up and gave me £90 in cash and I couldn't look at him! It was as if I was embarrassed to take it – I'd never been paid for playing football and it seemed like cheating!

I must have done all right in those three games because they wanted me to sign for them for a signing-on fee of £100 and £30 a game. There was talk of Dulwich Hamlet signing me for £150 and £20 a game, but it never got to the stage of an offer being made to me. Anyway, by then I was going to play in a triallists' Probables versus Possibles match for Greenwich Borough at Colliers Wood. Andy Gray and Alan Pardew played in that match, ironically, as both had ties with Dulwich Hamlet – Alan played for them at the time; and Andy had gone from there to Crystal Palace and wanted to get himself tuned up before starting pre-season. I scored a few goals in that game. It was then that Peter Prentice, the Crystal Palace scout, approached me.

I'm sure he had been watching me previously – I'd played in and scored in a couple of cup finals at the end of the season – and once he approached me, I thought, 'Woah! This is really it!'

I said I was really pleased and that he was going to have to speak to my Sunday morning manager because I hadn't signed with Greenwich and I was still a Ten-em-Bee player. I spoke with him for about half an hour. I told him what happened at Brighton and at Millwall, and how I was wary of getting my hopes up. I also told him I had a missus and a young kid, and I needed to focus on working and really wasn't sure if I wanted to think about professional football.

He listened to all of this, and he was great. Although I had been doing my best to convince myself I would be happy going to work at Tunnel Refineries every day and getting paid a few extra quid for playing for Greenwich Borough or Dulwich Hamlet, the simple truth was I really wanted the chance to set myself against better opposition.

I was playing for a club where I knew I was the top man, scoring goals every week, sometimes four, five or six goals in a game, and not thinking I was good so much as the opposition was rubbish. Was I just a flat-track bully in the Sunday leagues? I wanted to test myself against more than people who were putting out cigarettes as they stepped on to the pitch.

I shook hands with Peter Prentice and agreed to go for a two-week trial with Crystal Palace.

Technically from that moment on I was a professional footballer, but I never really felt I'd left Sunday mornings behind.

Ten years after I'd signed for Palace, when I was playing for Arsenal against Hartlepool in the League Cup at Highbury, one of their players tried to start on me when we were lined up in the tunnel. I wasn't looking at him so much as looking in his direction, but he thought this was a good opportunity to put his marker down.

He started staring at me and, playing the hard man, said, 'What you looking at?'

I replied, 'I dunno, really. I was just thinking how shit you look in that kit.'

'What the fuck you talking about?' he said. 'You're just a Sunday-morning player!'

'Yeah, I am,' I replied, 'but now look at me!'

And we went out to beat them five-nil and I got a hat-trick.

While that little exchange sums up how ineffective that sort of talk was to me, when he said that I never forgot it. I think to myself, 'Is that how people look at me? A Sunday morning footballer?' Maybe that's how I saw myself throughout my career, and I don't think it did me too much harm because I never lost my Sunday morning values. How I played was always about giving everything. A certain rawness of the Sunday league stayed with me throughout my whole career.

Chapter Fifteen

No Chalice at the Palace

I was invited to Palace for a two-week trial in August 1985, and at the end of it, on the Friday, played in a Crystal Palace XI against a local semi-pro outfit called Kingstonian. I must have done well because on the Saturday we played a behind-closed-doors game against Coventry and I was signed right before that game. On the Monday I reported for training. I was training with the first team straight from the off, which was quite surprising for me but I felt OK among them, mostly.

Steve Coppell gave me a deal for three months, which was actually the best thing that could have ever happened to me. I think if he'd signed me for a year right off the bat, I would have had a different attitude to it. It was long enough to give me a taste of what life could be as a footballer, but short enough to make sure I kept working and didn't get complacent.

That was either a masterstroke by Palace, or they literally could not afford a longer contract until they could see exactly how they could use me. They needed to tie me down quickly because they knew that Luton were interested – they'd asked me to come up for two weeks after the Palace trial.

One of the first things Steve Coppell said was that I looked like I needed some food, and after I signed I had to eat potatoes, steaks and bananas. This was a good example of how they were looking at my potential as much as anything else and were prepared to invest in me.

That made me feel good, but I was left wondering why Brighton couldn't have done that. Down there I played against their first team and scored goals, so what would it have cost them to have given me longer? If they'd offered me twenty-five quid a week I would have taken it.

As it was, after being given just three months I was convinced Palace would send me back to the building trade at the end of it so I was determined to have a blast before that happened. I played with pure freedom, didn't care if I was playing in the reserves or against the first team, and it was enough to get me taken on even though I would be twenty-two that November.

Technically, the three-month contract was the beginning of my life as professional footballer, but it wasn't something I fully came to terms with for quite a while.

After that Coventry game I was on the bus going to Morden to get the train to Forest Hill, thinking, 'Is that it?' I phoned my mum and said, 'Yeah, I'm a professional now', but after wanting so badly to be a footballer for fourteen years since the age of eight, it now all seemed to happen too quickly. Maybe I felt like that *because* I'd been waiting that long. For me there was no build-up to it where you go away and learn to be a professional footballer and focus on it. There was no ceremony . . . two weeks before that I'd been a builder, now I was a professional footballer.

To me, a doctor's a professional, a lawyer's a professional, they go away to university and study for ages to earn the right to be called a professional, yet it happened to me overnight. I hadn't done anything. As far as I was concerned, I was still a builder who played a bit of football, a professional in name only.

I didn't feel overawed about training with the first team because, on the one hand, I knew I'd done enough in those two weeks to earn my place there – they'd seen me around and I'd mostly earned their respect. When they saw I'd been elevated, they knew what I could bring. On the other hand, I wasn't getting above myself, because I knew from experience that it doesn't matter how well you *think* you are doing, it still might all come to nothing. A couple of weeks after I was signed I was sitting in a Jacuzzi, in the middle of the day, thinking, 'Don't get too used to this! You might be a professional, but all you really know is that you're a professional for three months.'

What I was doing and where my life might be going began to sink in properly when I started scoring. I'd come on for a couple of substitute appearances and played really well, then against Oldham I came off the bench, I set up the equalizer and scored a very late winner for us to win three-two. After that my name started getting thrown around in the newspapers – the nationals – and they're calling me 'Super Sub'. That's when I really began to acknowledge the fact I was a professional footballer.

All the same, at that point, although I was in it, I didn't know if I was truly going to be *in it* until I got the two-year deal. That's when I began to think, OK, this is starting to happen, I could be a footballer for a long time, although it took a while longer for me to stop worrying that somebody was going to come through like I came through and put me under threat. I was always on my toes.

It was at that point Steve Coppell gave me a talk, saying he thought I had it in me to go as far as liked, and I said to him that I *will* play for England, simply because I wanted to be the best that I could be. He replied that I would only play for England if I continue to work hard, otherwise they're hollow words. He said he thought I could make it to that level but he let me know that if I stopped working, it would all go nowhere.

He is such an intelligent bloke and I loved playing under him. He was always calm, thought things through properly and knew exactly how to handle each player, because he knew what was important and what wasn't.

I think the FA really missed a trick not appointing him as England manager. I don't know if they passed him over because he was too young, or because he wasn't a Yes Man. Most likely they just didn't fancy him because he was never the kind of person the FA would have taken to, but he was never intimidated by the players he had to work with and was easily smart enough from a football point of view to do the job.

I do punditry with Steve every now and again, and I'm never as nervous as when that happens because, like when I was one of his players, I just don't want to disappoint him. I don't want to get anything wrong or say anything that is going to embarrass myself. In fact, any time I'm in his company I just want to make sure he's happy with me.

People kept talking about 'professionalism', and in the beginning I wasn't sure what they meant by it. I knew I was working hard enough on my game because of the extra stuff I was doing after training. What I didn't understand, though, was how to be a professional footballer when I wasn't actually kicking a ball. The guys that came up through the youth and the reserves knew this because it was all part of their development, but a couple of weeks earlier I'd been in a labourer's job at Tunnel Refineries in Greenwich! What did I know about how a professional footballer carried on? The club car I was given showed how much distance there was between the world I'd come from and the world I was now in.

One of the other perks of being with Palace was they gave me a car. Brilliant! The problem was, I didn't have a driving licence – guys I hung out with on the North Peckham estate when I was a teenager had taught me to drive and I'd never had lessons or taken a test. It was something I'd never thought about and I had probably forgotten that I didn't have a licence.

I'd had the car from the club for a while before Steve Coppell found this out and told me not to drive it until I'd passed my test. Of course I did drive it. I used to park it away from the training ground. And of course he cottoned on. He caught me getting into it one day and literally made me hand over the keys, like a naughty kid, so then I had to take my test. Ron Noades promised me an Astra GTE if I passed, which I did, then after the play-offs against Swindon, he bought me a Mercedes 190E, which was probably my first big 'footballer' thing.

It was Mark Bright, when he arrived about a year later, who showed me about that side of professionalism. He was very professional: the way he carried himself, the way he behaved off the pitch, the way he spoke, the way he did his interviews . . . everything. He had come from non-league football to Port Vale and on to Leicester City where he'd been around guys like Gary Lineker and Alan Smith. He'd soaked up how they conducted themselves and passed it on to me. How to *act* properly, how to carry myself, not to be too loud, to never let people hear me swearing, how to act around the fans, how the way I dressed and presented myself should never be brash, always dignified, never giving it the big 'un. He would have freaked if he'd been there for that episode with the car. I can hear him telling me how unnecessary it all was.

While I know that I've still got my rough edges and always will have, rooming with Brighty for a few years did so much to smooth out so many of them. The only thing I didn't copy him with was the way he'd do media and interviews: his mantra was hands behind your back, stand up straight, look into their eyes. I just couldn't do that because when I was saying what I was saying, my body language just happened naturally – if it was after a game I'd done well in, I'd be buzzing about it and he'd be trying to calm me down.

Mark was another one of those people who showed up in my life with perfect timing, and I owe him so much for teaching me how to be a professional.

The first time I fully realized I was part of something so big was when we went on a club trip to Qatar just before the start of my first season: we were going through the airport all wearing the same tracksuits, carrying the same bags, there were fans there and quite a few cheers. That was my first real taste of 'I'm in the team, I'm one of them now.'

Steve Coppell had given us the talk about no one misbehaving, act professional, remember who you are and what you are, you're a professional footballer representing Crystal Palace Football Club . . . That's when I started to stick my chest out and think, 'Right, I'm going to make sure I behave myself, because I've got something much bigger than myself to live up to.' I felt really proud and I think *that* is when I first felt like a professional footballer . . . this is what happens to professional footballers.

I was in and around the reserve team when the trip was announced and everybody was desperate to get picked to go on this trip. When the list was put up on the notice board I couldn't get near it and somebody said to me, like they were amazed, 'Your name's on the board, you're going to Qatar!'

The first thought that hit me was, *on a plane*! I'd never been on a plane before. Then when I could get to read the notice, at the bottom it said to bring your passports in on such-and-such date. That was a problem for me as I didn't have one. You don't tend to need a passport when you're a kid growing up on the Honor Oak Estate.

Everybody else had one, and I was so embarrassed about it I didn't know what to do. I kept pretending I'd forgotten it. Then on the third day Peter Prentice called me into his office and asked me, 'Have you actually got a passport?'

Sheepishly, I had to admit I didn't. He gave me all the forms and I had to go up to Petty France, which I'd never even heard of, and sit around for ages in the passport office until I came out of there with a passport.

Qatar was amazing. Back then there was just this one unbelievable hotel, right in the middle of the desert – you go there now and this one looks about a million years old with the whole landscape totally crowded.

The trip was just an incredible experience, because it was the first time I'd left the country, the first time I'd been on a plane, the first time I'd been in a hotel room, and this one was just so opulent, they called it a seven-star hotel. The guests were dressed so fantastically, like I'd only ever seen on television. And it was so hot, the hottest place I've ever been to.

We went to a couple of souks, and that was amazing too, like something you'd see in a James Bond film – thousands of people, loads of noise and just about everything for sale. That was something that made me think: the souks were like stepping back in time, people were begging in the streets, but this hotel in the desert was the height of modern-day luxury, yet they were in the same country almost side by side. It was the first of the eye-opening things I saw when I travelled for football, like going to Russia or Poland or Albania, where you see real poverty that makes even the bad areas of London look wealthy.

Qatar was an extreme example of travelling, but getting to Palace was opening up a whole new world for me on a regular basis. Up until then, the only time I had left London was for the occasional football tournament, to see relatives in Hatfield or on the estate coach trips to Margate or Littlehampton or Camber Sands, and I used to *love* going on the coach. I used to sit at the front on all of those trips. There'd be food on the coach or we'd get fish and chips for the journey home. They were fantastic, and I think travelling by coach all over England with Palace brought back a few of those memories, because I usually enjoyed it. Coming back, we'd have a beer on the coach and if we'd won everybody was so happy and pleased with whoever had scored.

It was just one more thing that was coming to me as a professional footballer and, when I look back at those days, I know I was elevating myself off the pitch as well as a player. The world was opening up and I was experiencing things I'd either never thought about or simply didn't know existed – like Qatar. Six months previously I'd never even heard of it.

Another aspect of Life as a Professional Footballer happened a couple of weeks after I got to Palace, when Alan Smith, the reserve team coach, said we were all going for a spa day at this big hotel in Croydon. I had no idea what this was, except that we were told to bring swimming trunks and I had to go and buy a pair because, naturally, I didn't have any.

We were going for massage, stretching, sauna and Jacuzzi, in the middle of the day, when normal people were at work! There I was, just about coming to terms with getting paid for doing nothing other than playing football and training, and now I was sitting in a Jacuzzi waiting for a woman to come along and say, 'Mr Wright, your massage is ready.' They were calling me Mr Wright – I'd never been called that before!

Another weird thing: a woman doing a massage on me – what happened after a bit was I couldn't turn over and maintain my modesty so I had to tell her I just wanted my back and hamstrings done!

Then it was into the sauna, stretching, another session in the Jacuzzi and finish. I was home by three o'clock after having a day like that.

I honestly felt like I was cheating society! I thought, this isn't right, this isn't fair! So many people I know *work* for a living and I'm sitting in a Jacuzzi saying I'm a professional.

What I also couldn't believe was the attitude of some of the other reserve players who were strutting round giving it loads and speaking to people really offhandedly as they got their massages, like this was their right. I thought, I play with you lot, I train with you, I know what you can do, and there are players

I left behind in Sunday-morning football that are five times better, but they're out doing a day's work. I thought the club should make them try it. Ron Noades must have known somebody with a building firm and could have sent these guys off to do labouring for a week or more, make them appreciate what hard work is and how privileged they are.

I was always aware that, however hard I had to work at my game, it was never going to be as physically hard as a day on a building site. I took a pay cut to come to Palace as Tunnel Refineries were paying me £105 a week, and Palace were paying me £100 on that three-month deal. But then compare the amount of work I had to do compared to training, where I started out at ten-thirty and finished at twelve-thirty at the latest. Even if I stayed behind I was gone by five . . . that's when you realize how fortunate this life can be.

It was opening so much up to me and I was finding so much went on outside Brockley or New Cross, I almost felt guilty that I was able to do this. People from my area were just getting on with the same old, same old, and I was getting ready to get on a plane and go to Qatar. I was back living at my mum's and she'd moved from Brockley to Forest Hill, and if I popped over to Brockley, I almost felt embarrassed telling people what I did all day – 'Oh yeah, we did some training, and I did some work after training, I had to eat a lot of steak and potatoes, then I had to go and sleep . . .' Sometimes I just couldn't tell people what I'd been doing and what was going on.

Ridiculously, not long after I'd got myself into the first team at Palace I came far too close to throwing it all away, when the drug testers came to our game against West Brom. I'd been smoking weed since I was about seventeen, not in a smoke-myself-into-uselessness type of way, and I wasn't worried about becoming a drug addict. I was like the guy who enjoys a few drinks now and again, but is nowhere near being an alcoholic.

As a kid I preferred smoking to drinking when I went out. I'd been around weed smokers from a very early age, and recently it had become something of an end-of-the-week ritual – I'd go round my mate's mum's house, an older Jamaican lady who liked her spliff on a Friday, and we'd talk and have a little smoke. I always found it very relaxing after a week at training, and although I knew I had a game the next day I never thought anything of it. I was young, fit and probably thought I was untouchable. Before that when I played Sunday-morning games I used to smoke a little spliff on Saturday because it used to chill me out, especially for those big final games. Now, it didn't even dawn on me that I was doing anything wrong.

We beat WBA four-one that Saturday, the whole team came in to the dressing room still excited, and then the drug testers arrived. It's the first time I'd ever seen them and I panicked inside – I've been smoking cannabis, less than twenty-four hours earlier, and if that test comes back positive that's it. It is literally all over for me. I flash back to that same cold fear I felt when I got caught trying to steal from the sweetshop when I was a little kid. I'm practically paralysed while trying to act unconcerned. The guy says, 'Drug test, number nine.' Mark Bright. I'm sure he's going to call my number next, number ten. He calls, 'Drug test, number eleven.' Phil Barber. I sit down – more or less collapse – and think, 'Somebody's looking out for me, now I know it!'

What hit me the most is how much I would have been letting people from my area down. These are people who wanted to make sure I kicked on and they'd gone out of their way to keep me out of trouble. If I'd wanted to buy weed down there they wouldn't have sold it to me and they did their best to keep it from being around me – my brother-in-law at the time wouldn't even smoke in front of me. If I had got caught on that drugs test it would have been beyond them, they just wouldn't have understood it: '*What*!?!? You got into Crystal Palace and *you didn't stop smoking weed?*'

From that day to this, I never smoked a spliff again.

It wasn't all plain sailing in those early days at Palace. There was an established clique in the dressing room of older players who were coming to the end of their careers and seemed to deeply resent the new wave coming up at the club. They were led by George Wood, Micky Droy and Jim Cannon, who were ten years older than players like myself, Andy Gray, Tony Finnigan and Brighty, and seldom missed a chance to intimidate the new boy. Jim Cannon was the worst. The big Scottish centre-half had been at the club forever and behaved like the playground bully.

His attempts to bully me began when I was still on my three-month contract. I'd be used off the bench and was scoring a few goals. It was great, I was doing all I could to help the team and, while most of the guys were massively encouraging, all Jim Cannon ever had was a little dig or a snide remark.

'Yeah, you're just an impact player,' he'd tell me. I didn't even know what an impact player was, but Jim was there to explain. 'You just come on for twenty minutes, you can't do any more. You couldn't play a whole game.'

Of course this got wearing, especially after I started scoring. It seemed like every time I thought I was making progress he was there to knock me down, but I just got on with doing whatever the boss wanted me to do,

The mad thing was how he'd speak nicely to me on match days. I ended up feeling that he wanted to encourage me to make sure he got his win bonus – it was nuts. He'd tell me, 'Come on, you can do it today, come off the bench . . .' when the day before he was putting me down for being just a sub.

The only other time I can remember him being nice to me was when we played up in Grimsby and they'd give every player a massive fish to take home. He'd go round to everybody asking, really nicely, 'Hey, are you going to be taking your fish?' Even though I knew my mum would have loved it, I'd give it to him hoping to placate him or something. He'd take the fish, then on Monday he'd be back to his regular, miserable, bullying self.

In the canteen he'd always sit at the same table up near the buffet, usually with Micky Droy and George Wood, so you couldn't go up to get your food without walking past him, and he'd always make a remark about you or to you. It was like running the gauntlet, and before you went up all you'd be thinking about was what he was going to say. Sometimes I'd think, 'Shall I just go hungry?'

Then one day it kicked off in training.

We had a kind of young-versus-old game, seven- or eight-a-side, with tiny goals not much more than a metre across. Jim Cannon was in goal for his side and he simply positioned himself in the middle of it, standing right on the line and not coming out at all. How were we supposed to score? The only way to do it was to put it through his legs, which I did. Twice.

The first time everybody was cheering or jeering and I ran back to let the game re-start; the next time the reaction from the others might have been a bit louder and, as I ran back, he must have launched himself into the back of me. It was more than just a punch to the back of my head. As I'm going down he's grabbed me and started screaming, 'If you fucking take the piss out of me again, I'm going to fucking knock you out!'

Then it all went off as everybody rushed over. Andy and Tony steamed in and it was all Steve and others could do to pull it apart.

I was really shaken up by it, and Steve Coppell called me in the office. He'd had other problems with Jim Cannon – he and those other guys were older than the manager, which was something else that was making them resentful. Steve wasn't intimidated by anything, it was all water off a duck's back to him, and he told me, 'Don't worry, he's just an old, bitter and twisted professional footballer who knows he's coming to the end, and he can see that you have got this bright future. He's jealous of you, so do not take it as anything other than that. Keep doing what you're doing, keep learning, and continue progressing like you are, you'll be fine. Don't worry, you'll be here a lot longer than Jim Cannon will be.'

As it was, Steve got rid of him next season,

There was also a very weird situation with Micky Droy. When we played up north, especially midweek, the team bus would get back to London as late as two or three in the morning and drop us in Mitcham, where the players left their cars. After I had just broken into the first team, I hadn't been there long enough to get a club car and they weren't going to pay for transport for me, so the only way I was going to get home was with a series of night buses and a bit of a walk.

Micky also lived in south London, and because he was a professional – a team player – he felt he couldn't leave me there so he'd offer me a lift to Elephant & Castle. But he'd do it as begrudgingly as he could! He'd say to me, really gruffly, 'You going back to South London?' . . . 'Yeah.' . . . 'Come on.' And that was it: he wouldn't say another word to me in the car, then he'd stop by the Elephant & Castle roundabout and wait for me to get out.

To me, so new to professional football, it was nuts: he didn't seem to want my company, he didn't want my conversation – even if we'd just had a great win and I'd scored – and he definitely didn't give me any pearls of wisdom. Yet his whole sense of professionalism wouldn't allow him to leave me there – whatever he thought of me personally I was part of the same team, and what that taught me was the team came first, whatever the circumstances.

In the beginning, though, I used to be so intimidated just sitting there while he wouldn't even look at me, and it got to the point where, as the coach got closer to Mitcham, I'd be thinking, 'Oh shit, Mickey's going to give me lift!'

I was with Crystal Palace for six years from 1985 to 1991. I scored over a hundred goals for the club, got into the England team with them, played in an FA Cup Final and helped them get into the old First Division.

For my development as a footballer it was fantastic. Steve Coppell and the players around me helped me get from Sunday-morning football to the First Division and the England team and I will never be able to thank them enough for that. As important as that, however, was how my time at Palace encouraged me to grow as a man. I was introduced to a much wider world and helped to become a part of it.

I found out that dealing with success could be as awkward as dealing with failure, especially when it came to people I'd known for ages. I had gone back to living at my mum's in Forest Hill. I'd bought her council flat, which was the main thing I wanted to do when I became a professional: buy my mum a home so she would never have to worry about rent or being kicked out or anything. It was where she wanted to live. It was this great top-floor flat – kind of like a penthouse – and I got it for an unbelievable price. It seems a bit nuts that I was a successful footballer, and I was soon driving a nice car, but I was still living at my mum's. It was very cool there – my stepdad wasn't there any more so it was me, my mum and Morris, although he was in and out because he'd stay at his girlfriend's.

It was close enough to Brockley so I would still go down there. Although the majority of people were really proud, I started to notice my old friends looking at me or speaking to me differently, especially after the FA Cup Final. Not all of them, but quite a few were talking about how I was acting like I was better than I was, how I'd changed, but they were the ones that had changed. I'd always gone out of my way to be the same.

I'd go down to the Breakspear Arms, where my brother used to drink, meet everybody, buy drinks and everybody's cool. Then afterwards I'd hear that people are saying how I'm going there buying everybody drinks like I'm the big rich guy, when I'm just trying to be normal, knowing that some of the guys in there can't buy their own drinks. It would be no different if I had a regular job and somebody I knew didn't, I'd buy them a drink. Now I'd buy for everybody because I was trying to let people know I was still connected to the guys and the community.

I found out you couldn't win, nobody in that position can: if you buy everybody a drink you're a flash bastard; if you don't buy everybody a drink you're a tight bastard.

I stopped going down there regularly. I'd just pop in and make sure my brother had enough money to buy his beers, and if anybody wanted a drink my brother would buy them and I'd just give him the money back. I thought it was a shame it had to be this way, that there was some bitterness towards me because I had the chance and got out. Anybody else would have done exactly the same thing, if they'd had the chance to get out they would have, there's no glamour in staying there.

This isn't just Brockley, it's every working-class area in the country. The only people that glamourize those 'real' areas are people that don't actually have to live there!

Many people were so proud of the Brockley boys – me and Rocky – but it hurt that a few people stopped me going back there as often as I would have liked.

In reality, my Brockley life had moved on, which is why I so appreciated it when Tony Finnigan and Andy Gray started taking me to the sort of places where I could relax. Thanks to how they made me feel like I fitted in, I knew I was ready for that, just like I knew I was ready to move up a level as a footballer.

Chapter Sixteen

Uptown Funk

I've always loved music, although as a teenager even that could come with its own set of problems!

Where I grew up in south-east London, in the mid-1970s, it was all about Saxon sound system, which was getting really big around Lewisham and Deptford with artists like Maxi Priest, Tippa Irie, Papa Levi and Smiley Culture deejaying or singing. It was brilliant because they were fresh and they were London, so it meant something to me, but away from that I was starting to get a bit tired of the blues dance scene – pure reggae house parties and dances. I was fourteen or fifteen, going places with my brothers, and while I loved the Saxon stuff, elsewhere the music was changing and it was becoming much more hardcore and seemed to be relating to life in Jamaica rather than London.

When I first started to going to dances there used to be a nice mixture of soul and reggae. Now, as the vibe got heavier and heavier, dances started to get an aggressive, angry atmosphere. Singers like Dennis Brown and Sugar Minott were cool, I liked that sort of vibe, and I found Bob Marley uplifting, but as I got well into my teens I was feeling more and more like it wasn't enough for me. When I went to live on the North Peckham estate I started mixing with guys who took me to Jasper's, a disco in Bellingham near Beckenham, and another night at

Lewisham Way Boys' Club – these were soul and funk clubs and pretty much blew my mind.

The first time I heard James Brown – I couldn't believe it! When I heard that there was no going back! Straight away I knew this is where I wanted to be – everybody's like me, everybody seems to be feeling how I'm feeling; it's all cool . . . it was all so mellow, so far removed from the scene I'd been into before.

Things had been changing during those times. The National Front were on the rise in the area, the New Cross Fire was in 1981, so were the first Brixton riots, and people were getting vex. Understandably there was a lot of anger, and as the reggae music was getting very heavy and very Rastafarian, the dances were becoming oppressive, very segregated, far more men than women, and everybody seemed to be on edge.

Instead of giving people hope or inspiration, this music and the vibe just seemed to make people more frustrated and aggressive, and it always seemed like things could kick off at any minute – you walk down this corridor in this blues dance and step on somebody's shoes and you could get a beating or be stabbed.

I knew there were problems with what was going on around us – I was as frustrated as anybody else – but I didn't think that was the way to solve them. I had been part of that blues dance scene for ages, but as I started to develop my own character I was in these clubs thinking, 'What's going on? I'm not enjoying the music . . . I'm not enjoying the vibe . . . I'm not enjoying the way you dance with girls, real tight and rubbing up . . . Let me readdress this!'

That's why I got so excited when I went across to the soul music and rare groove scene: it had all the political statement stuff anybody could ask for, but that was only part of it, it was dance songs, it was love songs . . . it was uplifting in a way that people – black and white – needed uplifting after a hard week at work. The crowds at the clubs were far more integrated too, which didn't bother me at all. It was the first time I'd really mixed with white people, and it didn't make any difference to how I felt about myself – if anything, living in London, it made far more sense.

I understood that Morris loved the reggae and the blues dance business, but it just wasn't for me. Which you'd think would be the end of it. Not so. There's not many things more important to a teenager than what group you belong to – your music as much as your clothes or your haircut marks you out – but two conflicting styles within black London culture? It couldn't get much more serious than this! It's amazing that we didn't have enough to worry about and had to make up an extra layer of trouble for ourselves, but I was dreading telling Morris that I was a 'soulhead' now!

The ridiculous thing about it was that when Commonwealth immigrants came to Britain in large numbers, everybody partied together, so you'd get a dance in a communal hall or some-body's house that played everything – rhythm & blues, ska, soul, afrobeat, calypso . . . because it was all black music and could give everybody a boost by connecting them with home. Everybody was in the same boat so people tended to be toler-ant. In fact, people didn't really worry about what was what because it was such a relief to be able to have a drink and a dance and relax in their own space. Yet there I was, kind of scared about being in the house and saying to my brothers that I liked soul music and that reggae didn't really have an influence on me! That's how much things had changed in twenty or thirty years.

I was right to worry about it too. When I started playing music like Parliament-Funkadelic and Light of the World, my brothers and their mates started on with, 'What are you doing? You fucking banna!' 'Banna' was short for Banacek, a 1970s TV detective. I don't know how the term came to be used but it was pretty bad, an insult like Oreo or coconut – black on the outside, white inside, an Uncle Tom. They'd go, 'Look at you! Banna! Mixing with white people!' When I curly-permed my hair, they carried on like I'd bleached my skin!

There's no reason why every black person should be the same and like the same sort of music or dress the same. Even though I could understand Morris getting peeved that his little brother's striking out on his own, his reaction was a bit extreme. With artists like James Brown and Stevie Wonder there was plenty of black pride in soul music, and some of those lyrics were really uplifting, very positive. And, as I noticed more than anything, so many of the reggae tunes I liked were originally soul tunes that had just been ripped off from Philadelphia International or Motown, from everywhere. Around the end of the 1970s and the beginning of the 1980s, I noticed more and more of the reggae guys started coming into the soul and rare groove dances, simply because the music was better, and that scene started to gain real credibility.

Another, even more extreme reaction to us soulheads involved getting taxed – basically, guys would just hold you up in the street and rob you! You're walking with your afro and your nice clothes on and these real roughneck reggae boys would shake you down just because you're a soul man! They'd just go, 'Yo! Come here . . .' make you turn out your pockets and take your money. Sometimes they'd tax you for your jacket – if you had one of those pony-skin jackets that people were going crazy for back then, the chances are somebody would tax you. I even heard of guys being taxed for their shoes – Gucci loafers! It wasn't just soul boys who suffered either. My brother Morris got taxed in Edgware Road once.

There was this period when taxing the soul boys became what life was all about for some of these guys. We would get a bunch of reggae boys coming into the clubs like Jasper's or Lewisham Way Boys' Club just to check people out. They come in and look around to work out who they were going to tax.

I look back at that now and it makes me laugh – the importance that was put on music and me turning into a soulhead – but back then there was nothing funny about it! It was a commitment, and as good as that rare groove music was, sometimes it was hard work to be part of that scene!

My mate Johnny introduced me to the clubs where I first connected with those tunes and that crowd, but my real education in the music came when I used to go over to my aunt's in Deptford. The brothers over there seemed more mature for their age, more streetwise and more worldly, and they really knew their music, particularly Patrick Dyas's brother Danny. I used to go round to their house and we would smoke weed and play rare groove tunes. Danny had boxes of records and he'd play me the O'Jays, Teddy Pendergrass, George Clinton, James Brown, the Sound of Philadelphia, Michael Jackson's stuff before *Thriller*, Herbie Hancock, Steve Arrington . . . He would literally blow my mind with music!

Danny would play me tunes but he wouldn't tell me the names. He'd just stick a record on and say, 'Tell me what you think of this one.' And it would be brilliant. Then he'd put on another one, that was brilliant too! He'd get so carried away I'd have to make him go back if I wanted to find out the name of anything.

Once he played me a tune from Bad Bobby Glover called 'It's My Turn', and I just thought it was the best tune I'd ever heard. It was a beautiful song, the lyrics were great, all about a guy who's been messing around so eventually his missus has left him, now he's gutted and it's his turn to cry . . . the melody and the way Bobby Glover sings it, it's got so much feeling in it. He used to play the Prince album just called *Prince*, and there's one song on that album that will always stay in my mind – 'Still Waiting'. If I've got people round my house and I say I'm going to play a Prince song, they roll their eyes and are like, 'Here we go!' because they know I'm going to play 'Still Waiting'. It's just a beautiful song.

They're the kind of tunes I like: lyrical, melodic songs that say something. They might have a message or just tell a story, but much as I love the beat of a record, for me it's still all about well-written lyrics. Of course, there were a lot of reggae records I had heard that I'd think had a brilliant lyric, but once I went over to the soul side and started to *really* hear the lyrics, like those of the Isley Brothers, it went up to a different level.

I didn't buy many records when I was younger, but one I did buy was 'You'll Never Know' by Hi Gloss. I don't know why I loved that song, but I loved it so much. Everybody has tunes that make them just get up and on the dance floor, to stop their conversation or put down their drink – *their* song.

When we were younger my mum had a couple of songs like that and I didn't really understand it until I heard this tune. Now it's *my* song, and every time I hear it I'm gone, I'm on the dancefloor!

With tunes like these, if I was in the dance, half-charged, I didn't need to dance with girls. I was happy to follow the groove by myself, which is just as well. As I said before I was shy around girls, so if I was ever thinking about asking somebody to dance I'd try not to make it obvious to people around me. I'd sort of ease over there and be dancing by myself near her, so it wouldn't look like a such a big deal compared to walking across the club.

The thing about that, though, there was nothing worse than looking up to see somebody coming striding over and suddenly he's dancing with her! It was like, 'Oh!' and you'd just carry on dancing by yourself for a bit, then make your way back to your mates. I was often a bit too slow.

I was so young and trying to build up my confidence in those situations, and I couldn't deal with that kind of humiliation. I had this thing where I would only dance with girls that I knew, friends, rather than wanting to get off with them, and I knew they would say yes. If I wanted a really good rave, I'd dance with Joan Siley – she's a little bit older than me – and we'd do some nice dancing together. Not that close stuff, it was in and out with footwork and spins, lovely stuff to good rare groove tunes. I used to love dancing with Joan Siley.

In my early Palace days, I had to stop going to local places because, although I knew my crowd, these were open dances and it was all too unpredictable. The older guys would still be looking out for me, stopping me and saying things like, 'You shouldn't be here, you shouldn't be in a place like this. People are smoking weed, it's a free-for-all, anybody could be in here. You shouldn't be around this kind of vibe.'

They couldn't have been prouder of me – they might have just watched me on *Match of the Day*, and then when I came in a place it would be all 'Nice one, Ian.' Then after a while one of the guys would say, 'Yo, Ian, it's time for you to go now.' I'd tell them that I'm not getting into any mischief, that I've just come down to hear some rare groove music and have a dance. I'd say I didn't have a game the next day, that I've already played. They'd just tell me that didn't matter, that I shouldn't stay out all night because I needed to be at home resting, recovering from the game.

I used to think back to how the same guys said the same things to me when I was playing Sunday mornings, and I'd start cussing, thinking, 'I'm a professional now, I got there, and I'm still getting this shit!'

Really though, they were being even more protective of me, saying now that you're a professional you have to act that way. As well as the fitness angle, they knew that as a Crystal Palace player I couldn't afford to even be near anything that might have gone off in those places. I'd always leave when they told me to, and then sometimes I'd hear a few days later there'd been a fight.

It would have done me no good to have been around such things, and I am eternally grateful to those guys for continuing to look out for me the way they did. They know that, but I still can't say it enough because they were keeping me out of the type of very tricky situations that are so easy for young players that have grown up in inner-city environments to fall into.

Too often, a young player's friends, the guys he grew up with, will put pressure on him to carry on hanging out with them at these kind of places, nagging him about 'keeping it real'. Too many youngsters are terrified of being talked about as 'rich and switch', carrying on like they are suddenly too good for the people they grew up with. But the bottom line is, when you have any sort of profile you can't afford to be caught up in things that are beyond your control and will show you and your club up in a negative light. As I say, a man will be judged by the company he keeps.

Also, if you're hanging out with all sorts of ruffians, people in the dressing room won't want you around them, and that will translate into a reputation for you as being trouble, whether you deserve it or not. It's seldom a case of rich and switch: usually it's more a matter of moving on as your circumstances change.

What this meant was that, although I never forgot where I came from and would still drop in and drop out of some of those places, it came as quite a relief when I started hanging out with the boys at Crystal Palace and being taken to these places up the West End. These were clubs – Browns in Holborn, Crazy Larry's, the WAG Club – where I could go and really kick back because I knew it wasn't going to kick off in there, the music was always brilliant and the places were always comfortable.

There was a core of us who used to rave together – Tony Finnigan, Andy Gray, Mitchell Thomas, Mark Bright once he'd joined Palace, myself and sometimes Garth Crooks. After we'd played on a Saturday, because we'd have the next day off, we would go up the West End, usually to Browns.

The music was fantastic, all funk and rare groove, and we really used to dance down there. There'd always be a few other foot-ballers – Gazza used to drop in – and London-based music people would go in. George Michael and his crowd would be there, and the emerging black acts had made it their spot, so we'd be hang-ing out with people like Jane Eugene and Carl McIntosh of Loose Ends and Leee John and the other lads from Imagination.

It wasn't like I'd felt I'd *arrived* or anything like that, but I was in a place where my face fit, totally, so I could relax and get completely into the music. The whole thing was a world away from my background of Brockley blues dances and clubs in the back of pubs!

Back home, it got so that the only things I could go to were family functions like christenings or birthday parties where it was safe because I'd know everybody in there. But there were some seriously good raves, especially if my ex-brother-in-law Johnny Sutherland was doing the music. He has got the most extensive rare-groove collection probably in the whole world – I don't care what anybody says, if I had to bet my life on a rare-groove challenge, I would put Johnny Sutherland in my corner. He has got the lot.

On Boxing Day, if we were playing in London – I couldn't do anything on Christmas Day because we'd be playing the next day – afterwards the whole family would be at Johnny's and we'd be playing rare groove until the early morning. It was always fantastic.

The first person I got in with at Palace was Tony Finnigan. He was totally cool, so was his mum, and I used to go to their house and hang out with them. At this point, my entire world wasn't much bigger than Brockley, Deptford and New Cross, so my social circle was the people who lived there. There was I having this ridiculous battle between reggae and being a soul boy, agonizing about getting a curly perm or not, which I thought was all so important in my life, and then I met people like Tony Finnigan.

He was worldly, cultured, he knew his roots in Jamaica, he knew who he was over here too, he was soul, he was reggae, he was everything . . . He was London and understood what the new generation of Londoners was, and was so totally confident in himself. If I could have picked somebody to teach me about being worldly or being properly streetwise, it would have been Tony. Once again, the right people have been in the right places at the right time to allow me to learn and grow.

It was a slow burner with Andy Gray because he was already the forward there and didn't know Steve Coppell had plans to move him back into midfield. I think he thought I was a threat to him. He was alright, though, and we became really good friends. He was an unbelievable foil for me. Andy was very streetwise – an aggressive, in-your-face black guy, Cockney accent and all, who didn't take any shit.

I feel like my personality was in between Andy and Tony. I had a bit of each of them to start off with, and I learned a lot from both of them.

We'd go out on a weekly basis with Mitchell and Brighty. At some of the clubs I'd hear tunes I could remember from way back, like Parliament or Earth, Wind & Fire, and I'd never, in my life, seen dancing like I saw in those clubs. I saw these black guys dancing to jazz/funk with total freedom and putting down some unbelievable moves. We had moves, but we would just get out of the way and literally stand and watch these guys for ages . . . it was so brilliant, so vibrant.

When I first started going out with them I didn't really have much of a dance style, so I'd just copy whatever I thought looked cool when other people were doing their stuff. Usually that was Tony, because he was a beautiful dancer. He could just stand there, didn't even have to move much of his body, but he'd have the whole rhythm of the tune right there. That's what I used to try and copy, and I still dance like that to this day if I go out and the tunes are right. I learned from Tony that I could just stand there on my own and just do the moves that make me feel good and it would be cool.

We'd all be on the dance floor, four of us, but not Mark Bright. Brighty didn't dance. We'd be putting down some serious moves, and he'd be standing on the edge doing his own uncomfortable out-of-rhythm moves, kind of bobbing from side to side.

Of course we'd tease him, but never too much because he'd had a very different upbringing to us. I don't think he had too much dealing with the black side of his culture as he was growing up, and raving simply wasn't part of his background. He was a bit uptight, and so didn't have a relaxed approach to the rhythm like we did. We'd always make sure we didn't overdo the teasing because he's such a lovely guy and he was our mate. He always contributed to the vibe we had going when, because he was from up north, he might have been a bit overwhelmed by us full-on London types. But that was Mark, he took everything in his stride.

That was something that, when I came through at Palace, I found hilarious – black guys with northern accents. I hadn't had too much contact with black people from Birmingham or Manchester, and I am so totally London-centric that listening to guys like Carlton Palmer or Dave Bennett or Mark Walters used to crack me up! When Chris Kiwomya was at Arsenal, he was pure Huddersfield, and actually used to call people petal and flower! 'Y'alright, flower?' he'd say! The only black man I'd heard talk like that was Charlie Williams, and he was a comedian. However, Chris always said the accent worked for him down in London, especially when he called the women petal or flower.

Hearing them took me back to the first time I can remember hearing anybody with a northern accent, which was when me and my brothers saw the film *Kes*. We loved the accent and laughed our heads off trying to speak like that: 'Noo, going ta Sheffield, meet girlfriend.'

So when I first heard a black guy speaking like a Yorkshireman or speaking with a Brummie accent I couldn't believe it! We used to slaughter those guys about their accents, especially on the pitch. Then you'd go into the players' bar after the game where we're all dressed in cutting-edge London style and they're all there in full northern-black-man clothes. And you'd know they put in extra effort if they were coming to Selhurst Park! We'd look at these weird-looking trousers and dodgy shoes and really feel good about being Londoners, because we were leading.

Brighty had some strange clothes when he first arrived at Palace, so of course he got teased mercilessly about that, but so did I when I turned up to my first game. Tony and that lot were killing themselves laughing at me. I actually felt OK, but when I looked at myself up against them I was like an old-time sticksman – one of those ruffian guys you get in blues dances, trying to steal purses! I was wearing Farrah slacks, in burgundy, multi-coloured Bally shoes, probably with a little chain across them, and I may even have been wearing a suede-fronted cardigan. They were decked out in linen this and that – suits and shirts and trousers – and immaculate brogues! Once Tony stopped laughing he knew he had to take me under his wing and get me kitted out.

This was something else about Tony Finnigan, he was impeccable in every way. He was metrosexual before the word was invented, and in 1985 he was using Clinique everything, cleanser, soap, moisturizer . . . You could go to his house and you'd find a stack of GQ magazines that would go back forever, so he knew about clothes and style. Even if you see him now, thirty years later, he's still one of the most stylish dressers you'll ever meet. He was perfectly turned out every single time.

He took me shopping down to Covent Garden and South Moulton Street. Linen shirts, linen trousers, linen suits, just really classy-looking stuff, classic English clothes, and we'd get brogues from Church's in Bond Street, and I still get my shoes there. We'd go to Browns in our really cool suede Church's shoes and linen suits, looking amazing. We'd get on the dance floor to some serious rare groove music and I used to think that life couldn't ever get much better than this.

Music in dressing rooms before the games was just starting to come in when I was leaving Palace, and they used to play some pretty pumping tunes in the Arsenal dressing room. You couldn't play any silky soul or rare groove. It would be a case of hip hop or deep garage tunes that everybody liked – or more or less everybody because whatever went on there was always somebody who'd say, 'What is this fucking shit?'

I had my own musical ritual for driving up to an Arsenal home game too. When I left my house I'd be playing soul and rare groove music – the Isley Brothers, Harold Melvin & the Blue Notes, Bad Bobby Glover . . . that sort of smooth stuff. Then as I started getting nearer to the ground I'd gradually pump up the funk and the tempo. When I turned into Avenell Road, where all the fans were milling bout and I was going to turn into the car park, it would reach a crescendo with 'Firestarter' by Prodigy blasting at the highest volume. By the time I got in the dressing room I was pumped and ready to go. All I needed was a top-up of whatever banging tunes they were playing there.

When Wimbledon came to Highbury they would literally bring the noise. As they got off their coach outside the stadium they'd be pumping out music from a suitcase-sized ghetto blaster. Walking up the stairs to the marble halls they'd all be dressed differently – this one would have a tracksuit on, this one had jeans and a T-shirt, this one had a suit on and so on – like they obviously didn't care. Their music would be playing as loud as can be, instantly making you wonder, 'What the hell is that?' and, immediately, you're thrown. Somebody would ask them to turn it down, but even if they did they would almost immediately turn it up again. It's what they did, upsetting their opponents by knocking everybody in the place off their axes right from the start.

How many times did Wimbledon come to our place and cause us problems or beat us? That was because they got us so bothered before we even kicked off – 'How fucking dare

Wimbledon come to Arsenal and act like that?', we'd be think-ing, when we should have been thinking, 'Let them carry on, we'll just do what we do. We're better players so we'll beat them on the field.' Wimbledon beat us off the pitch which, too often, enabled them to beat us on the pitch. The most annoying thing about it was it was actually some very, very good music! Hard-pumping, bass-driven tunes – whoever was doing it was picking some really cool stuff.

Nowadays there has to be meaning to my music, and after thinking long and hard I've decided the two greatest records I've ever heard in the whole world are Louis Armstrong's 'It's a Wonderful World' and John Lennon's 'Imagine'. Those two records resonate with me more than any other tune I've ever heard. I just think that's where I am now: if somebody said I had to pick two then it would be those for the way that they're sung and the meaning in them.

My love for rare groove music hasn't diminished, but my tastes have broadened out. I've got a hard drive that my mate put 46,000 tunes on, every genre of music you could think of is there, and at the time of writing I am waiting to move so I can wire it up into a really cool system and start blasting. When I do, I'm pretty sure the first tune I'll play will be either Hi Gloss's 'You'll Never Know' or Bad Bobby Glover's 'It's My Turn'.

Chapter Seventeen

'You're at a Big Club Now!'

My earliest memories of being an Arsenal player weren't as positive as they might have been – I was at David Rocastle's house watching the six o'clock news on the day I signed. My transfer had become a news item, then it cut to a series of clips of Arsenal fans who all seemed to be saying, 'What did we buy him for?'

I could understand their point – sort of. It was September 1991 and in the last couple of weeks the team had scored five against Sheffield United in the league and six against Rapid Vienna in the European Cup. They were scoring goals for fun, yet they'd just paid a club record fee of £2.5 million for a striker? Of course they were going to think they didn't need me.

Then I caught myself. My signing to Arsenal was on the six o'clock news and then the ten o'clock news, that's how big a deal it was, and that's the size and stature of the club I was joining. I just sat back and thought, 'What a great experience, make the most of this moment, slow down.' Because the most remarkable thing about it was the speed with which it happened.

When I'd left my house that morning I was a Crystal Palace player and very happy to be one. There'd been no talk or rumours or whispers about any transfer, so I really didn't see it coming. Back then, without all the media attention, transfers weren't those long drawn-out sagas, and when they appeared to come from nowhere to the general public they were coming from nowhere for the player, too. I think we'd played Villa on the Saturday, had Sunday off, and when I arrived at training on Monday Peter Prentice told me the boss wanted to see me.

I went into Steve Coppell's office, sat down and he looked really solemn. He straight out said, 'We've accepted a bid from Arsenal for you.'

That was frightening. I froze. It was that Mars bar/drug test moment all over again. I kind of stammered, 'What? When's that? When do I have to go?'

'Today.'

I felt like I was in shock and I replied, 'I can't, I've got to buy my mum a television!'

Which was true. I had promised to pick her up a new TV that afternoon. Steve just kind of shrugged and said that would have to wait because I had to go for my medical straight away.

He was brilliant about all of it. I know he didn't want me to leave and the club had given me a very good new contract when we went up in 1989, but he wasn't going to stop me going. In fact, he wasn't even going to give me the 'Are you sure about this?' speech, because he's the type of guy who wouldn't stand in the way of anybody's development. Ron Noades tried to get me to stay by offering me more money, but it seemed like Steve had already resigned himself to my going.

It was nine-thirty in the morning, and while I was driving across London to the Whittington hospital in Archway for the tests with Arsenal's medical team, it began to fully sink in. It had all happened so quickly, I didn't get the chance to think about it until then.

When Steve told me I had to go he also told me I couldn't speak to anybody at the training ground so I didn't say goodbye to anybody there – I couldn't even go back for my boots. They had to send them on. The one thing I did do, which I really shouldn't have but I was so excited, was phone David Rocastle.

'Rock,' I said, 'I'm going for the medical at Arsenal, but you can't say anything to anybody.'

He sounded as excited as I was but promised he wouldn't tell a soul.

It felt like the longest ever medical. It never occurred to me I wouldn't pass it, because all I'm thinking is, if I pass this I'm going to Arsenal, *the* Arsenal. The last time I saw them was at the end of the previous season when I went to watch them beat Manchester United three-one and take the title. Now I was on the very edge of joining them.

I got through the medical, and had to go straight over to Highbury to physically sign the contracts – this was it! I went there with my agent, Jerome Anderson, and that was when he took me out into the directors' box and let me gaze down at Arsenal Football Club.

As I was soaking it up he was telling me how, if I could do here what I did at Palace, commercially I would go through the roof, that what it would bring me would mean I'd never have to worry about money again.

'Being at this football club,' he said, 'means you will achieve your goals.'

I wouldn't say I was really listening because I was so taken up looking around. While he was probably talking about monetary goals, I was thinking about footballing goals. I've never done anything purely for the money, and this was definitely no exception.

'Fine,' I said, 'let me sign and let me go home, you can do the stuff to fill it all in.'

I signed a blank contract. It was only afterwards that I learned I'd only be earning £700 a week more than I had been at Palace.

People said I must have been crazy to have done that, saying my agent and the club must somehow have been in cahoots; my wife at the time simply couldn't believe it – she ridiculed me! It was like, '*What*? You signed for *that*?!? You left Crystal Palace to go to Arsenal for just £700 a week more?'

Although I did get a twinge of, 'Oh God, have I made the right decision?' they were completely missing the point. I didn't go to Arsenal for the money: I went to play football with the reigning champions and to win things.

I went there in 1991–92 and won the Golden Boot in that season with twenty-nine goals; then in the second season I won the FA Cup and the League Cup; in the third season we won the Cup Winners' Cup when it was worth winning, although I was suspended for the final; we got to the final of the Cup Winners' Cup again; then won the double in 1998.

That was what I went to Arsenal for and I totally got it.

As soon as it was done and I was out of there, I phoned Rocks again and went up to stay at his house, which wasn't far from Arsenal's training ground at London Colney. We sat up practically all night just talking about Arsenal, discussing practically every aspect of the club and the people who were there.

Of course, I was nervous I was remembering Charlie Nicholas coming to the club from Scotland to a big fanfare and it didn't happen for him – I think I managed to bring up every striker who went anywhere and it didn't work out for them! Very calmly, Rocky said, 'Ian, you're going to be great here. You keep scoring, especially in the derby, and you'll be a legend at Arsenal. Forever.'

I don't know if he was saying it just to make me relaxed, but it worked, I was convinced I was going to be all right.

What I didn't find out until later was George Graham had thoroughly checked me out with the players who knew me, the guys who knew me from England and, of course, Rocky. He'd spoken at length to Tony Adams about what I was like to play against and what my attitude was in training. He'd asked Merse what I was like to play alongside and talked to The Goalie about my finishing. He'd asked Rocky what I was like as a character, because he knew me better than anybody. This had been going on while they were scouting me, and I remembered Merse and Rocks telling me that the boss liked me, but I don't remember taking any notice of it.

The next day I went in for training and could immediately see I'd moved up a level, and this wasn't just because the guys I knew from England made sure I knew it – when I showed my face I had Merse and Tony Adams shouting stuff at me: 'Oi! Wrighty! You're at a big club now, you better get your finger out!'

In that first session the ball was shooting about like it was in a pinball machine. It was electric. I was trying to play against Tony, Bouldie, Dicco and Nigel and thought, 'OK, now I get it.' Even Paul Davis and David Hillier in the midfield were impossible to get anything from . . . with all due respects to Palace, this was a step up in quality in every department.

Even when we'd finished, we had our own separate baths, each! That first day at Arsenal training was magical. It's days like those that I really wish I could have again. As I was driving home, all I could think was, 'Bloody hell, I'm at Arsenal.'

I made my debut really soon after that on 25 September 1991. It was in a League Cup game against Leicester that I wasn't meant to play in. I was going to be on the bench, then Alan Smith went down with his ankle before the game so George Graham came to me really late in the afternoon and said, 'Wrighty, you're playing tonight.' I don't know if he kept it from me so as to avoid me feeling the pressure of starting.

Like the training, this was fantastic too, again a definite step up. I didn't have to cover nearly as much ground as I had done at Palace. It seemed like every time I looked the ball was there and I'd just got to go *'Bang!'* I'd never had so many touches in a game, made so many runs or looked so sharp. Of course the Leicester fans started singing 'What a waste of money', which was when I scored.

The ball came across from Paul Davis and I kind of slipped, my arm went on the floor, and as I got up I whipped the ball around and it went in. I thought, this is amazing! I ran towards the Leicester fans to say, 'Go on then, sing!' Sure enough, they stopped singing it.

I really couldn't have asked for a better debut.

My Crystal Palace journey had been incredible: from 1985 until we finally went up in 1989, sometimes there were only four or five thousand people watching us against teams like Shrewsbury and Plymouth. When I hear about Palace fans getting plaudits for being the best in the country, I remember how loyal and noisy those fans were even back then. Establishing the partnership with Brighty was something we both worked very hard on, and it was brilliant to see that pay off when we started blasting. And, of course, there was the FA Cup Final and getting into the England team.

I needed that journey to take me from Sunday-morning football – I'll always be indebted to Steve Coppell for taking a chance on me at age twenty-two. However, by the time this came around, I felt ready to make that move up.

Ironically, I came close to becoming a Spurs player. I'm pretty sure Arsenal only started seriously watching me after the FA Cup Final in 1990, which was a year or so after Tottenham were showing interest. Mark Buxton, Spurs's chief scout under Terry Venables, had bumped into Mark Bright somewhere and told him that Terry Venables was keen on me and asked him to find out if I'd be interested in coming to Spurs.

When Brighty told me I was like, 'Yeah!' I would have loved to have gone to Spurs, which is the truth. They'd had Glenn Hoddle, one of my heroes, and at that point they had Chris Waddle, another player I love, they had Gazza, and they were about to sign Gary Lineker, plus one of my best mates Mitchell Thomas was in the team. It was an extremely attractive proposition, and I was simply excited that anybody was making some noise around me. At that point, Arsenal were nowhere near my radar and I didn't think they'd even be looking at me, so if Tottenham had come in at that time, I would have joined and I know I would have been a legend there too.

In the end they signed Paul Stewart from Manchester City, who had been brilliant in our league that year, so that got scuppered. There wasn't anything made public about their interest in me at the time, so I often get asked, usually by my Spurs-supporting mates, would I have played for them? Of course I would have, but that was before Arsenal. Once I went to Arsenal and understood what playing for the club meant, there was no way *ever* I would play for Spurs. There's nothing you could have offered me to make me cross over.

Part Three

Life Goes On

Chapter Eighteen

The Whistle's Gone

I left Burnley in June 2000. I'd decided two years previously that was when I was going to retire, wherever I was playing – it worked out well. I felt like I'd gone out on a high with the club going up and me doing my bit to help them. I thought I felt ready to retire, as I'd achieved pretty much all of my ambitions in football, but when the reality set in it was a hard one to take. Waking up one morning to fully appreciate I wasn't a professional footballer any more – and never would be again – was difficult.

It was in July that it really hit home. This is when pre-season comes around and everybody's getting ready to go back: then, suddenly, it's the first game of the season, the sun's out, there's new boots, new kit . . . everything's new, everything's great. I remember not doing anything – not having anything to do – and feeling something's not right, something's missing. What I did to cover up feeling that way was act like I was really pleased I didn't have to do any of it any more, then I went on a prolonged holiday. Just because I could!

This is the immediate reaction most players have to not playing any more – especially the ones that quit quickly and at the top, rather than spending years fading down the divisions. They do that thing where they take a look at themselves in the mirror and, as the lightbulb pings above their heads, they say, 'Hang on a minute! I'm free! I can actually do *anything* I want!'

This can be a real big deal. For all those years, maybe since they were teenagers, footballers' contracts would have meant there were so many things they weren't allowed to do. I can remember reading my contracts and being astounded at what I wasn't allowed to do because it would have put me 'in harm's way'. I wasn't allowed to ride a bike, they even questioned us driving ourselves to the training ground, and we used to joke that we'd be in breach of contract if we were doing anything other than walking at a reasonable pace!

You really do belong to the club for the duration of the contract, and the club even holds your passport – you hand it over on the first day of pre-season, then you get it back after the last game. Although that in itself isn't such a bad idea as footballers are always losing things, being able to go where you want sums up that new-found freedom. So while the prolonged holidays happen mostly because you have no reason to rush back, they also seem the appropriate way to celebrate.

While you get this new-found freedom, however, there can be quite a trade-off involved. A club like Arsenal will do every-thing for you, so at the same time you'll be losing what was really a support system. Suddenly having to deal with the organ-izational side of life for yourself, and not having your days planned out for you, can be a bit of a culture shock.

I was always quite happy with having everything taken care of because I'm terrible with any kind of organization – I'll leave my house and have to go back three or four times because I've forgotten my phone, I've forgotten my wallet, I've forgotten the door keys . . . I'm always losing my phone, and I would have lost my passport on a weekly basis.

Dennis Bergkamp could have carried the whole team if he'd wanted to!
© Barry Coombs/EMPICS Sport

In the Arsenal changing room before the 2015 Cup Final against Villa, and, no, I didn't bring my boots.
© Stuart MacFarlane/Getty Images

Singing with Lionel Ritchie on *Friday Night's All Wright*, one of the highlights of my TV career.
© Ken McKay/REX/ Shutterstock

Sir Trevor McDonald, a true gentleman who had a profound effect on my TV career.
© Ken McKay/REX/ Shutterstock

Back on *Match of the Day* after all that went on before – how lucky am I?
© Photoshot

(top left) Goals from Scholes are wonderful things – against Moldova in 1997, me and Sol Campbell let him know that.
© Colorsport/REX/Shutterstock

(middle left) If ever there was a player who made my life as a striker easier, it was Dennis Bergkamp.
© Colorsport/REX/Shutterstock

(bottom left) Goooaaalll! Equalling Arsenal's goal-scoring record.
© Colorsport/REX/Shutterstock

(below) Glenn Hoddle, an amazing coach, gave me my England career back.
© Daily Mail/REX/Shutterstock

(top) Wembley 1998 – I might not have got on the pitch that day, but I was still going to enjoy the moment.
© Bob Thomas/Getty Images

(above) The other half of the 1997/1998 Double: *(left to right)* Adams, David Seaman, Lee Dixon, Martin Keown, David Platt and me.
© Michael Steele/EMPICS Sport

(right) Victory for Arsenal against Everton in 1998.
© Colorsport/Stuart MacFarlane

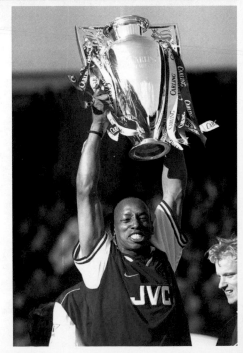

Arsenal's greatest ever player *(left)*; Arsenal's greatest ever signing *(right)*.
© Mark Thompson/Getty Images

Me and Tony before a charity game in Trafalgar Square in 2013.
© Christopher Lee/Getty Images

With David Dein – Mr Arsenal – at the 2005 Capital FM awards.
© Richard Young/REX/Shutterstock

When you get to know him, Arsène Wenger has a brilliant sense of humour.
© Michael Regan – The FA/Getty Images

Tony is still one of the funniest blokes I know.
© Author's collection

(top right) After I retired, I threw myself into golf to satisfy my competitive nature. © Warren Little/Getty Images

(above right) I did my *Top Gear* lap in 1:47.08. Clarkson said he'd never seen anybody drive so fast and so aggressively.
© Author's collection

(above left) Family fortune – with Nancy and the girls at the European premiere of *Kung Fu Panda 3* in 2016.
© Retna/Photoshot

(left) From Brockley to Buckingham Palace – receiving my MBE in 2000.
© Photoshot

Lee Dixon's testimonial vs Real Madrid in 1999 – such was the reception I got at Highbury, Dicco thanked me for letting him play in my testimonial! © Colorsport/REX/Shutterstock

To suddenly have the structure you've had in your life removed and to start fending for yourself can cause problems for quite a few footballers once they stop playing. Many players have had everything taken care of for them for practically their whole lives, so they don't even know these things *need* to be taken care of. I was really lucky because my wife took over and did all of that for me. She still does. She literally runs my life to the point she might as well be called a football club!

There wasn't that much I wanted to do that I hadn't already been doing, because like so many other players I had been doing stuff I wasn't supposed to. My big thing was motorbikes.

I've been a massive motorbike fan since I was a kid – and, quite understandably, riding one was pretty high up the list of contractual no-nos. I bought one in 1996, a Harley Davidson Heritage Softail, a serious piece of machinery and a massive bike.

We almost always used to play on Saturdays then, and my favourite way to relax on a Sunday was ride it around the M25 or go somewhere with my mates who were also into bikes – sometimes we'd do a hundred miles to somewhere, have something to eat and do the hundred miles back.

It was a genuine escape from having to think about all the stuff you have to think about leading up to, during and immediately after a game – especially playing for George Graham! Just bombing round on the bike, totally in charge of myself, was fantastic.

Arsenal never knew I had it, although I nearly gave myself away after I'd been riding for a couple of years, when I asked David Dein if I could get insurance on a motorbike through the club. I really wanted to find out if there was any way I was going to be allowed to have one. He didn't even answer me.

He just started laughing because he thought it was hilarious that a footballer should even be thinking about owning a Harley Davidson motorbike. He just looked at me as if I was crazy and eventually said, 'Why would you even ask that?' I can't remember what I said, but it certainly wasn't that I'd had one for the last two years.

So it was a bit of a weird one, because although I was free to do anything, there wasn't that much I felt I was missing and I had to do as soon as I stopped. Sure, I could ride openly now – I could ride the bike across Europe, and me and my mate Eddie used ride all over Europe on our Harleys. We could ride across America if we fancied it, and I used to spend quite a lot of time over there. I remember Tony Adams was always very keen to go skiing – obviously something else that wasn't permitted. I tried it a couple of times and, I don't know if it was my upbringing, but I never felt like I fitted in. Back then you didn't see too many brothers from south London going on ski trips and I simply couldn't get into it.

I threw myself into golf, which was really cool because it's one of those sports that, if you want to do really well at, you have to totally dedicate yourself to. I got lessons from one of my best mates, Tony Healey, a teaching pro, and with my attitude and what I'd been doing for the last fifteen-odd years, golf was good for me. I could get into it in the same way as I worked at my finishing – I literally practised golf all day – and it was good for me because the improvement was easily measured so I could see my progress every time I played or went to the driving range.

Also, it was about the only thing I could actually do to give my competitive juices the fix they needed. Although my ankle wasn't fused yet, it was in a bad way and hurt so much there weren't many other sports I could play.

That is something I'm sure every footballer thinks about when they retire – the pain and how they don't have to put themselves through that anymore. I wasn't pain-free just because I wasn't playing any more, and I knew I'd have to have my ankle fixed at some point, but I remember the relief I'd feel at not aching as much as I did on an everyday basis.

It's not unusual for footballers to work at keeping fit when they stop playing and training. I didn't even bother to try, though. I had a good metabolism, so during the first two or three years after I stopped I was never more than a couple of pounds over my playing weight of eleven stone seven pounds, and I really enjoyed eating whatever I wanted. I enjoyed drinking too, not abusive drinking, just being able to enjoy a good bottle of wine or something like that without having to think about it.

I could stay out for as long as I liked on any night of the week, as well . . . I did a load of those sorts of things, just because I hadn't been able to for the last decade and a half. But all the time I'm doing all of the above, all I'm thinking is, 'I miss football *so fucking much*!'

You're not even allowed to try and forget what you used to do either. When I had just finished, I was at the height of my fame and my chat show was going really well, so I still had all the same recognition factor. Once the season started, I couldn't go anywhere without people doing double-takes and saying, 'Hang on a minute . . . shouldn't you be playing football?'

Any time there was a game involving Arsenal, even though I'd left them two years earlier, people would say, 'What you doing here? Shouldn't you be kicking off in a minute?' This happens to every former player, and I'm sure it can get a bit wearing to some, but these are the people that cheered you on when you were playing and now they're just showing they haven't forgotten you. The higher profile you were, the longer it lasts. Then when somebody else takes over your role at the club you're most associated with – for me that was Thierry and Arsenal – you kind of fade away. This is natural progression, and never a problem for me.

The fact that I was already in television with the chat show took my mind away from leaving football. I was still learning a new skill and fitting into a new world, so I didn't really have time to pine for football. I had to do a lot of reading, looking at scripts and preparing for interviews, and because it was light entertainment not football punditry I was completely removed from football.

It seemed as if I had a fantastic new career. I was doing interviews with Denzel Washington and people like that on my *Friday Night's All Wright* show, I had these great bands on, I gave Beyoncé and Destiny's Child their first platinum disc on my show, but while I fully appreciated how privileged I was to have that opportunity, it didn't even come close to how much I missed football.

As a footballer the best part of your life is playing – that sounds obvious, but you'll always be a footballer whether you're still playing or not – and if you're doing it properly then all the different aspects of it take up all of your life. When it stops there's bound to be a big hole, and because of the nature of football and the team spirit, when I had to leave it behind I was a bit lonely.

I tried to replicate that dressing-room situation with the television production teams, but while they were great I couldn't quite do it. This came as a bit of a surprise, because I assumed it would be easy to copy that kind of thing as the team-building exercises that happened in offices all seemed geared up towards that.

Back at Arsenal some of the lads used to call the training ground the office. They'd talk about it as 'going to the office' because, to them, it was just like any other workplace. I looked on the TV production offices like that, and in theory it was the same: you make a few good friends, but you might not like everybody; you've got people who are very intense; you've got people who mess about all the time; then you've got the in-betweens; there's always some people who are antagonizing other people all the time . . . you've got banter and teasing and in-jokes going on all the time . . . everything that happens in a production office should be the same as a dressing room, but it isn't.

Maybe it's because it's all blokes in a football club's squad, or maybe it's because so many footballers have been pretty much cocooned in that environment since they were kids, but being part of a football dressing room is like going to school. It's like going to a brilliant school, the greatest school in the world! I'm sure some of our behaviour was pretty juvenile, but it was who I was, and I loved it!

Having retired, I know I felt a bit . . . if not exactly resentful, then I was hurting that I wasn't part of all that any more. I used to think about this a great deal, perhaps more so as Arsenal were doing so well and were the team of the moment.

Had I gone into football punditry as a route into television I would have remained part of that world, because although I would have been a step removed from the actual dressing room, I'd be with footballers all the time, I'd be watching football with them, reading about it, talking about it . . . Even the rhythms of my life wouldn't have changed because I'd be working when footballers are working, I'd be on holiday when they're on holiday, so I'd still feel as if I was involved as a footballer because I would still be doing the same hours that they're doing. Everything would have still been planned around match-days, and pre-season still would have been special.

I would have liked to have done my coaching badges right after I finished playing, too. That would have been the right time to do them – I was fresh from playing, relevant to young players coming through, and I had enough money to take the time out to do them. I didn't do anything related to football, however, because I had a management company that convinced me to stay as far away from it as possible while I was doing the light entertainment.

They were trying to reinvent me from being just a footballer to push me towards the light entertainment, which was where they believed the real money was coming from. This why they lined up the deals for me even before I finished playing.

It wasn't right for me. Listening to them left me brainwashed, and I went along with it because they were supposed to be working in my best interests. I had an agent, Jeff Weston, who worked for the company, Jerome Anderson Management, and he *acted* like he was somebody who cared about me, but all he did was use me as a cash cow for him and the company.

I know ultimately I've got nobody to blame but myself, but these were people who I should have been able to trust because we were supposed to be working together, with me out front, either playing football or on television or whatever, and them being able to operate in the areas I don't understand. That's what agents do and they get very well paid for it.

I won't dismiss anything I did in light entertainment because it was a genuine privilege and so much fun. In fact, I enjoyed more or less all of it. My character got me through it. I've always liked meeting people – just liked people, really – and I had the brashness and the confidence to pull it off, but I was a football person when all was said and done.

I should have been in football . . . I should have been coaching someone, somewhere, because my expertise was in respect of playing football, not light entertainment.

I kept the same friends from my playing days, but the reality of it was they were still professional footballers and by then I was a television person, acting like I'm really happy with it. 'Oh, I'm in television now, and it's brilliant . . . Got my own show, and everything's great! . . . Television's great!'

But the simple truth was I'd rather have been doing what they were doing. I could always hang out with the guys, I could phone the same people or go out to dinner with them, but, in the end, they were still playing and were still in their professional-footballer mode doing their stuff, while I was a television person.

This really was a weird one, because while I was happy to see the team do so well during that time and was proud that Arsenal was my club, I was envious of Lee Dixon, Tony Adams, Nigel Winterburn and The Goalie, who were still there in that whole set up for all those years after I had stopped. I thought, 'Why couldn't I stay at Arsenal for longer? Is it because they're defenders they were able to?'

Dicco and I are the same age – he's only a couple of months younger – yet he stayed on for four more years. The Goalie and Nigel too, although Tony's a few years younger. It used to come down to me thinking, 'How come I'm so old?'

Not only were these guys going on after me but they'd started earlier as well – Nigel had youth-team football at Birmingham, Lee came through the ranks at Burnley, Tony was an Arsenal schoolboy, and Dave Seaman came through at Leeds. They'd played when they were kids, played through successful professional careers, and now they were still playing and I was not! Why couldn't I have been part of that whole set-up for longer than I was?

That used to irk me quite a bit, and would set me thinking about all the time I'd missed when clubs had passed me over as a teenager. I got a bit bitter then, for the first and probably the only time. Not with those guys, because they're some of my best mates. I found myself *hating* the people who rejected me when I was younger.

It didn't really make sense, because if I had got signed when I was younger, maybe I would have finished earlier. Would I have played until later? Would I have made it to Arsenal? I don't know . . . I just needed somebody to blame for the fact that I wasn't playing football, I wanted to be and I couldn't for whatever reason.

Those are the moments in which I'm sure a little bit of depression crept in. Although I can't pretend I was completely satisfied with so much of the television work I was doing, I feel now that it was having that stuff to do at that time, when I missed football so much, which stopped me from slipping into the depressive mode that lots of footballers go into.

It's not at all unusual for footballers to go through what I was feeling and suffer quite badly from depression after they stop playing. Obviously it helps if they've got something to do, but even that might not be enough.

256

Lee Chapman had gone down the restaurant route with his wife, the actress Leslie Ash, and he told me how, in spite of that, he got depressed when he stopped playing. I met him at his place in Soho, Teatro, and we had an unbelievable chat in there. He told me how much it affected him just to have so much of his life taken away from him. Lee was doing well with the restaurants, yet he still missed football to the point that he found it so hard to deal with.

For a footballer it's like having a tap turned off and everything he's done since he was a teenager or younger has had to stop. And not because they want it to stop, either. It's a massive gear change, which is why players miss it so much and it's all they can think about. No wonder it's going to have such a deep psychological effect – there's more than a few go off the rails, usually with drinking too much, but it's not something that gets too much publicity.

As well as missing everything about football to such a degree, there is also the very big worry of earning a living when you stop playing. There's a huge amount of professional footballers in the UK, I think currently it's around 4,000, and the vast majority aren't David Beckham. In reality, many of them don't earn a great deal more than people with regular jobs. During their careers most footballers won't have earned anywhere near a fortune, then they'll finish at around age thirty-five and will have another fifty or sixty years to live. Pensions aren't worth peanuts, and you couldn't take one at thirty-five even if it was enough.

Football only really prepares you for football, but when you pack it in there are only so many coaching jobs to go around. If you can't coach or don't get the opportunity to, then what do you do? The punditry jobs are limited too – really it's only a couple of dozen ex-players make a living at it – and even to do that you need a particular personality.

This is why you have to worry for the players that don't have the business acumen to branch out like Lee Chapman did, or have character or the skills to be able to go into something else. Andy Linighan, who scored the winner for Arsenal in the 1993 FA Cup Final replay, is a plumber now – he's very happy running his plumbing business – but he was apprenticed with a plumber when he was starting out in football, so he was well prepared. Andy's in the minority, though.

Even if you do get into coaching or the media, you still have to try and preserve your money for as long as you can because at any stage it can finish – whatever contract you're on could be your last just because nobody fancies you any more. Somebody can join a club as a coach, then the manager that hired them gets sacked and they get their contract cancelled too. Or a pundit could have a slip and say something inappropriate on television, and it's all over! Every contract can be voided and then you're finished, so you always need to look at ways to make sure your money lasts.

You're not immune from this even if you were at the top end during your playing career. Every single footballer has to try to make investments that, while they're never going to give them the lifestyle they had – that would be impossible – will ensure a certain amount of money in the future. They want to know they can survive for the next ten or fifteen years – enough to pay for the kids' education, to make sure they can keep their house.

Even then, no matter how careful players think they're being, it can all go wrong. You can be told it's a sure thing to invest in this or that, then fifteen years later, just when you feel everything's all right, you're told, 'Well, actually, the investments didn't work out and there's nothing to left in the account.' Or there's HM Revenue & Customs coming at you from every direction.

Knowing what I know now, if I had to go through it all again I'd buy one house every year, which I could have afforded, would have made me money while I was playing and given me a good investment for retirement.

You have to remember footballers are just like everybody else: we have divorces; we have people who are gamblers; we've got people who turn to alcohol; we've got people who spend too much and their money just runs out. The real difference is so many footballers won't be able to earn anything from football after their late-thirties, and that is a huge contribution to why so many former players become depressed.

It's a very real problem, but one you won't hear much about because, for the most part, people aren't bothered — it's not a story that's going to sell papers because people don't seem to be able to feel any compassion for former footballers. The general public won't feel any sympathy with them over depression: the attitude is, they're rich and they're privileged so what have they got to complain about?

Stan Collymore talked about how earning £100,000 per week doesn't make you impervious to depression, that it happened to him and could happen to anybody. He's unusual in that he came out and talked about it – Clarke Carlisle didn't, and he drank too much and tried to kill himself. Dean Windass was depressed *while* he was playing and recently told the BBC he should have been an actor he covered it up so well. Then after he retired he took to drink and thoughts of suicide, finally getting help from Tony Adams's Sporting Chance Clinic.

The problem is that when footballers come out and talk about depression, instead of getting the kind of support they ought to be getting, they're going to get slaughtered – especially on social media. It's all, 'What's your problem?' . . . 'You earned all that money, you should be happy!' . . . 'What you got to be depressed about? Try bringing up three kids on factory wages!' . . . It's a very closed-off attitude, and footballers know that.

It's the same inside football too. In general, you've got a society in which men put up barriers around themselves and won't even admit to being depressed, let alone talk about it. Then you take that into the ultra-macho world of professional football . . . There's no way anybody is going to open up about the fact they're a depressive and therefore vulnerable – nobody's going to ask anybody for help in that culture. So you've got all that to deal with in the game that should be helping you, then in the outside world you've got the stigma of being an ex-footballer to deal with, so nobody's taking you seriously.

The bigger clubs are trying to do something about this. They'll do their bit but they don't like to make a fuss about it, although every once in a while something comes out in the media – like Clarke Carlisle or Kenny Samson's problems. Arsenal tried to do a lot of things with Kenny, and I know that Sporting Chance has tried to help him. No big club is going to turn their back on a former player, but the smaller clubs haven't got the resources to do too much, yet their players have got exactly the same problems.

I don't think there's enough being done in this area to give players and ex-players somewhere to go for the kind of help they need and deserve. This is where the Professional Footballers' Association, the PFA, should come in. I don't think they do nearly enough to ensure the wellbeing of players after they finish playing.

We have to pay enough money to the PFA during our careers, and they get a cut of the TV money, but it seems to me they don't instigate the sort of help so many former players need. Take Tony Adams's Sporting Chance Clinic: after his own problems, he's gone away, he's sorted himself out and built the foundation – the PFA should have done that. They've jumped on the back of what Tony has done, but they should have put something like that together in the first place. They only do just enough to get themselves noticed. And that's about it.

There are serious health issues among former players that are the result of playing professional football – depression is just one of them – but instead of looking at what they can do to help them, the PFA just seems to sit there. Gordon Taylor has been Chief Executive since before I was playing: he's in charge of one of the greatest and most powerful organizations in the world, and I don't even know what he does, apart from turn up at functions every now and again, show his face, do his spiel and go.

What annoys me most about the PFA is that they don't work hard enough to let members know what is available to them, and a lot of footballers or former footballers aren't really capable of finding out for themselves – often because it just doesn't occur to them this help is available. It's not enough to say, after an event, 'Oh, they could have come to us for help, we make all these provisions . . .'

I'm sixteen years retired and the PFA have never approached me in any way, other than to do publicity work for them, or sent me anything to let me know they could do this or they could do that for me. My ankle's fused and I'm sure I would have been entitled to have had the operation paid for by the PFA, but I've never been told what I could get from them. As it was I could get my ankle done on a private health plan, but very few players are as fortunate as me.

The PFA doesn't seem to offer help unless you're phoning them up and chasing them about it. They don't push their services enough – if they worked as hard at that as they do at getting in touch with former big-name players, myself included, asking us to go here or there to promote the PFA, I'm sure there wouldn't be nearly so many former players with difficulties.

Retiring in your thirties wouldn't be the easiest thing for anybody in any profession to cope with, and because of the massive changes to your life that are involved, quitting football can be particularly challenging. I had my own problems, but I was able to get through them thanks to people around me and my getting back into football through punditry.

When I started doing that, after the light entertainment, and found out how much I enjoyed it – not just because I was around football again, but having to think and to have something to say about football – I became a much more relaxed, happier person. But I was very fortunate that everything fell into place in that respect and that I've got the character to do it. Too many former footballers don't have my opportunities and, if so little is done to help them, it's storing up trouble for the future.

Chapter Nineteen

Him Off the Telly

I was still playing when I started the chat show *Friday Night's All Wright* in 1998. I was at West Ham and it had never been in my thinking to do anything like fronting a light entertainment show.

My agents came to me when ITV local news got in touch because they were planning a series of interviews with sporting people – cricketer Alec Stewart and golfer Lora Fairclough were a couple of them – and they wanted me to do some of them. I must've done well, because off the back of that they gave me a couple of other sports-related things to do.

Then all of a sudden the light entertainment people asked me to come in to sit down and talk about making some sort of pilot show. They wanted a chat show that would attract a younger, hipper audience, with the plan being to only show it in London. That's when we came up with idea of having deejays, putting people in the cages, the nightclub-type idea, a live audience . . . all of that stuff.

It was great, contributing to all of that, helping to shape the show: they said they wanted some music, I said why don't we get a DJ? They asked, 'Who?' I said, 'Who's the best? Get the best.' So they went for Pete Tong – of course, it helped that he's a Gooner. Then we got Paul Oakenfold in there some of the time. It was unbelievable.

Lennox Lewis, who was then the Heavyweight Champion of the World, was my doorman. What was very funny was how he got into it and started to act like a nightclub bouncer, so if Denzel or somebody came to the door to get on the set he'd stop them and have a few words. Ridiculous, really.

They got these vintage cars, put them on low loaders and filmed so it looked like I was driving them up and down in London, which was really quite cool. Actually, the whole thing was very cool.

Then we had to get some guests, which, for a pilot of a show that is only going to be broadcast in the London region, isn't as straightforward as it might seem. We got the boxer Prince Naseem Hamed and Tina Hobley from *Coronation Street*, which was great, but we needed a real headline kind of guest. Amazingly, we got Lionel Richie. He simply liked the look of what we were about and said he'd rather do my show than *Parkinson*. That immediately gave the show some clout – once Lionel Richie signed up they had to take it national.

It was still only a pilot, though. They said if it goes well they'll make a series, so all London Weekend's top brass came down to the gallery to watch what was going on.

On that first show I had no autocue, and so badly wanted to get it right I stayed up until three or four in the morning trying to learn the intros – I put Post-It notes with my lines written on them all over the place, where the camera couldn't see them. We had a live studio audience there; I had all the gear on; my mate Ric Blaxill, who I did *Top of the Pops* for, was there as producer/director; everybody's hyped up and ready to go . . . three times the camera came on, three times I came out and messed up the lines. It was just nerves.

Everything was so daunting, I look back now and I can't believe I got through it: there are multiple cameras; I've got to remember which one to look at; I'm trying to remember the words and my memory's not great like that.

We got through that show with me thinking, 'This is it! That's my television career started and finished in the same night! I'll never come back on again after this.' It was a nightmare, and I could imagine how frightened they were upstairs with them investing so much in somebody who's never done this sort of thing before *and* it's going out nationally.

I was expecting it to get panned in the press the next day, but everybody loved it. They loved Lionel Richie and that I did a little bit of singing with him, they loved Prince Naseem who seemed really relaxed talking to me, and there was a lot of fun with Tina Hobley. The executives at London Weekend must have loved it because they decided straight away they're going to make a series.

The only person who seemed to have a problem with it was Michael Parkinson. He slaughtered me in the press after that first show. He steamed into me about me not being a 'proper' journalist, that I wasn't equipped to do the job, made a big deal out of the fact I had Post-It notes all around the place . . . all that sort of stuff.

I was shocked more than anything else by how horrible he was being about me. Michael Parkinson is The Man when it comes to chat shows, the one everybody aspires to be because of what he's done and who he's sat down with. Him going out of his way to belittle me would be like Pelé having a go at me for trying to play football. It just seemed so bizarre. We had totally different shows catering to totally different audiences. Mine was a young, lively crowd – the show reflected that by trying to be as much fun as possible – and I was learning my way with it.

It might have been Lionel choosing my show rather than his that set him off – I did hear Parkinson said he'd never have Lionel on his show again – but I definitely wasn't someone for him to feel threatened by. Later, I found out he did the same to Jonathan Ross, so maybe he has difficulty accepting there's room for more than one sort of chat show and more than one sort of chat-show host.

All the same, it wasn't very nice. What really helped me through it was a phone call, straight out of the blue, from Sir Trevor McDonald. He was amazing. I didn't know him, but he got my number and just phoned me up to say he saw the Michael Parkinson thing and he was destroyed by it. He told me how proud he was of me, how I mustn't conform or change anything about the way I did things. Then he said, 'If other people don't like the way you're acting then that's their fucking problem!'

That shocked me as much as the Parkinson comments – *to hear Sir Trevor McDonald swear*! One of the most eloquent and dignified men in the world . . . that's how seriously he was taking this. He also gave me some really valuable advice: 'Whatever gets you to get them on that seat so you get to speak to them, you do it, but one thing I will say to you is make sure you know what you're talking about. Give yourself more knowledge of what you want to speak about, you can't do any more than that. Whatever you have to read, however much you have to study, make sure you do that. Do not give people the opportunity to try and discredit you.'

He told me to just enjoy what I'm doing. He said if it lasts a year, if it lasts ten years, just enjoy it, take it as an experience.

That is exactly what I did, I didn't see it as anything other than, 'Wow, this is brilliant!' I was thinking, 'I've done the football, I'll do this now. I'll learn a new game, do it properly and go from there.'

I had a blast. I had Elton John on the show – he was really funny – Denzel Washington, Annie Lennox, Mariah Carey, Will Smith . . . Destiny's Child, when Beyoncé was still with them, came on and I presented them their first platinum disc for the song 'Bug a Boo'. They didn't know it was coming and they were absolutely over the moon . . . Lionel enjoyed himself so much, we're still friends today.

Once we really got going, everybody wanted to come on the show because it got a momentum of its own: the first thing an artist's management would ask is, 'Who's been on it?' and because we could drop a big name right from the off they'd agree to let their artists on. Then it becomes a matter of, 'Oh, I saw your interview with Mariah' . . . 'I saw your interview with Elton John' . . . so by now they're approaching us. You get management companies or PRs who look after more than one person, so they want to bring others on and it all snowballs. Also the record companies looked at my audience demographic and straight away realized it was a great show for certain artists.

But the best thing was that people who had been on always said it was interesting. Guests would say they enjoyed the crowd being right there, they enjoyed the questions coming from a different angle, which was because, as Parkinson so helpfully pointed out, I wasn't a journalist and I was genuinely asking them stuff that I wanted to know.

It wasn't particularly easy. They didn't give me an autocue for the first three weeks – no, I don't know why either, probably they wanted to keep it spontaneous – so I'm trying to remember my lines and what to say and I've got the director constantly in my ear going, 'Energy, energy, energy, we need energy . . . We have to record this again, record that again . . . Energy, energy, energy!'

I would get nervous. I wasn't scared of the audience; I just didn't want to be the person who messed up in front of those big stars. The closer I would get to the show the more nervous I would get, and when you're nervous on television people can see it – I wouldn't even like to watch those early shows back! I had to learn the lines and remember everything I'd learned about the guests so I knew how to talk with them, then follow the direction, look into the right camera, all of that.

Even when they got me an autocue I still had work to do, in spite of it helping me take my game up to another level. It was like Sir Trevor had said, and it was something I knew from football: leave no stone unturned in trying to be the best at what you are doing. I realized I had to learn exactly what was on the autocue, so I knew what was coming, then I could look away and come back without losing my place and not look like I'm obviously reading from something.

Simply knowing the autocue was there gave me a lot more confidence to remember things, and once I got that first paragraph of my autocue right, *Bam* straight into the intros, '. . . *and we got that and we got this . . . Ladies and gentlemen, my first guest . . .*' *Bang*! We were flying. I knew then how good this could be.

The great thing about the calibre of guests I was getting was they had been doing this sort of thing for ages, and they wouldn't let you mess up in an interview situation. They always knew how to cover something up. So many of them were incredibly supportive, especially the Americans. Lionel Richie was amazing, he knew it was my first show and told me all sorts of things, saying how you've got to make sure you get this right, because as a young black guy getting through into the mainstream you can't afford to fail.

Same with Will Smith. I was really excited about interviewing Will Smith, then at about three o'clock that afternoon we got a call saying, 'Will's got to do it *now*! – If he's not out of there by four, four-thirty, he can't do it.' So there's no public audience because we recorded at seven-thirty. We had to email round the building asking anybody who wants to see Will Smith to come to the studio *right away*, so the audience was all people from the offices.

I got changed, got my stuff together and we did a fantastic interview, then we had a great chat in his dressing room afterwards. We talked about going forward and being the best you could be, *aspiring* and being a role model through hard work and proving it can be done.

Denzel came to my dressing room after we'd finished filming, too, and we just talked about how it is for black people, how you have to work twice as hard, and then you have to make sure you get it right because there'll be no leeway. He put the emphasis on not losing sight of who I am, too, even though I was blasting a path that was so important and had a greater responsibility. This sort of thing was really empowering, especially as I was so new to it all.

It was crazy that I was still signed for West Ham when all of this was happening.

I'd joined West Ham thinking I only had a couple of seasons left in football, so even back then I was kind of half-thinking about what I was going to do after that. Then all of a sudden the offer to do the news interviews came about. It didn't take much of my time, so nobody at the club thought twice about it, and I thought, 'Great, I think I've found my next career.'

When the idea of the chat show came up, I started figuring that was what I wanted to do when I stopped playing, so if Harry and West Ham had said they had a problem, I'm pretty sure I would have retired there and then. He was fine with it, though. He didn't seem to care as long as I was still scoring goals.

Strangely, it was David Dein who had the most to say about it. He called the agents in and said he thought it was immoral that I was doing the show and playing football at the same time. I guess he was still looking out for me and wanted to make sure I wasn't being exploited. I feel sure that had I still been at Arsenal, Arsène Wenger wouldn't have been too keen on my doing it.

The bottom line was that when I went to training or was in a game, nobody could question my level of intensity, and the show didn't interfere with my match-day preparation. We recorded the show on a Thursday, I finished training between half twelve and one o'clock, two o'clock at the latest. I'd always stay at the training ground as long as anybody wanted me to, but I was past the point where I'd stay on to work on my finishing. I'd go straight to the television studio instead of going home or to play golf or something. I'd find out who we were going to have on, go to the meetings, do all the stuff, then we'd record that evening to go out on the Friday. After I'd done the show I'd go home, sleep, go to training on the Friday and play the game on Saturday.

It never caused me a problem in respect of it affecting my game. It was much easier than people might think because of all the time you get off as a footballer. I used to stay up quite late at home reading scripts or researching guests we were going to get on, but that wasn't making a difference – I could have been staying up that late watching television. Also, at that stage in my career, some of the time I didn't train at all, or I just did weights and gym work – Paolo Di Canio was there at that time doing the same thing, mostly weights.

The thing is, I was scoring goals and West Ham finished fifth that year, the highest they'd finished for ages, so nobody there had anything to complain about.

I did two series of *Friday Night's All Wright*, which seemed to be going very well, then ITV started messing about with the *News at Ten*, and suddenly I've got the news bulletin in the middle of my show. Literally, I've got to stop for the news and say, 'After the News we've got such and such . . . so don't forget, come back . . .' It killed the show stone dead. I couldn't work out why they would even think about leaving me in a time slot that was going to be affected like that. I had something that was going brilliantly – the audience figures for that time of the night were amazing up until that point. Then the figures fell, and they just kind of got rid of the show.

I was very disappointed because to me it seemed like one of those decisions made by television executives who think they know everything, but haven't got a clue what people really want. The cool set *got* that show, it had a big audience and people would stop me to talk about that rather than football, which I found a bit weird at first.

After so long playing football you get to think the whole word revolves around football to the point at which if somebody doesn't recognize you, you think, 'What's wrong with him? Doesn't he watch football?' It took some getting used to that there were different people out there, but it showed me how much people seemed to think of the show. People still talk to me about it: 'Yeah, I used to watch that show, it was really good. What happened to it?'

The love for it was there and ITV couldn't boast about having a successful show in that time slot before that – or for a long time after – so you'd think they would have tried to grow it, give it more of an airing. Instead they went totally the other way. They killed it.

Television is so cliquey, popularity goes up and down, people fall in and out of favour for no obvious reasons, and I was never part of the in-crowd. The executive in charge, David Liddiment, was a typical TV person inasmuch as in the beginning they get you in and they've got all sorts of big plans for you. Then something shinier comes along and they can't seem to remember they ever knew you. I guess, to him, my show was expendable and they didn't seem bothered that it was getting hammered through no fault of its own. Maybe I was kidding myself a bit about how well we were doing, but I doubt very much if they would have allowed anybody more established than me to have the news put slap-bang into the middle of their successful show.

I'm still very proud of *Friday Night's All Wright*: it was something I'd fallen into, but I learned a great deal and I was able to do well on the force of my personality and I met some amazing people.

I left ITV after that and went over to the BBC, where the thing that got me most interested is they said they wanted me to do a chat show – brilliant, because I felt *Friday Night's All Wright* was kind of unfinished business. I did a pilot of something that was going to be called *Wright Here Wright Now*, with Victoria Beckham and Audley Harrison as guests, which went OK but it wasn't *Friday Night's All Wright*. It took a while for them to tell me, 'Er, no, we're not doing that anymore . . .'

In 2001, they got me to take over from Ant & Dec when they left *Friends Like These*, which I really enjoyed because it was a good show and they'd left a good audience and a good vibe. But after that it was all downhill.

I had a three- or four-year contract with the BBC, so they had to find other things for me to do. In 2003, they got me doing this National Lottery show *The Wright Ticket*, followed by *Wright Around the World*, in which contestants won a trip around the world; and there was something called *I'd Do Anything*, and that really made me ask myself, 'What am I doing here?' Maybe I saw the title as some kind of writing on the wall.

When I was told about that show the format sounded fantastic. People would face their worst fears and do something really brave to win a once-in-a-lifetime experience for a friend or a family member, which was all fixed up without the recipient's knowledge. I thought this was a good idea but they managed to turn it into a series of shit dares. We'd just started to see the beginnings of the *I'm a Celebrity Get Me Out of Here* type of thing, and that was what they were starting to go for here. It became all about seeing people having to eat bugs or spending the night in a room full of cats or having snakes run over their legs. It was ridiculous, and I was dying!

It was around that point I started thinking I didn't want to do this any more. I felt like I was turning into this kind of diluted, watered-down, professional presenter. The type who will do anything just to stay on television and have no particular strengths, so nobody really takes any of what they do too seriously.

The chat show had been good but that was becoming a distant memory, and once it was gone I *really* missed football – that might have been a lot of the reason why I couldn't settle at any of these things. I missed football *people* because, whether I got on with them or not, I usually trusted them and most of the time knew where I stood with them. I think, pure and simple, I was fed up with the people I had to deal with in TV light entertainment.

The biggest thing I'd learned during those years was how people talked so much nonsense to you that you wondered if even they believed it. After the first series of *Friday Night's All Wright* I had everybody upstairs at ITV all over me: 'Oh, it's brilliant, you're going to do this, you're going to do that, we're going to take it to America . . .' All empty. Every single thing empty.

I went to the BBC and they're the same: 'Oh, we're changing the look of the Corporation and we want to bring in this kind of show and this kind of presenter and we want you to do this . . .' It was all rubbish.

When you're doing well you're everybody's best friend and everybody's claiming they had a hand in your show; then when something new comes along they would drop you off the roof of a building and not think twice about it. I started realizing that most people in light entertainment television had two ways of dealing with people: they either thought you could help their career and they were all over you; or they thought you couldn't, so they figured it was OK to be rude to you.

I wanted to start edging over towards football again, but the agents I was with wouldn't hear of it. Those guys were still convincing me not do anything to do with football while I was doing light entertainment. At that time, light entertainment was where the money was, so after I finished playing they wanted to make sure I kept earning for them – that's why I didn't do my coaching badges right after I finished playing.

When *Friends Like These* was winding down in 2003 I thought the best way forward for me would be punditry, which would at least combine television work with football, but they steered me away from it. When I looked back at it I realized they wanted to reinvent me as this prime-time-friendly-Mr-TV-personality, and not bamboozle this new audience that I was a footballer.

As I said earlier, it's a confusing enough time when you finish playing, and I know I allowed myself to be brainwashed after the success of *Friday Night's All Wright* and went along with it as a means to an end. Once I started to realize this isn't for me and made it known I was unhappy, however, my agents should have listened to me and done something about it.

You would think in the long term it would make more sense for them to keep their client happy, because I was earning a lot of money for them, but they weren't advising me or even properly consulting me. Not once did I have them say to me, 'Ian, what are you happy doing? What is it you'd really like to do?'

Really, they didn't give a damn about the fact that deep down I was pining, and very unhappy that I wasn't in football. What they should been doing, as my management company, was everything they could to help me get back into football in some way, to get me involved with any form of punditry. I suppose my presenting *Gladiators* in 2008 was some kind of connection to some kind of 'sport', but that wasn't what I was looking for.

This was just about money, though, them filling their pockets, but everything I've ever done simply because it was driven by money has never worked out for me. And true enough, when I carried on down that light entertainment line as it was successful enough in the beginning, but it went badly wrong.

I should have listened to Denzel. I had lost sight of who I am.

It wasn't all a waste of time or unhappy, though; I was still very aware of how privileged I was to be earning a living from being on television and had some incredible experiences.

I went across America on a Harley Davidson for one programme, that was very cool; and I went up the highest mountain in the Arctic, which was great because it was real stuff, real endurance, a real testing of will. It was the hardest thing I've ever done in my life and is what completely finished my ankle and my knee.

Then there was *Surviving the Kalahari* in 2002, which was just frightening! It was totally for real, out in the Kalahari Desert – me, a boy from Brockley! – camping close to a water hole that wild animals were going to heading for. When I think about it, it was crazy.

I had to go through the day collecting wood, and it had to be the right sort of wood, because your fire had to burn all night, otherwise the hyenas and wild dogs would close in on you – you could hear them! The guide told me my fire was wasn't big enough, my wood was burning too quickly and that I had to really ration it. What do I know about making fires?

That was the first night, and as I was trying to sleep I could hear lions and other animals at the watering hole, so I stayed as close as I safely could to my fire.

Then, as if I wasn't frightened enough, the next night I got a call over the walkie-talkie to say there's a breeding herd of elephants heading straight towards me. Apparently my camp was right on their line to the water hole and if my fire wasn't big enough they'd trample right through my camp. I'm like, '*What!?*' I had to throw myself out of my sleeping bag and run round gathering up every single piece of wood I could find. It worked because the elephants went around my camp – close enough for me to clearly hear them and see their silhouettes. It was terrifying, but I loved that sort of thing because they were tests and had a sense of purpose about them. I think the public liked them for that reason, too.

The other show I did that really meant something to me and people seemed to enjoy and talked about was *Football Behind Bars* in 2009, where I worked with twenty-two lads at the Portland Young Offender Institution in Dorset. I enjoyed trying to do something good for a group of boys who really were disenfranchised, as they were in there with no respect for anybody or anything. Even each other.

The only way I could reach them was through football, and then use what football can do as an education – teamwork, helping your mate, you run for your friend because if you run ten yards you're going to save him running forty. I was trying to get into their minds those kinds of things, ideas they could apply to their lives when they got out: there are laws, like there are rules in football; you can play brilliantly but you might not win and you have to swallow that; football is all about team-work, life is all about co-operation . . . that sort of thing.

The first game we played was against the warders – the screws – and the way some of them talked to the boys wasn't nice. One of them, Barry Clark, was amazing, a good, fair, honest screw – he's still my friend now, and the same with a guy called Brownie. But the rest of them treated the boys really badly and there was nothing they could do about it.

That first game was literally bullying. The screws would foul and cheat, elbow and kick . . . everything. They got away with it too, not only because one of the screws was the ref, but the boys couldn't do anything to a screw because they'd have problem when they went back on the wing.

When the lads came off they were crestfallen. The screws had thrashed them, eight-nil I think, and I felt sorry for them because they felt degraded because of all the fouling. It made me want to cry to see people do that to other people, and there's no recourse.

I told them, 'See what's happened? This is how life is for you right now, and you brought this on yourselves. They do what they want with you. Now you've got to build yourself up through what we're doing and you're going to earn their respect, because they're not going to just give it to you. Exactly like you'll have to when you're back on the outside. You're going to have to start to sacrifice. If you do not, you will continuously be in this situation and people like that will carry on treating you like you're nothing.'

During the series we had a blind football team come in so we could show the lads what teamwork was all about, what communication was about, and how much it helps. We got victims of crime coming in, some of the boys, especially the ones who were in there for drugs, didn't realize there were any victims of their crimes, so it helped them understand responsibility.

As the series went on, they got better and better. Then they played the screws again, who tried to do the same things, but the boys *battered* them, about ten-nil. They'd used everything they'd learned about teamwork and co-operation, and, of course, the football stuff I'd taught them as well.

Afterwards I talked to them: 'Did you see what you could do because of the way you are now? You're standing together; when they're doing their bullying and their intimidating, you've got people who are backing you up, people who are supporting you. Together – you beat them together. And that's how it works in life.'

I told them to look at the screws and see how angry they were. I said, 'That's what you've done to them by smiling, playing your game and showing them that you're better than they are. You see how they are, that is exactly how they are and that is how they're going to stay. They need you lot to be underneath them, not thinking you're better than they are, because that is their power over you. They can take everything else from you, but you can't give them that. You've got to stay proud and dignified in what you're doing and how you are. You don't want to be in here so this is how you've got to conduct yourself on the outside.'

That series was one of my most fulfilling things, because I know there's eight or nine of them from the team who never went back, when the statistic from there was 70 or 80 per cent re-offending.

There was talk, before the production got going, that if it proved successful then together with the Home Office we'd set up football programmes in other young offender institutes, with me involved. Naturally I was very keen, but it was exactly that – talk. It was just about doing the show and getting me to do the show, and that was a huge shame. They wouldn't do a follow-up show either. I would have loved to have started with a team photograph, and then followed the success stories of these boys who got their lives together. People talk to me about the show a lot, and always ask what happened to the guys, but I guess somebody decided it wouldn't be 'good television'.

When I think what could have been done and what the executives said they'd do, I feel a little bit used, and if the guys accused me of using them, there wouldn't be much I could say.

If anything was ever going to convince me to get out of the light entertainment, it was *Live from Studio Five* in 2009. I never wanted to do it, but it seemed to have been carved up already by my agents and the production company. My big mistake was that I succumbed to the pressure put on me to do it.

The premise was that I would head up what would be mainly a lifestyle show; the girls would talk about stuff and I would go out and do bloke stuff. So although it would be entertainment-driven Justin Bieber-y stuff, there would be a good balance. They told me I'd be on the road doing stuff and I was quite happy with that, but after the first month I knew that wasn't going to happen. They'd scrapped that idea, so I found myself in between the embarrassingly poor Kate Walsh and Melinda Messenger, and they got a lot of reality TV stars on there . . . I hated the show. *Hated* it.

There was one time when Ricky Gervais was on and he said to me, totally incredulously, 'What are you doing with these two?'

And I had no answer. I just shrugged my shoulders and said, 'You tell me!'

If what he'd asked me hadn't already hit home, it did when one of the questions the production team had Melinda ask Ricky was whether he'd sleep with me, Kate or Melinda if he had to choose between us . . . I thought, 'Has nobody who's part of this show got any dignity?' Ricky just sort of palmed it off, but for me it was the most embarrassing moment of my TV career.

There was a great deal made in the press about the rows, and the reports were probably all true. Everybody was rowing with everybody else all the time; sometimes people would be nice to your face, sometimes they wouldn't bother. It was a horrible atmosphere.

The big row I had was over promoting a show called *Don't Stop Believing*, which was like a truly awful *X-Factor* wannabe. It was so bad I told them I would do nothing in respects of promoting that show. I said let the other two do it, because I refuse to plug a show that terrible. Of course, they told me it was in my contract to promote whatever they told me to, and therefore I was in breach of contract, but by then I was past caring.

That was it. That show, with that production team, made me say, 'That's my lot. Anything to do with television or light entertainment is over.'

Nothing could make me do anything on television in that kind of format again – there isn't enough money in the world. I had a contract for a year. I started on 14 September 2009 and I left on 13 September the next year. It was put about that I'd thrown a strop and diva'd off, or that they sacked me, but if either was the case would I have seen my contract out to the very last day?

It was the beginning of the end for me and my agents, too.

*   *   *

I really wouldn't do it again. Even though I was very proud of what I did with *Friday Night's All Wright*, and when I started with ITV I thought that was it, I was going to go on to be a massive talk show host, learn what I was doing, go to America, all that sort of stuff. During the series, I was getting all the big guests and I had the big dreams, but I realized that with the big stars come these big demands and all sorts of uncertainties. Will Smith, all of a sudden he wants to do it a three o'clock . . . Mariah Carey, all of a sudden she wants her room decked out in certain things, to sit on a different seat when she's being interviewed . . . all sorts of stuff.

Then there is all this vagueness all the time: Are they coming? Ain't they coming? They said they were coming, now we've just got a call to say they're not, but we're hanging on hoping because we've got to do the show. I don't want to deal with that kind of stuff. Maybe it's because I'm older now, but I just couldn't take the uncertainty.

The agent I have now, who I am incredibly happy with, says I shouldn't do anything that's not football-based.

He says, 'That's where your expertise is, that's where you should be learning, don't let anything detract you from that.'

The bottom line is that even when I was flying on *Friday Night's All Wright*, I was always a footballer with a chat show, never a chat-show host that played football.

Chapter Twenty

Agents of Doom

There was a Champions League game in 2015, Monaco versus Valencia, in which the same agent, Jorge Mendes, represented sixteen of the twenty-two players on the field. Yes, it's an extreme example, but at the same time it shows just how much power agents have within the game now.

This isn't just another rich footballer having a rant about having to give up 20 per cent either, although we'll get to my problems with agents in a minute. These days, with the notable exception of Barcelona, big clubs won't make any kind of moves without dealing with the so-called super agents like Mendes, Kia Joorabchian or Pini Zahavi. They're making fortunes while they practically run the game, as they represent managers and coaches as well as players. And this can't be good for football.

Look at Eliaquim Mangala and Nicolás Otamendi, the two Manchester City centre backs: both Jorge Mendes players. Mangala is the second most expensive defender in football history; the other had only been a year at Valencia, did very well, the club made it public they were desperate to keep him, then all of a sudden he's at Manchester City. Between them they cost City over £70 million, yet Vincent Kompany gets injured and that defence falls to pieces like a house of cards.

If I owned City, no matter how much money I had, I'd be

asking what has happened to our scouting system? I'd be saying, 'Wait a second, I've given you all that cash to buy these two and there are Leicester with a player who's come from Nottingham Forest and another who got released by Stoke for free, probably earning a fraction of what those two are on, yet they've won the Premiership and they've conceded fewer goals.'

The big clubs wouldn't even look at Wes Morgan or Robert Huth, because instead of scouting players they'll get on the phone to one of these agents and say, 'I'm looking for a top player in this position . . .' And if the first agent hasn't got one he'll get on to another agent who has – it might involve some moves among other players – but if the club truly has the ear of the first agent, they'll get their man. That's why so many big transfers seem to come out of the blue and so often don't appear to make sense – they're being manipulated by agents who have no particular loyalty to any club and are doing what's best for themselves.

I'm not having a knock at all agents and saying they don't deserve their money, because there are some very good agents out there but there are more bad ones than good ones. The most worrying aspect of all this is further down the game with individual players. Pretty much every one of them has an agent now – it's the new normal – and while this is taking control away from the clubs, in too many cases it can do the players' careers more harm than good.

Things hit a point a while back, when I was still playing, that players started assuming they should have an agent – if they didn't, then either they're not very good or they're missing out on something. It was still a relatively new thing and players loved the idea of having an *agent*.

There was a lot of ego involved, because agents did things for you: you could phone them up twenty-four seven and it was all, 'I need a car': *Bam!* There it is . . . 'I need some clothes': 'Don't worry, we'll sort some out and send them round . . .' 'I want to go to that restaurant': 'No problem, they'll be expecting you . . .' That's very flattering to a young guy, who might still be living at home with his mum.

When I first signed with Jerome Anderson Management they promised me 'Anything you need, no matter what time, day or night, call us and we'll sort it out – whatever it is.' They had people whose only job was to make sure everything was cool in my world. They practically followed me everywhere I went, and this guy Jeff Weston was always on the end of the phone for me.

In the beginning, there's definite kudos, so in my case there was a lot of, 'Hey! I got an agent!' . . . 'Yeah, my agent will sort that out.' . . . 'Talk to my agent.'

Laziness figures in all of this too, and it can make you feel big to have somebody running round after you, so you don't really look at the situation too closely.

The real big thing they're supposed to do is negotiate the best contract for a player at his current club, or when he moves clubs – not necessarily the most money, but the best deal and the one your career will benefit from the most. Likewise with the commercial side: an agent should make the connections for their clients, then make sure they're getting the best deal and building the right profile. Then if they're 'management' rather than just an agent, like mine was, they might well look after a player's finances as well.

They go berserk if you do a deal with or even talk to somebody about doing a deal without them involved – the worst thing you can say to an agent is, 'Yeah, I've done the deal. It's

OK, they only wanted . . .' That agent will then get in touch with whoever and go crazy. 'He shouldn't be talking to you . . . he doesn't understand the facts . . . he could be in breach of contract and what you've agreed to is null and void . . .'

Then your agent will be in your ear telling you how you could've got yourself stitched up, that the only reason they came to you direct was because they didn't want to pay the right amount of money. It'll be, 'Leave it to me, I *know* I can get you this amount. That's what you have an agent for.' They can't afford to have somebody say to you, 'What are you paying an agent for? I want you, not your agent, and I'm going to pay you this.'

Which is a very good point. I didn't have an agent when I signed for Palace. I got one while I was there and people were saying to me all the time, 'What do you need an agent for?' Mark Bright in particular, and I remember a conversation I had more than once with Tony Finnigan: 'Really, what does your agent do for you?' . . . 'I phone him up and he . . .' 'And he *what*? You carry on playing like you're playing, you're doing more for him that he is for you.'

Of course he was right, because the ridiculous thing about it is, on the purely practical side, nobody needs an agent – there's nothing an agent does for a player that a solicitor and an accountant shouldn't be able to do.

A good solicitor should be able to go through any contract offered by the club or sponsor and explain what it means, and get anything you're not happy with changed. There are so many different law firms that specialize in things like that, and if the player's regular lawyers couldn't do it they'd find someone who could. Then you'll only pay him or her for their time on that particular job, not for the life of the contract.

Likewise, a good accountant should be able to handle your money, advise you on how best to look after it and make sure you pay all your taxes when they are due. Again, you'll pay a set annual fee, not give them a percentage of that money.

With the commercial side of things, it's not actually that difficult for a decent player to get sponsorship deals for himself – I look back on my time when it was going well for me, and it wouldn't have been hard for people to get in touch with me directly. It would have taken Nike no more than two or three phone calls to get through to me and ask me if I wanted a big pile of money for wearing their boots, and a bit more money to wear the rest of their gear and appear on their posters. What do you think I'm going to say? I wouldn't have needed *advice*.

Then the bigger a player gets, the less he'll need somebody to find these deals for them because the companies will come looking for him – most sportswear companies aren't waiting for a team of agents to tell them it would be a good idea to have the current England centre forward wear their boots.

The only decision to be made with sponsorship is whether or not a player wants to get involved with whoever, which ought to be up to him anyway; then he gets his solicitor to look over the contracts.

It ought to be the same thing with changing clubs, too. If a club is interested in you they make the approach to your club, then it's up to you to decide if you want to join them or not, and for what money. When it comes to getting paid, a player can find a lot of stuff out for himself, or have a family member or friend do it, by just doing a little bit of digging around.

It's all available at the PFA. They won't tell anybody who's actually earning what, but a player can find out what somebody of his stature at a particular club ought to be getting, in terms of wages and bonuses, then negotiate from there. Personally, I'd like to see the PFA take that a bit further and appoint somebody to negotiate on behalf of players.

Really, as regards contracts and money, when a player gets an agent all they're doing is giving that person the opportunity to be a middle man, to make money for themselves. Which, in the majority of cases, is all they do. They've almost become a thing in their own right – being there just to be there and get paid for it. When I look back at it now, my agents were making a fortune off me commercially, *and* making money off my contract. I did use to think, 'What do you do apart from answer the phone and fix up little things? You're like a glorified hotel concierge. You're not advancing my career or making sure I've still got one.'

In an ideal world, the less said about my first agents the better, but I believe it is important to use my experiences with them as an example of how even a successful player, at the top of his game, can get taken advantage of. So imagine how easy it would be for that to happen to a young guy just getting into life as a professional footballer.

So much of this ought to come down to taking responsibility for yourself and your career, which used to be the case for most players up until the 1990s or so. The situation now, however, is that it wouldn't occur to so many players *not* to have an agent, and although there's enough managers out there that aren't at all happy with this, they have to accept it.

Youth team players have agents now, kids below them at the academy too, because agents know any potential talent has to be tied up early doors. And this is where it starts getting really unhealthy.

Agents will hate the idea of anybody that could earn for them slipping through their fingers, so they're prepared to take what seems like big gambles on very young players. What happens is agents will talk to senior players they've got on their books and ask who the most promising academy and youth players are, the ones most likely to succeed. Then, often as not, they'll ask that same senior player to make the first approach to the kid's parents.

It makes anybody sit up and take notice when a big star phones up one evening, saying how good he thinks their son is, what a future he has, and does he have representation? No? 'Well, can I recommend my agent . . .'

In many cases, if any deal comes off from this, the player who made the approach will get a kickback, or sometimes a percentage of the deal itself, so they could be earning for a long time by doing this.

Jerome and the others from my former agent's company would say to me, 'We just need you to speak to a few players . . . So why don't you get the ball rolling . . . and then you can get this and that out of it.' The idea was, 'OK, you're at this level now, so we can use you to try and rope some young ones in – those that will look up to you as a player.'

They'd want me to get in touch with all these young black players for them, talk to their parents. I made a few phone calls for them – I spoke to Jamal Blackman who's at Chelsea now, Blair Turgott and a couple of others – but I never felt comfortable doing it because I didn't believe in my agent.

I would always say to the parents, 'Listen, I'm speaking to you because I'm with this company and, yeah, they might have done this and that for me, but I also did this and that for myself. My advice to you is to speak to as many people as you can and use your instincts to make a decision. Just because I'm phoning you, do not think it's gospel. I'm just saying you need to get the right kind of representation for your son. It's not that, all of a sudden, these agents are going to get your son playing for West Ham or Arsenal. If he's that good, anybody else could get him there as well. What they're doing at the moment is they want your son to pay them – but really, what *exactly* are they going to do for your son? Those are the questions you've got to ask, because they haven't done that much for me, I did most of it for myself.'

Particularly with black players, I'd tell their parents not to pay any attention to what race the agent chasing your son might be. Many, many slick young black guys have set themselves up as agents and will approach black parents or players talking about 'Aw, bruv, who you gonna go to? *The Jewish man?* I look after my own, trust me!' and will browbeat kids into signing with them because they feel they're letting their own down.

There's just as much chance of them letting the kid down, either through skulduggery or incompetence – probably more so if the only thing they could offer in the beginning was, 'You and me both black.'

That sort of thing really gets to me, because they're using some pretty serious emotion to swing a deal that should be strictly business. I always make sure I let people know that a black agent can take money off you with no concern for your future, just as easily as a white agent or a Jewish agent.

After the initial contact has been made, the agent will then get onto the kid's parents, ordinary people who all of a sudden find they've got a really good little player on their hands. Agents will be coming out of the woodwork. They'll all be talking about what he can earn, or, rather, what they can get him, and how he won't get any of that without an agent. This will be quite easy for them to believe, because by now everybody else has got an agent – as I said, it's the new normal – and the parents of a kid that young could well still be in their twenties themselves, without a massive amount of life experience.

Agents will be prepared to put their hands deep into their pockets, but it will start with something as easy as football kit. They'll ask the kid what his favourite boots are, then next day there'll be boxes and boxes of that brand gear turning up at the house. That will be enough to get an eight- or nine-year-old kid on their side, which will help with the parents, and won't have cost them a penny – they will probably have a top player sponsored by that company, and will have told them this could be the next big one, and they'll need to get him quick. Of course, the company's going to come up with the latest tracksuits, boots and trainers, and a bag to put it all in.

It starts as simply as that. Then if the kid really starts getting good, the stakes go up to get his signature as the agents go to work on the parents.

'What car do you want? . . . No problem, will somebody be in to take delivery on Wednesday? And one for his mum too?'

Then if getting him up to training is a problem, 'Don't worry about it, we'll send a car for him . . . or, better still, if his older brother can drive we'll buy him a car and pay him to bring the lad up to training.'

To get a genuine Premiership hopeful signed up, an agent will pay his parents' mortgage off or buy them a house, they'll give siblings jobs – even if it's just giving them a wage packet for doing nothing . . . whatever it takes.

It seems like a massive amount of money to lay out for a

player who might not make it, but when you do the maths it only takes one to get through to pay for loads that don't.

Nineteen year-olds are on £30,000 a week now, then if a player makes it as a first-team regular in even a mid-table Premiership side, the next contract is going to put them on £50,000 a week, which is over £2 million a year, not counting bonuses or what can be earned from sponsorship deals.

At a top Premiership club this could double for somebody who's not even a regular starter, not to mention transfer fees of £20 or £30 million for often very average players. If he really hits the heights, that agent will have a £50 million player on his books, who could be earning £200,000 a week – over £10 million a year – for maybe ten years. And the agent is taking 20 per cent of that, all the way down the line.

Suddenly their investment of making sure your dad's got a nice car, your mum's got a job, your brother's got a job, the family's got a decent house, is no money at all in the grand scheme of things.

It is like the agency *buys* the player – which is happening literally with third-party ownership – and then needs as big a return as possible. At some stage we're going to get a foot-baller earning a million pounds a week, so there is a real para-noia in that world as agents are desperate to hang on to their cash cows.

I've had players come to me, especially young black players, asking me for advice about playing or about anything else, and within days their agent is on the phone to me: 'So what did he say? . . . What did he want? . . . What was he talking about?'

And I always say we were talking about football, that's all we were talking about, but all they're thinking is, 'Hang on a minute,

Ian Wright's trying to nick my player. He's going to try and nick him and give him to his agent, so he can get the kickback.'

It's easy to say this is a good thing, as an agent will handle all of the other stuff and leave the player to concentrate on what he does best, playing football, and regardless of what his agent is getting he's still earning a fortune. But being an agent is about more than just counting money.

A good agent ought to be guiding and advising the player on where they should go or what they ought to be doing to grow their career in a way that is right *for the player*. A player, or his parents, have to look closely at a prospective agent and ask themselves, 'Why did he want to be an agent in the first place? Is it the Porsches and the Lamborghinis, or did he want to help somebody?' There are enough people who want to do the latter out there, and there's enough money in the game for them to do very well by doing the right thing.

On the other hand, a not-so-good agent will often go for the biggest fee and the highest wages – it doesn't matter if that's the best move for that player's development. And it is very true that some agents might even deliberately unsettle their players and agitate for moves.

At the moment, that tends to happen more with foreign players in the English leagues, because there is less long-term attachment to clubs, they have already made one big move just to be here, and their European or South American agents are operating internationally. That doesn't mean it doesn't happen to English players – it is definitely on the up – but you can guarantee any overseas player that has a decent season will suddenly be 'linked' with big continental clubs.

At the time of writing this might be happening with N'Golo Kanté and Riyad Mahrez of Leicester, Romelu Lukaku too, while Dmitri Payet was given a massive new contract with West Ham only a year after his first one, presumably just to make sure he stayed there.

What happens is the agent will be in the player's ear saying Real Madrid or Paris St-Germain are interested, how they can get in there on whatever wages, and then they put that out to the media who will go with it, reporting that 'an insider says . . .' They go back to the player, and stories like this play a part in convincing him he's got the chance to be at a bigger club, so whatever happens it's at the back of his mind, 'I could be winning the Champions League instead of wasting my time here.'

The chances are something like this is just a tactic for negotiating a contract renewal, but straight away it's undermined the player's relationship with his club. And his relationship with the fans too, because they think they're going to lose a favourite, or he's unhappy playing for them, and it's all about getting more money or belittling their club.

Many transfers are motivated by the fee itself and what the agent's cut might be. Agents hard-sell glamorous players to club chairmen rather than coaches, who will go for the deal because it's exciting and, from a purely business point of view, they see the player as an asset that will increase the value of their club.

It's not unusual for players to be dropped into a coach's lap, sometimes against his wishes, and he has to accommodate them regardless of whether it's good for the player or the team.

Agents will often start offering their player around several clubs to play them off against each other, saying, 'If you don't buy him then your bitter rival will.' Or, it might be a case of one agent saying to another agent, 'Arsenal like our player, but they've already got your player in that position. Could you move yours on so mine can come in? I'll give you a piece of the deal.' They agree and *bang* the deals are done.

Too often when you see high-priced players suddenly switching clubs and it doesn't work out on the pitch or they're obviously not happy, it's because the transfer was purely down to agents and their own greed. This loss of control was why so many of the old-time managers hated agents.

Alex Ferguson had no time for them and would move players on if their agents started having too much influence. George Graham was the same; that's why he threw Jerome Anderson out of his office that time he came round to Arsenal claiming that Parma were interested in me.

Where an agent really needs to put the work in is when a player is coming to the end of their career, and the contract leverage and commercial opportunities are starting to wind down, and also after they retire if they are still representing them then. Too many will only be there when the player is virtually selling themselves, and haven't got the drive or the connections to make it happen for him when companies and clubs are no longer queuing up. Or, like with mine, it could be a matter of companies simply not wanting to deal with the agent, regardless.

When it came to doing commercial deals and I would hand it over to my agents after the initial contact. Jeff Weston would come in and put so much into the deal it would start to become awkward. I think people didn't like dealing with him because he made the process so laborious and arduous, and if a potential sponsor had a choice the chances were they'd go elsewhere – we lost deals because people didn't want him around the place.

Especially when things started winding down for me, when I wasn't so commercially viable in people's eyes, it didn't take much for people to go and deal with somebody else's agent.

I had all sorts of arguments with the agency. They were never proactive while I was doing well, because people just kept coming with more and more stuff for me, but once it started to wind down they still weren't doing anything.

I'd try and talk to them about creating opportunities for me and all they'd say was there was nothing they could do. I couldn't believe it! After all the money I'd made for them over the course of more than twenty years, Jeff Weston actually said to me, 'Well, you're getting older now, it's not gonna happen for you so much now, so I don't know what you're going to do.' Really, all they're thinking about is, 'Who can we get to replace the big earner we're about to lose?'

Back then, almost anybody could set themselves up as a football agent. You didn't need to do a course or take badges or anything like that. This is why you get complete chancers overseeing £50 million deals, just because they're the player's cousin or their best mate from school. All you need is the connection to the first player and then the others start to fall into place. This is why I advise young players' parents to check out agents so diligently, because I didn't.

When I signed for Palace I didn't have an agent. I'd been there for a couple of years when the Watford goalkeeper Tony Coton introduced me to Jeff Weston at an end-of-season Division Two versus the Army match I was playing in. I went to meet Jerome Anderson and that was it. They already had David Seaman, Charlie Nicholas and David Rocastle, which was why I went there. Jerome Anderson used to be the stadium announcer and play the records at Highbury on match days, which is how he got in with Arsenal players to start off with, and Jeff Weston used to be in the music business. The closest he'd got to football before this was he had something to do with that song 'Diamond Lights' by Hoddle and Waddle.

I don't know what they did for me except answer the phone and show up at contract negotiations where, essentially, I was always going to get what the club had already decided to pay me. I wasn't angry about that at the time, because I was playing football for a very a good living and always seemed to have enough money for anything I wanted. I wasn't happy about things when I was coming to the end of my career, but what did leave me mad was what happened when I finished.

I wasn't sure what I was going to do, as I wanted to do my coaching badges at some stage because all through your career people say, 'Do your badges because you're never sure what's going to happen later on.'

To be fair, Jerome was always keen on me doing the coaching badges, but never quite enough to say to Jeff, 'No, let him do them then we'll get into television later.'

Then, of course, once they started seeing the figures that the television people were offering it seemed that they forgot all about the badges and pushed me towards that. They must have looked at that and seen that this was the best way to make money out of him now.

I thought that if I was going to go into television, surely I ought to get a television agent. I wouldn't speak to my agents for a while, but they were literally bombarding me with phone calls: 'ITV want you to do this . . . BBC want you for that . . . they love you and they want you to do this . . .'

People frequently ask me why I didn't go into management, especially seeing how there are so few black managers, and often I have said to myself I should have been more forthright. I should have insisted, 'No, I want to do the coaching badges.' So I've got to take the blame for that, but when you're dealing with agents who can be very persuasive and all they're seeing is pound signs, it's hard to stay strong.

Then I started doing *Friday Night's All Wright*, and once that started going well and got some decent plaudits, they said, 'See . . .' And I just got wrapped up in it.

I've got a great agent now: Steve Kutner. We have a fantastic rapport and he treats me with respect so we have a real good professional arrangement. He recognizes what I need, what keeps me happy and what my strengths are – I love the fact that he won't let me do anything that isn't football-related – unless, of course, it's something I really want to do, and then we'd have to have a proper conversation about it first.

Although I have very few regrets, sometimes I look back at all those years I wasted with Jeff Weston and Jerome Anderson with a tinge of resentment. I'm twenty years older now, too, so it's much easier to make more considered decisions.

The point is, football has come so far down this particular route it's impossible to imagine a situation where there aren't any agents, and that their power won't get any stronger. Most managers these days have had to accept them and have adapted their working methods. This is why I can't stress enough to young players and their parents, be very, very careful about who you sign up with.

Chapter Twenty-one

Not as Simple as Black and White

I played professional football for about fifteen years and have been retired for about as long, which means I've been a footballer for around thirty years – as I said before, there's no such thing as an ex-footballer. In that time, there's been a great deal said and written about racism in English football. I've seen and experienced changes in attitude, and the question is, 'Have things got better?'

The answer to that has to be, 'Yes and no', with the split being between the game's players and administration, which, ultimately, is not so different from so much else in this country.

During my time as a footballer, I believe people in general – especially in London – have become less bigoted. I put this down to two things: the crackdown on racially offensive behaviour in the 1970s and 1980s; and a generation of white kids coming through who had grown up with black kids and Asian kids and found out for themselves that they didn't have anything to be scared of – that essentially there are no differences between, if you like, them and us.

On the pitch, on the most obvious positive level, there are many more black players in the divisions than there were thirty years ago, and in all but a few cases they are so natural a part of clubs' squads it's not even talked about.

This really wasn't the case when I started in the mid-1980s, and a lot of other players were still looking at black footballers as exactly that – *black* footballers, who were somehow different from them.

It was really a generational thing. Remember, this was a time when people were still throwing bananas at black players. You didn't have to look very far across a dressing room to find characters who saw the game as being all about white guys and nobody else. Simply because, when they were coming up, it had always been that way.

Attitudes were seriously shifting during the first part of the 1980s, through to when I got to Palace. Men like Viv Anderson, Des Walker and Paul Ince had destroyed that myth that black players were Fancy Dans, all right on the wing, but 'haven't got the bottle' to be any use anywhere else.

Black players regularly featured for England by then, and the new wave of players coming through not only included so much young black talent, but white kids who didn't have such a racist attitude towards them. Sometimes it seemed like the old guard were having everything they thought they knew stripped away and it must have been frightening for them.

There was a definite racial undercurrent to the problems with the old firm at Palace, because, basically, they were bigoted and so many of the new guys were black – myself, Brighty, John Salako, Andy Gray and Tony Finnigan.

Tony really summed up what this cultural changing of the guard was all about: not only was he well dressed and sophisticated, he was really intelligent – *fiercely* intelligent would probably describe him up better. He was well read, knowledge-able and extremely articulate. He knew his own mind so well he could argue with anybody about practically anything with-out resorting to shouting and waving his arms about.

Back then, if you were in a professional football dressing room and you were obviously smart, you'd be treated with suspicion and hostility. Like Graeme Le Saux – just because he read the *Guardian* and did crosswords he got talked about no end.

Tony was smart and black, so they'd level the old cliché at him, that he had a chip on his shoulder. There was nothing at all chippy about Tony Finnigan. He was a frontrunner in this new wave of eloquent, confident black players who felt at home in any company, but being like that in the early 1980s meant so many of the established characters were straight away going to call him 'uppity'. I had my fair share of that too.

None of it was very nice. In fact, it could be pretty horrible. The reality of it was that I couldn't do anything about it other than be myself, and the same with the other guys. We were the force that drove that Palace team on to promotion to the First Division, and whatever those guys thought of us they were reli-ant on us for their win bonuses. And they knew we knew that, so for all their attempted bullying they couldn't stop us feeling good about who we were and what we were doing.

This really was the bottom line: yes, that kind of nasty, personal racism was wrong; and no, it shouldn't have been allowed to go on; but when you were on the end of it the most important thing was to win in your own mind. You couldn't afford to be bitter about it. Indeed, you didn't think much beyond that particular situation. You needed to come out of it with a bit of swagger; if you came away feeling beaten – *oppressed* – you'd probably lost more than that particular round.

We were sharp young guys, getting everything we could out of being professional footballers in London, we were having a blast, and those old bigots had to deal with us more than we had to deal with them.

Historically, this is why things like blues dances and sound systems became such a big deal among black immigrants in London in the 1950s and 1960s: people who would be barred from so many pubs and dancehalls would dress up beautifully and go to their own functions. It was a way of showing their pride, that whatever was thrown at them, at work or in the street or from their landlords, they were there and going to enjoy themselves on their own terms.

Picking on young black guys wasn't limited to football either. In some parts of London, it was almost a sport.

There were no night buses back then and nobody had a car, so you were always walking places and you were going to get chased at some point or Old Bill was going to give you a hard time.

The skinheads, once they got to a certain age, had those Cortina Mk IIs and they'd cruise round the area just looking for trouble. When I was a teenager, running from skinheads was a regular occurrence, and not just for us! They chased the hippies . . . they chased the heavy-metal kids . . . they chased the punks . . . they chased the teds . . . they chased *everybody*! They were totally equal opportunity thugs! Then when they ran out of people to chase they chased each other, if they supported a different team or were just from a different area. So although they'd be shouting 'black this' and 'black that', we never took it personally.

We used to go to Jasper's club in the Squire pub near Beckenham, which was a notoriously racist area. It was a soul and disco club – Chic and all of that late 1970s music – and like most soul clubs in London it had a very mixed crowd of black and white kids. Black guys used to go down there to dance and were the coolest characters in there, so of course they would get among the white girls.

The problem was the club was at the back of this pub that was full of completely racist white guys from the ages of eighteen up to about forty. Seeing black guys with white girls would drive them insane! Any black guys coming out of there would have to run the gauntlet, and some nights they would literally chase you home. You'd have to fight your way out of there, then you'd be hiding under cars or jumping into people's gardens just to get away from them.

If I'd just gone to the library and then gone home every day I probably could have avoided most of this, and while it wasn't exactly funny – if the skinheads caught people they'd beat them up – it was what went on. Often older black guys off the estates, kids' brothers, would get together and have a go back. It was just part of the adventure you had when you were growing up.

We always thought we were fast enough or smart enough to get away and looked upon it that if you did get caught it was *shame*! It was like you'd brought shame on the community because you weren't good enough to get away – it was bad enough getting a beating but your friends would never let you forget it.

One of the worst things that used to happen was we'd get away from the white guys chasing us, make it into our own area, just starting to feel safe and the police would stop us! Some of my friends would do their nuts about that: 'I've just been fucking chased, like two or three miles . . . I've just got away, now you're stopping me because of *what*? What you stopping me for?'

I'd always keep quiet under those circumstances, because the police down there were no joke. There were all sorts of stories about brothers being thrown in cells in Ladywell police station, having a wet mattress put on top of them and then being beaten with truncheons. The word was it hurt like hell, but the bruises didn't show because all the damage was done inside.

Also, once you got sucked into the system with arrests and court cases and all of that, you could be fitted up to the degree that you won't get out for a long time. Most of us were scared of the police and tried to avoid any dealings with them.

How it seemed to work, though, was they seemed to know who the real villains were, so with the rest of us it was just the sort of low-level harassment designed to piss you off and make sure you knew who was in charge – it was bullying just because they knew they could get away with it.

Sometimes, however, they kind of had a point. I remember when I started getting the most hassle from the police was after I bought a car, a Vauxhall Viva – that was when I had no driving licence or insurance, and the car had no tax or MOT. There'd be about seven of us in there, the stereo cranked up, weed smoke blasting out of the windows. I'd get pulled and my first reaction would be, 'What you picking on us for?'

It was how you thought back then, because you were always getting picked on by Old Bill, but I look back at it now and think, 'What was I doing?' *I* would have pulled that car over if I'd seen it, and I wasn't even a copper!

The way me and my mates used to deal with the police when we were teenagers wasn't really much different to how we handled those older guys at Palace: by not getting bitter or angry about it. We'd just accept it as something that was likely to happen every time we stepped outside your door – there literally was nothing that could be done about the police, so don't let it put you off your swagger.

We'd be stopped on the street, questioned, made to turn out our pockets and then sent on our way, and we'd be laughing about it because we were on our way to a club. We'd be going to have a great time, drinking, dancing, maybe even end up with a girl . . . what were those coppers going to do? If messing with us is really the best they could do for entertainment, who's the winner here?

There's no way I'm OK about them or anybody else behaving like that, but at the same time we knew we had to get on with our lives. People ask me if we were angry about it, and get confused that we weren't. Back then, all these well-meaning people had this caricature of the angry black man, downtrodden and having no fun, but that simply wasn't us, or even most black people I knew.

There was a lot about our lives that was unfair, but ultimately we were pretty cheerful about most things, and certainly didn't hate white people – of course we made jokes about them – but we hung around with black people mostly because of where we lived. We weren't fighting down Babylon because, really, we had more exciting things to do, things that defined us as ourselves and not in relation to anybody else.

There was a real problem, though, with what became the race relations industry, around the second half of the 1970s, when we began to get pigeon-holed as all the same: angry, frustrated, poor, probably badly educated – there was a whole educated, aspirational black middle class out there that wasn't being acknowledged, and still isn't. People were always asking, 'Tell me, what's your problem? . . . Why do you dislike this and dislike that? . . . Why have you got this chip on your shoulder?' That was not only insulting – nobody would dream of assuming all white people were the same – but it held us back.

It's no different to those dark ages in football when it was taken as read that any black player was only good to run down the wing and do some tricks, but wouldn't show up when it came to the hard work. That stereotype may have been overcome, but now in football, the glass ceiling is stopping so many black players making the next step to becoming managers or coaches. It's the same thing.

The generation of players with the old–school thinking, like I came up against at Palace, has been dying out, meaning life has got much easier for black players, and, *finally*, clubs have stopped looking at us as being something different.

The reality is nothing much has changed beyond that, and there's a massive imbalance when it comes to management and coaching. You only have to look at the benches on a Saturday afternoon, and in most cases the only black faces you'll see are the substitutes.

The statistics speak for themselves: I recently read that around 30 per cent of professional footballers in this country are black; the PFA reckon 18 per cent of those on their coaching courses are black; yet when you get to who has got the jobs in coaching or management, that number drops to 3 per cent. That figure includes managers, assistant managers, academy managers, youth team coaches, goalkeeping coaches, fitness coaches, physios and technical directors. The only black guy I know at board level is Les Ferdinand, who is Director of Football at QPR.

This is because nothing's changed at the top. The people who have the real power in English football – the FA, the Premier League, the Chairmen's Association, the Referees' Association, the League Managers' Association, even the PFA to a large extent – are exactly the same people, or the same sort of people, who have always been there.

In June 2016 I read a statement by Heather Rabbatts, the FA's independent director and a very principled person, that she was considering quitting her post because she was 'very frustrated' and 'very disappointed' that attempts to reform the organization were being blocked. She has been great at the FA: in 2013 it was only because she really took them to task when they picked an all-white panel to look into the future of the national team, that they gave Rio Ferdinand a place on it.

In 2016, Greg Dyke revealed that he was stepping down as FA chairman because his proposed changes to make the FA more diverse and more accountable were unlikely to get past the FA Council. Two years ago, Lord Herman Ouseley resigned from the FA Council because it wasn't reforming in the way it needed to.

In my view, except for in the dressing room where the actual football *players* are, attitudes haven't shifted in the thirty years I've been in and around the professional game. It seems to me the generation that was playing when I started out have now risen up to executive levels in the game, and brought their outdated way of thinking with them.

The standard excuse used to be there was a lack of 'qualified black candidates' for coaching and management roles. That is blatantly not true now – there are so many very well qualified black coaches out there it's almost a joke. That comes down to what my generation were taught as kids by our immigrant parents: you'll need to be twice as good as the Englishman to be considered for the same job, so you'll need even more qualifications. But even in spite of this they're not getting the opportunity.

Take Chris Ramsey. His philosophy was that nobody was going to tell him he wasn't qualified enough, so he made himself into what is probably the most qualified coach in the whole world – he got a university degree in Health, Physical Education and Recreation; he got UEFA badges; ten coaching diplomas; he's done courses on anatomy and rehabilitation . . . he must have intergalactic coaching badges he's got so many!

In fact, Chris is so well qualified he sets the tests for the pro licence, yet he was out of the game for a while, then had to go to America to get into coaching. Once he got his opportunity back in England, he became one of the most valuable guys in the Premiership with ten years at Spurs as Head of Youth Development, keeping things steady under all those different managers. Harry Kane, Ryan Mason, Danny Rose, Nabil Bentaleb . . . so many of that young Spurs team worked with Chris from the moment they came to the club. Ledley King talks about him as one of the best coaches he's worked under, and the reason Tim Sherwood did so well is because Chris, and Les Ferdinand, were there alongside him.

All he needed was opportunity, but even then that might not be enough. Take Eddie Newton. He took up the coaching reins as second in command to Roberto Di Matteo at Chelsea, and had worked with him at Milton Keynes Dons and West Brom before that. Eddie coached Chelsea to winning the Champions League and the FA Cup in the same season. Now, Di Matteo gets all the credit for that and Eddie has ended up looking after the loan players.

And what more has Chris Hughton got to do to prove himself? The way he's been treated at different clubs for whatever reason, or sometimes no reason at all, is not because he's been poor: he won the Championship with Newcastle to bring them up; he took Birmingham to fourth; Norwich finished eleventh in the Premier League under him; and he took Brighton to the play-offs in 2015–16. Given what he's had to work with, he's been an unbelievable manager, because he served an apprenticeship under about ten different managers at Tottenham and learned from all of them. Yet clubs don't seem to have shown him much loyalty and have shown him the door prematurely.

All managers are under pressure, but the pressure for a black manager is crazy. Sometimes things don't work out, like with Paul Ince or John Barnes, but the issue is that black managers are not given the chance to prove they can handle that pressure. Don't forget, most of these guys came up with crowds making monkey noises at them so they know what pressure is!

The thinking from too many chairmen and executives has come back to that nonsense that all black people are the same. Like they used to say we couldn't play in a certain way, they're now saying we don't make good management material

– whatever that is. Worse than that, they are so-called proving it to themselves by saying because so-and-so didn't work out at wherever, they don't want to consider a black candidate because he won't be any good either.

Really, I think it's just their way of keeping things as they've always been. They – old white guys of a certain class – have always been in charge and see anybody who's not like them as some sort of threat. Now, when they see a younger generation out there that doesn't think like that, they're petrified, so they make sure they pass their power down to people who are exactly the same as them.

It's not just in football, it's in the government, it's in the BBC, it's all over the media and big companies in general . . . I ask myself why Parkinson slammed me and my chat show like he did? Did he do it to Alan Carr or Graham Norton? Maybe the establishment are protecting themselves, and the organizations that should be doing something about it don't seem to care at all.

Black English players get racially abused in Europe and UEFA hands out fines of a few thousand euros. When that director at Crystal Palace was caught exchanging racist and homophobic texts with Malky Mackay, who was in line to become their next manager, the League Managers' Association's reaction was it was just banter. Then when the chairman of Port Vale said he wouldn't consider Jimmy Floyd Hasselbaink for the manager's job because some of their supporters wouldn't want a black man in the job, nobody said a word.

If somebody like me makes too much noise about it, they'll just palm it off as me having a chip on my shoulder, but really any decent person can see this sort of behaviour is disgraceful.

Personally, I can't understand what they're so scared of: we're just the same as them, we love the game, and all we want is a good life and for our kids to do well. It's like that scene at the end of the film *Trading Places*. Eddie Murphy's character has made a shedload of money for the firm and he's obviously much smarter than Dan Aykroyd's character who has screwed up badly. One of the two old guys that run the company says: 'Do you really believe I would have a nigger run our family business?' and the other replies, 'Of course not, neither would I.'

Ignoring so many talented people can't do the country as a whole any good and it's definitely not helping football if another Chris Ramsey doesn't get an opportunity.

It's exactly problems like this that the Kick It Out campaign ought to be worrying about, because as long as nothing is changing at the top of football, nothing is going to happen further down. I've got no time for the Kick It Out organization because, with situations like this still going on, I can't understand, deep down, what they do.

They give out some T-shirts, and they get involved with conflicts that have happened on the pitch, which to me comes across as distracting from the real issues. Of course, those incidents of racial abuse should be stamped out, but by presenting it all as individual racism and ignoring the institutional racism they won't move anything forward. Those confrontations might make the papers for a few days, and get Kick It Out's name mentioned, but then they will be forgotten. Or they present black players as continually in conflict, which tends to get them palmed off as chippy and not taken seriously.

I won't support Kick It Out, and I get accused of being selfish because of this, but the simple matter is I don't agree with what they're doing. I sometimes wonder if it's just there as a showpiece for the FA and PFA to demonstrate they're doing something about racism in the game, and not expected to achieve anything that would really change things.

There has been talk about introducing a Rooney Rule here, which arose in the American National Football League where shortlists for high-ranking jobs have to include at least one minority candidate. It's been fairly successful over there, but that's a different situation where in so many other walks of life there are black people in positions of real power – they've got a black president! Also, black people's commercial power is widely acknowledged, so there's the advertisers to be considered.

Over here, these things aren't really the case, so the only way the Rooney Rule would work would be if people wanted it to, but it's clear that the powers that be *wouldn't* want it to work. Can you imagine somebody who is bigoted to start off with being faced with a black candidate they *have* to interview, but have got no intention of giving it to him? They're going to be so resentful the poor candidate is going to have even less chance, if that was even possible!

What else happens is somebody will be given a position of authority just so a black face can be paraded in front of the media to prove there's no bias. The big trouble with this occurs because these guys are assumed to be representative of the rest of us and are usually sent to deal with any race issues that might come up. As their main objective is to maintain the status quo and keep whatever bullshit position they've been awarded, frequently this does more harm than good, as their opinions are taken as gospel – 'Well, that's what a black guy's said, so it must be right.'

Also, just to make sure nobody misunderstands what side they are on, they can often be more intolerant than the white guys. This is nothing new, either. It's been going on since slavery days when black people were used to help control other black people. He may be a fictional character, but Stephen, played by Samuel L. Jackson in *Django Unchained*, is a great illustration of the sort of behaviour that's still taking place today in organizations like the FA or Kick It Out.

I can't line up with any organization with big policies that I don't agree with. This is not because I don't care but because I won't be anybody's ventriloquist dummy – my name's Ian, not Stephen.

It's never particularly nice to be racially abused on a football pitch, but most players will either ignore it or sort it out themselves. It's like with the trouble we'd get from the police or the skinheads: you find your own way of dealing with it. Then if it's high profile the media loves it and can play on that whole conflict business until what started off as a spat becomes a full-blown race war.

That business with me and Peter Schmeichel was a case in point, showing how players react to situations and each other, how the papers operate, and how the PFA *doesn't* operate.

It started in November 1996 during a game up at Man United when I went in for the ball. He thought I was a bit late, he grabbed the ball, jumped up and yelled at me, 'You fucking black bastard.'

I didn't really see it until I watched the football that night, where it was there for everyone to see his mouth going, plus it was in the newspapers the next day, where they were saying they employed a lip reader, not that you needed a lip reader to understand what he was saying. I thought, 'Right, let's see what they do about this.'

It turns out to be a blatant case of sweeping it under the carpet. Gordon Taylor, the PFA and whatever faction it was of Kick It Out . . . none of them did anything.

Of course, the papers were still making a big deal of it, Alex Ferguson was supposedly keeping me and Schmeichel apart, and apparently Incey was trying to broker something. Then Ferguson got Maurice Watkins involved – he was a solicitor and a member of the FA Premier League Legal Advisory Group *and* a Man United board member. All the time, I had said nothing, but because Manchester United just wanted to protect Schmeichel in case something happened, this was all going on – so it festered and festered.

Then came the so-called tackle that shamed football. It was when Man United came to Highbury the following February. To be fair, I did go in hard on Schmeichel. I got booked and the United players swarmed round me, but Schmeichel made a meal of it, got up and carried on. Of course it's being played up by United and everybody else as a potentially career-ending tackle, but afterwards he never missed a day's football.

The papers, though, were loving it – Arsenal/Manchester United . . . black/white . . . striker/goalkeeper – they really wanted to keep it going, with the racial bit being the most sensational. I wouldn't talk about it, because there was nothing to say, but that didn't stop the press. One journalist even tried to make out the confrontation happened because of his Aryan looks!

It would have been laughable, except to keep it on the back pages they started writing stuff like I said he called me something racial again, as my excuse for the Horror Tackle. I didn't and he didn't, but it got really got me angry because now it had become another incident where white people were able to say, 'He's played the race card.' I don't play the race card, I don't need to and I never have.

Even Alex Ferguson joined in. After the second game, I met him at a reception given by Tony Blair in Downing Street and he pulled me aside and said, 'I never had you as a race card player. I never had you as that.'

That particularly upset me, as I've always liked him, and I would have liked to have thought he'd know I wouldn't do that. I told him I didn't, but I don't know if he believed me, because it had already been in the paper. Or he might just have been saying it to unsettle a rival team's striker – either way I lost a bit of respect for him that day.

Peter Schmeichel and I are friends now, we've done punditry together, but back then it's fair to say we didn't like each other. That was mostly because I wanted to score against him – I never did in a competitive game – and he wanted to stop me. It wasn't a racist thing, and what he said to me was what goes on in football matches: players will say all sorts of things to try and get an edge, things they wouldn't be too proud of if they stopped to think first. That doesn't excuse it, but the point is we would have sorted it out between us. The PFA did nothing, although I think Schmeichel got a small fine from the FA after the first incident.

For several months, the whole narrative about race and football got switched to a conflict that never was.

*   *   *

To find a solution to race problems that in many respects haven't got any better in the last thirty years, the race relations industry – because that is what it is now, an industry – is going to have to start listening. They need to talk to the people who are really affected by racism, and respect what they actually want. They should listen to intelligent people in the game, both black and white.

They're also going to have to realize that one size doesn't fit all and every racial situation is unique, and therefore must be looked at differently. It's like Malcolm X and Martin Luther King: very different, but each man's approach was right in certain situations. We are not all the same person, and won't all react to everything the same or want the same things out of life, and we won't all go the same way about getting them.

What we all do want, though, is opportunity.

Chapter Twenty-two

Kids 'n' Play

I've got eight kids with four different women, two I married and two I didn't: Shaun and Bradley's mum is Sharon; my third son is Brett; Deborah and I got married in 1993, and we have a son, Stacey, and a daughter, Bobbi; my daughter Coco was born in 2006 and I support her but play no other part in her or her mother's life; and I married Nancy in 2011, and we have two daughters, Lauren and Roxanne.

I didn't set out for it to be like that. I wanted to get married just once and never planned to have so many children in so many different circumstances. In fact, because of our upbringing, me and my brother always used to say we didn't want kids at all, but as we were growing up, the examples that were everywhere we looked were of guys with kids all over the place. It's difficult not to be taking that in on a pretty deep level, even if you don't realize you are, and that's the real problem with the so-called Vanishing Black Father: it's self-perpetuating.

When I was younger I used to go around with Shaun and Bradley's uncle, Norman, Sharon's brother, and he had girl-friends and kids everywhere. I kind of absorbed that and it almost felt like that was what people did. This one's sleeping with that one, he's got kids with her, her and her, she's got kids with him and him . . . You go to Jamaica it's the same thing.

I'm not saying it's the best way to live, and, really, I just fell into it rather than made it a choice.

When I was seventeen or eighteen I was going out with a girl called Sonia, who I loved. She got pregnant and unfortunately lost the baby. When I was eighteen I started seeing Sharon, so all of a sudden I've got a son, Shaun. The three of us are together for a bit, then Bradley comes along, and in the space of two and half years I've got two kids. Sharon and I split up for a while, and I started seeing someone new, which made me realize how much I was missing Sharon, then my new girlfriend told me she was pregnant, with Brett.

I'm twenty-one with three kids, I'm back living at my mum's, I've not signed for Palace yet so I'm working as a labourer on building sites, and I don't really know what's going on.

I needed somebody, at some stage when I was younger, to explain to me there was another way. Like so many young men in my environment, I just needed guidance and I didn't have it.

This doesn't mean that, where possible, I don't make as much time as I can for my children, do everything I can for them or love them any less. Often, it was they who taught me about life and what I needed to do.

I'd left my home very early because my mum was a nightmare, and when I started to see Sharon, everything seemed right: she was from the area, she knew where I was coming from, she's a decent person from a good family.

She already had Shaun, and I think because my own child-hood had been so chaotic this stable, loving environment really appealed to me. I'm sure taking Shaun on was the direct result of the way I was treated by my stepdad. I thought to myself that

I would not want anybody to treat somebody else like that so I was going to look after him. That was about the only positive I got from my stepdad, that I would always see Shaun as my son, not my stepson, not my adopted son, but my son.

In my eyes there was never any difference between Shaun and Bradley, I treated them exactly the same, but that wasn't always the case with my family. My mum and my sister would always be getting at Shaun and complaining that I was spending what money I had on him when, as they'd say, 'he's not even yours'. He'd go round to see my mum, and some of the things she'd say that made him cry were so nasty – he was just a little kid, and we used to have to get back in the car and go.

When we had Bradley as well, I'd buy stuff for everybody for Christmas and my sister would say, 'Why's Shaun getting so much, why's he getting the same as Bradley?' I saw them as exactly the same, but because Shaun was the eldest he'd get stuff that we'd then pass on to Brad, so of course the others would start on with 'Why's Shaun getting more, when he's not your son?' Then once Shaun started to do well, they were all over him.

It's nothing short of shameful when you look at your own family, you see them like that and think to yourself, 'You horrible, horrible two-faced people.'

Brett's mum was virtually the same: she would actually say to Brett, 'Shaun is not your brother, so don't call him your brother.' Shaun is such a mellow guy. He sees all the other boys as his brothers – it was Shaun who bought Brett his first car.

As good as life with Sharon was, and she's a wonderful woman, I think I was too young for this sort of responsibility, and attractive as the reasons for the relationship were, they weren't the right ones. We just fell out of love and I left when Bradley was five.

It was a shame, and she did a fantastic job bringing them up without me being there. People have nothing but lovely things to say about the two of them. Their mum is the most pleasant, placid woman you will ever meet. so cool, so calm, and both of them have got that side of her. It showed up as soon as they started playing football, because neither of them had a malicious or vindictive vibe to them – not like I used to have. I would leave my foot in on people just because I could.

Deborah, who I married, was a completely different kettle of fish. We'd been going out for while, then we got engaged, but I wouldn't say I was fully committed to the relationship at that point. That was entirely down to my selfishness because I was having too much of a good time: I was flying at Palace, I was on a good contract so I had a bit of money, I had a nice car, and it was cool to be living at my mum's because the flat I'd bought for her was nice and, really, I was only there to sleep.

I still saw myself as single. I was going out with Mitchell, Brighty, Andy Gray and Tony Finnigan, and we'd be wearing our lovely clothes and handmade Church's shoes, hitting the rare groove clubs.

It wasn't as if I was putting it about or anything, it's just that this was a kind of perpetual lads' night out and I felt that, with those guys, in my mid-to-late twenties, I was just starting to get properly introduced to the world – I said it was selfishness! Even my mum was telling me, 'What you settling down for? This is when you should be doing what you're doing as a young man.' She might simply have been being contrary, though, because she never liked Deborah.

I had bought a lovely house in Warlingham in Surrey, for no other reason than Ron Noades, the chairman at Palace, used to keep saying to me, 'You need to start getting property, buy property. Just have it! It doesn't matter what you do with it, just have it.' Which was more or less what I did, as I had no intentions of moving out of the cool gig I had at my mum's!

I was still living there when Deborah and I got engaged, but as soon as I bought the house she started putting me under serious pressure: 'Look how long we've been together . . . Why haven't you moved me in yet? . . . What have you bought a house for if we've got engaged and we're not even living in it?'

The truth was, I was probably going to rent it out, but she was on my case, on my case, on my case and we moved in, with, literally, only a mattress and our clothes.

Once we started living together it was, 'We've been engaged for so long now, why aren't we getting married?' That was more like a nudge than any sort of serious pressure, because I loved Deborah and, in spite of all the fun I'd been having, I wanted to get married as much as she did. I was thirty years old by then, and starting to think that settling down was the right thing to do at that age, so we got married in 1993.

This was around the time footballers were beginning to earn big money and we were hearing about these girls who just want to take it from you, so the thing was to settle down but with the right one. I thought Deborah was that woman, because we'd known each other practically since we were children – she was in the same class as David Rocastle in primary school. She was from the area, so she understood all of that, and she worked in a bank as a personal banker, so I thought she'd know what to do with my money. As it turned out, that last statement was true, but not in a good way.

Too often, with Debbie, there were issues with the other kids. I've got a lovely picture of me in the local park, taken the day after the Cup Final with Palace – I'm with Shaun, Bradley and Brett, and my little nephew's on my back. Any time anybody noticed it and said, 'And how are the boys?', she was always quick to reply, very pointedly, 'They're not all my boys!'

When I was very much at the height, Shaun and Bradley used to come over to stay with me every other weekend, which could be quite difficult when I had to go to play football. It meant Deborah had to look after them, and while she was always very nice to them, there were still problems because quite a few times I'd come back to find there'd been a big argument of some kind. It meant I didn't spend as much time with them as I would have liked because it worked out better if sometimes they didn't come over for the weekend.

I never had any problems with Shaun and Bradley's mum when picking the boys up or taking them for the weekend or in school holidays at short notice. I'd phone up and Sharon was always great about it: 'Yeah, come and get them, they'd love to see you.'

After I split up with Deborah, I'd want to see Stacey and Bobbi and she'd tell me, 'Well, no, we're not ready yet, our minds need clearing.' For six years I didn't get to spend any more than an hour at a time with them, which of course I was unhappy about, but could understand her anger because our marriage finally collapsed because of my infidelities.

★   ★   ★

This was the most shameful part of my life, because it was just *wrong*. Yes, Deborah and I had disagreements, mostly over my other kids, which I admit did used to upset me, but beyond all that she was a wonderful woman and it wasn't fair to cheat on her.

I think we always wanted different things, as she was much more for settling down, building a home and staying in – hence all the pressure to move in together and to get married – at a time when I was travelling the world and getting swept along with all sorts of new experiences. All the same, though, I had no excuse.

It happened when I was on the television show, after I'd finished playing, and was triggered by a combination of things: I desperately missed football; the show was a success and I was starting to believe I was something special; there was a massive amount of socializing and drinking and late nights around the TV production; and with so many single women it would get pretty flirtatious.

Being in such a male-dominated environment for so long, then going to one that was predominately women was a real shock for me – especially one with such self-assured, casually sexy young women of all shapes and sizes. I was never that confident around women, and growing up with my mum and my sister I'd never had this much attention from women before and I found I really liked it.

The drinking and the banter with the production team was all good fun, but underneath it all I often felt a bit lonely because it wasn't really my world – whether I knew it or not, I was still a footballer. I'm not sure what I was looking for, maybe I was just attention-seeking, but in some cases it didn't stop at the flirting and the joviality. As I said, these aren't excuses for how I behaved, simply the set of circumstances.

Of course, all this stuff got out into the press and that was it, my marriage was over in probably the worst possible way. To have your dad leave in that manner and for it to be so public was never going to be good for the kids. Stacey was nine and his sister Bobbi was five, and it was hard for them. I can understand why, in the past, they've both shown their anger toward me. When I was only able to spend so little time with them for so long, naturally there was going to be a bit of the relationship that was going to die.

Stacey used to go to Whitgift School, a very sports-centred private school in Croydon, where he played rugby and had all these Hooray Henry mates. When they go for it they *really* go for it, and one day when he was about fourteen or fifteen he came in steaming drunk, bouncing-off-the-walls drunk. His mum phoned me up and I went down there from where I live in north-west London and tore into him about sorting himself out and not disrespecting his mum like this. He just came back at me with, 'You can fuck off! You're not even here, you can't tell me what to do!'

Although I was so angry and he was so drunk, I could understand where he was coming from – when you've got a mum that can, and will, continually throw infidelity at your dad, of course I'm going to be the one that gets the blame, and I'm wholeheartedly taking it.

In the past, we've had massive problems with Bobbi and Stacey in respect of my second wife Nancy and my two little girls, too. I don't think Deborah ever truly came to terms with what happened and that, eventually, I moved on.

Stacey had to see things for himself with regards my actions. He's now at the stage of his life where he can understand, without me trying to explain, how things work, what happened with me and his mum and how I'm trying to be. These days, I love being in his company, he's such a wise kind of guy. He just wants to relax, spend time hanging out with me and see the girls.

He's a rugby player, and the biggest person in the family – he's six foot two and weighs about eighteen stone. Massive! He's a prop forward and played for Whitgift when they won the *Daily Mail* RBS Cup at Twickenham, so he gets to wear this fancy jacket.

Stacey went to Durham University for a while, then went to America to try his hand at American football, realized it wasn't going to happen because his knee and his back wouldn't have been able to hold up, so he came back, got his head down, and now he's at Nottingham University. We've had a couple of arguments, but he's kicking on and going for a really good degree in Business Studies. He's realized you can't be angry for ever. I've had to wait many years to have this sort of relationship with him but now I have, it's worth it.

It's more difficult with Bobbi, because she and her mother now live in Los Angeles. I didn't have any say in the matter. It's not difficult to understand why not, but it's hard to try and build a relationship with her when all I get from her and her mother is, 'She's going to this school, she's going to that school. I need this much for this and I need this and that.'

Bobbi phones me up every now and again and mentions 'co-parenting', but it feels like the co-parenting only comes into it when she and her mother want something. Otherwise they don't have a lot to do with me. She's only seventeen, though, so I know I'm going to have to wait a while before we can talk like I did with Stacey, and I'm looking forward to that.

I'm so pleased Shaun and Brad made it in professional football, simply because it's the greatest profession in the whole wide world. It is such a genuine privilege just to be able to have playing football as your job, but to make it into the Premiership where you earn great money, you have a very comfortable lifestyle, travel all over the place first class, train at the best facilities . . . that's fantastic.

It wasn't the case that they were always going to go into football just because that's what their dad did, especially Shaun, because he was so small, he was minute – I struggled to get in because I am small, but Shaun is no more than five foot six. He was so robust, though, we used to call him Rubberman because of the way bigger players seemed to bounce off him. While Bradley was never the quickest player he's always had good technical ability and a real footballing intelligence.

I know when you watch your own kids you like to think, 'Oh yeah, they're pretty good', but I did think they had something and they were both prepared to work at it, so I was really happy when they made it.

Brett, my other son, nearly made it too, and he was very unfortunate not to. He had good feet and was a very good finisher. He was an out-and-out striker, more in my mould than the other two were. Again, very small and very slight, but he's got more of my persona and could get angry when he was playing.

He made it to Reading when Steve Coppell was there. Steve liked him and he got into the reserves, but Brett was always sick

– he was severely asthmatic. He worked hard at it, then he went down with irritable bowel syndrome and it scuppered him. He had to give it up.

Since then he's carried on working hard and done well in estate agency, but I wonder if he's a bit bitter about how his chances in football came to an end. He'd seen how well his brothers have done and he'd set his mind on a professional football career, so for a while after it was like an itch that couldn't be scratched and he found it difficult to settle. I do feel for him, because he was a very good player.

With Shaun and Brad I was never ramming football into their heads, although because I used to talk about it so much and because playing for Ten-em-Bee and then for Palace obviously made me happy, that must have had an effect on them.

We had a game we used to play in the living room of this little flat we lived in, with one of those little soft yellow balls. The two of them would have to try and run past me while I would blast the ball at them and try to hit them. Of course they'd end up shrieking and Sharon would tell us all to calm down.

When Brad was very little and I was in the bath he'd come in to eat the soap suds, and I'd talk to him about how Daddy was going to be a footballer. Same with Shaun. When I went to trials I'd tell him where I was going and ask him if he thought I was going to do all right – he'd always say 'Yes.'

When they were playing school football, I'd have to watch them from afar because by that time if I turned up pitchside it would cause such a fuss. I wasn't one for coaching them, although sometimes when they'd come over and we'd play football in the garden I'd tell them they couldn't come in until they'd done fifty keepy-uppies. I wasn't serious, but to their credit they would actually do it.

When I'd drive them to and from matches, the only advice I'd give them was, 'Make sure you don't give the ball away and enjoy the game.' I'd tell them to try and score a goal and if they do it's even better. Shaun was never too bothered about scoring, but Bradley liked to and he was good at it from back then.

I thought it was great when they were both taken to Nottingham Forest as boys, not simply because they'd actually made it on to the first step of the ladder, but, at a smaller, lower profile operation than one of the London clubs, they had a much better chance of being developed properly. At a club like that there isn't so much pressure for instant success, so it's less likely expensive signings are going to be brought in ahead of homegrown players. There'll be less competition within the club because they won't have the budget to take on players they aren't completely serious about. Also, as Ian Wright's sons, it helped them to be away from the limelight associated with a bigger team.

Crucially, it was in Nottingham not London. They were living on the same estate we all grew up on in Brockley, and at that age, early teens, it was important for them to come out of there, move right away and live in their digs. It made better people of the both of them.

They're good lads in the main, but they were mixing with the kind of boys that end up in prison, cause loads of problems, do this, do that, and there's stabbings and all sorts of negative stuff going on. Because of some of those environments, and how so much of the rest of the world will look at you if you're from a particular situation, it's easy to be forced to see yourself in a certain way.

It's just how the world has become since I've grown up – people seem less likely to judge you on the strength of your character, and it'll be, 'Oh he's this, therefore he must be that.' It's *really* hard for black boys to grow up in London unaffected – sometimes I look back and think, how lucky am I?

That said, however, I feel that those early years in Brockley have left Bradley and Shaun much more grounded than they might have been. They've got a certain street knowledge which makes them understand stuff, and very little fazes them as their natural reaction is, 'OK, that's cool, I can deal with that.'

But even all of that is not going to protect you all the time. Just like what happened to me when I found myself running for my life because those guys had snatched the trays of rings, it can simply come down to the company you're keeping.

Bradley joined Southampton in 2006, where he got mixed up with some idiots. Him, Nathan Dyer and some other guy were in a nightclub in Southsea in 2008, and Brad was standing by a door watching the other two going through people's stuff. I've seen the CCTV footage, and while he's having no part of what's going on, he's still there, so when they get arrested it's guilt by association. Nathan Dyer pleaded guilty and Brad's case went to the Crown Court, where it was dismissed, but I believe the whole thing damaged his career in England.

From the very beginning he was telling me he didn't do anything, and I believe him because he's been brought up much better than that and there have never been thieves in our family, but because he's running with these guys he became inextricably linked with this crap. I never saw Nathan Dyer's name in the press nearly as much as I saw Bradley's, yet on the film I saw Nathan Dyer's hand in someone's bag.

Like any other father I explained to him you'll always be judged on the company you keep, and if you choose the wrong people it will be your downfall. Thankfully, after that incident, he began to listen.

That was the beginning of the end for him in English football. He went from there to Plymouth and because of their financial problems at the time he was hardly getting paid – I had to pay his wages some months.

He scored goals there, then went to Charlton where he scored a load of goals and the fans loved him, but their manager Chris Powell still let him go. I believe he was still tainted by that episode in Southampton and people constantly saying he was a thief even after the case was dismissed.

Going to the USA in 2013 was the best thing he could have done. Darren Dein, David Dein's son, had a lot to do with it because he's Thierry Henry's agent and Thierry was already there. In fact, I owe Thierry a huge debt of gratitude for all he did for Brad at New York Red Bulls.

Brad went there for a virtual pittance compared with what English footballers earn, and after an initial period they were going to let him go – I think he had difficulty settling in New York – but Thierry said to give him a chance, simply because he knows how to play the game. Thierry was brilliant, literally like his dad or his older brother, and on the pitch put chances on a plate for him, which allowed Brad to grow to the point that when Thierry left he could kick on and become the MLS top scorer.

Shaun went over there in 2015 because he needed a change. For whatever reasons, after a good career with Manchester City and Chelsea, he wasn't playing much football in England. He had Premier League and FA Cup medals but like Brad he had slipped down the leagues and was at Queen's Park Rangers, hardly getting a game and people talking about how he's just there for the wages.

He was disillusioned and said, 'Dad, I want to go to the MLS now. I don't think there's anything left for me in England.' I told him, if that's what you've got to do then that's what you've got to do, as long as you work hard when you get there. New York Red Bulls was the obvious first choice, because of Darren's links and Bradley already being there.

They both absolutely love it over there. They're living in Harrison, New Jersey, both settled, playing great football and being loved by the fans – it couldn't be better. With the emergence of the American game and the way it's going out there it's fantastic. They've got a lot to offer not only as players but with the young Americans that are coming in, as Shaun and Brad can give them what they've got, *and* show them what you have to do to be a top player, how you train and how you work, rest and play.

I often find myself thinking how I would have loved to have had that sort of opportunity when my playing days over here finished – to go somewhere like New York and carry on playing football for another few years would have been brilliant. As it was, I was just too early for that, like I was just too early for the real big Premiership money!

With those two doing so well over there I couldn't be happier. I've seen them both represent their country – Shaun as a full international, Brad at Under-20 – but nothing makes me so proud as watching them at Red Bulls when Shaun puts the ball over and Bradley finishes.

★   ★   ★

The kids have been the one constant in my adult life, and the only real regret I have is not spending as much time with them when they were really young. Bradley was five when I left. Now my daughters Lauren and Roxanne are six and four, and if I'm not with them for long enough it's horrible, I don't like it.

I love my wife Nancy so much, and this time I'm sure I'll get it right. I'm more than thirty years older than I was when I got together with Sharon, and I've come to terms with a great deal about life and about myself. I'm a different, calmer person. I realize now how important it is that you find the right person, because once you get into a situation where you have kids . . .

Part Four

Wright Now

Chapter Twenty-three

It's *Match of the Day*

When, at the start of 2015, the BBC asked me to do an FA Cup game – Manchester United against Arsenal – I did it, had a good laugh with Gary, Alan Shearer and Roy Keane, and thought, this is great. Then off the back of that they offered me *Match of the Day* again. And that was it. I was back in and I could hardly believe it.

After all the stuff I'd said about them and the BBC, they've let me back into the fold. It's fantastic, because in the world of football punditry in this country, being on *Match of the Day* is the equivalent of playing in the Champions League.

I've got some brilliant people I deal with at BT Sport, and they are catching up with *Match of the Day*, but as they'll admit they've still got a long way to go. When I do the internationals for ITV, like at the Euros in 2016, they've got a fantastic production team and I cannot fault them, but the BBC still edges it just because it's the BBC.

Also, for anybody who's at all interested in football in England, *Match of the Day* is an institution. When I was fortunate enough to get back on it, I had to look at myself in a mirror and say out loud, 'You lucky bastard!'

★ ★ ★

It really was a shame my first stint on *Match of the Day* ended the way it did. It's been fairly widely reported that when I first got on the show I was so overwhelmed I told Des Lynam, the presenter at that time, it was my Graceland. In the same way Elvis fans make the pilgrimage to his former home as if it was a shrine, *Match of the Day* meant that much to me.

I'm sure it means the same for anybody who's been playing top-flight football and has spent so long seeing themselves on it, but it was made even more emotional for me because of my childhood. For a kid of that age who was crazy about football, not being allowed to watch it by my stepdad was sheer torture, which sometimes used to come back to me while I was watching as an adult. To then actually be on it, to be part of it, was a kind of closure on that because it proved to me, unequivocally, all of that hadn't held me back in any way and I knew I'd got past it.

Then as a player I felt as if I'd *arrived*, that the game I loved thought enough of me to have me talked about on the BBC. I'm sure every player that gets on there to talk about football experiences that 'Oh my God! I'm on *Match of the Day*' moment.

When I got on there as a pundit, I was still playing. At the time I was starting to build a television career on the strength of my personality, all of which contributed to the persona I presented from the start on *Match of the Day*. I saw it as being banter-driven because that was how footballers talked to each other, plus I seemed to be doing all right winging it on the other shows I was presenting.

I was having a laugh and I was loving it. I would be sitting with a couple of other pundits and when first Des, and then Gary Lineker, talked for a bit, I'd be thinking, 'OK, they're coming to me last, I've got time to come up with a quip.' I'm pretty sure I thought I had to impress or maybe compete, and the way to do it was with a joke or a crack.

I don't think I was really too comfortable with it, and maybe I was starting to get a bit worn down by the criticism I was getting. Perhaps I was thinking, I've been doing this for a while yet I don't feel there's been any progress. In fact, there were times when I seemed to be going backwards, because the BBC puts such an emphasis on doing things correctly. Someone would come down and say, 'Oh, you don't finish off your sentences' . . . 'You're dropping your Ts' . . . 'You're not saying your aitches properly' – I've always had a problem saying my aitches. It felt as if after every show went out, somebody there was complaining about something.

I started to get more and more insecure about what I was doing – I'd had a successful chat show without worrying about these things, now I was starting to question myself a bit, which was when I started losing my confidence.

My reaction was to really steam into the *Match of the Day* executives in 2008, accusing them of treating me like the court jester, that they weren't taking me seriously and so on and so on. It was pretty strong stuff, and must have come as a quite a surprise because suddenly I'm shouting about how I want to be taken seriously, when just the previous month I had appeared happy to do it so light-heartedly.

I realize now that blasting off about it wasn't the right thing to do, but I was a bit wrapped up in myself back then, and probably frustrated that the programme I most wanted to be on wasn't working out too well for me.

It finished me in football punditry for a quite a while, as I went through a phase for a few years when nobody on television would touch me. After that outburst at *Match of the Day*, the BBC wouldn't have me – understandably so – then not long after that the guy who had been Head of Football at the BBC, Niall Sloane, was made Director of Sport at ITV, so now ITV didn't want me either. And Sky weren't interested because they saw me as a BBC person.

I wasn't just out in the cold. I was in the Arctic Circle.

Getting back into it was quite a process because I had agents who were determined to keep me on the light entertainment road and wanted me to have nothing to do with football, but I was helped by some people who were really good to me.

During that time, TalkSport were amazing. I'd been doing the drivetime show with Adrian Durham before I'd left *Match of the Day* and, in spite of all the fuss around me in the papers, they were happy for me to carry on. Bill Ridley, the Programme Director there, and Adrian were fantastic, never less than fully supportive. People can be negative about Adrian as a broadcaster and a presenter, but I think he's brilliant to listen to. He was a joy to work with and really gave me a boost when I needed it.

That kept my name afloat talking about football, which was vital because it allowed me to keep on working and think about how I was approaching things while staying on the football broadcasting radar. As I result, I went to work as a television pundit on beIN Sports's football coverage – they're part of Al Jazeera and broadcast football all over the world. That was great, very low-profile, so I was away from too much pressure as I worked to evolve my on-screen style.

Another reason I did it was that Al Jazeera were in the same building on London's South Bank as some of ITV Sport, and the same crews were being used for both channels. It meant I was working with ITV technicians and directors, who, pretty soon, were talking about how Wrighty's back, and he's doing his stuff and he's pretty serious about it now. Of course, this got back to the producers and senior producers, and while I didn't get anything out of it immediately, they knew what I was doing and how I was doing it.

I got some traction with radio during that time, though, and how that came about did a great deal to shift my thinking.

A really bad side effect of me doing that *Live from Studio Five* show in 2009–10 was that it messed up my relationship with TalkSport. I didn't want to do the show and thought – or hoped – that I wouldn't be able to because it would clash with me doing my stuff on the radio. My agent Jeff Weston pointed out to me a clause in my contract stating that if I was doing that radio show and a TV gig came up, I could take the television show instead. I didn't want that but feel that Jeff pushed me into it.

Right after I finished with *Studio Five*, Absolute Radio offered me the opportunity to have a show on the weekend, talking about football. This was fantastic because Absolute is a music station, but Paul Sylvester, Head of Presentation, figured I'd fit in with their listener profile. That gave me the chance to really get my confidence back and got me through some tough times. I'm still doing it, too, so it must be working.

A good friend of mine, Simon Cross, who used to produce the BBC radio show I did with Brighty, had helped me get in with Absolute, but he did much more than that for me when he phoned me up in 2013 with another idea.

He told me he had his own independent radio production company and asked me if I wanted to do a show for him on

5Live, which, of course, is the BBC. I wanted nothing to do with the BBC, because I was still pissed off with them because they were pissed off with me – that's how grown-up I was being!

Quite rightly, Simon took no notice of such behaviour and said to me straight: 'Ian, I guarantee that if you read that piece you did slaughtering the BBC now, you'll be embarrassed by it. Properly embarrassed. So get over it and take this chance to get back in there.'

He was right, and I started thinking that, if I was being completely honest with myself, I had been a bit of prick around that time. So I said, 'Let's do the meeting with them', and it finished up with me on the *606* phone-in with Kelly Cates.

Things immediately started picking up for me, and I love that show. Sometimes I have to tell some home truths – most frequently I have to let Arsenal fans know that just because I give Tottenham credit or give Chelsea credit or Man United credit, doesn't mean I love them. Some of the fans are *so* closed off in their opinions it's almost embarrassing! I argue with some of them, I don't argue with others . . . it's brilliant.

People say one of the things they love about listening to the *606* show is hearing me sniggering and giggling in the background, which also upsets a load of other people. That's the great thing about the freedom we have on that show; I'm not doing it to undermine anyone or anything but some of the things that people say are literally laughable!

Around the same time, I got back into football television, but again I took the scenic route. ITV were making a documentary about Laurie Cunningham, and the feeling was they had to have Ian Wright in it, if for no other reason than people would ask why not.

Niall Sloane approached my new agent Steve Kutner and said they wanted me to contribute to the film. Kuts said yes, but you've got to give him some kind of game to cover. I'm sure Niall ummed and ahed about it, but in the end ITV put me on an FA Cup game, MK Dons against QPR.

I just did what I do, but because I'd been thinking about it and working out what I needed to do to be a good pundit, I said what I wanted to say and it was funny, it was concise, it was informative . . . it had everything it needed.

The reaction to me being on there was really positive, which was great because people hadn't seen me on television for a while. Then it just kicked on from there. They gave me Brentford against Chelsea, then the internationals, and I was back doing football punditry.

One of the most pleasing things about doing this work for ITV was getting back with Niall, because when he was at the BBC and I was just starting to do punditry, his mentoring of me was so helpful.

He'd tell me, not in a snide way, how I should speak, in respect of working out what I wanted to say and how I wanted to say it. He'd talk to me about how I dressed, and it really was what I needed. Now, through his having me back on ITV, I was getting the chance to prove there was more to me than there had been when it came to football punditry.

The BBC had it both ways: they'd seen what I was doing on the ITV games; and I was working for the Corporation on 5Live, which was going really well. Through the radio show, I kept getting calls from within the BBC asking me to do *Football Focus* and a few other things. I always said, 'No'. Maybe I didn't think I was ready to go back on to BBC television, or maybe my ego was making me think that I didn't need anything else after doing matches on ITV, or maybe I was still being a bit stroppy in some kind of hangover from my falling out with them years ago . . . I don't know.

Then they talked to me about *Match of the Day*. I pulled myself up at that point. I figured a lot of water had gone under the bridge and by then I was prepared to swallow my pride – after all, it's *Match of the Day*!

Perhaps the personnel at the BBC had changed so people there didn't have any baggage from my last stint on the programme. But I'm sure the main thing was they were listening to *606* and realized I had a different approach to what I was doing now.

The thing about production teams is they're not at all starstruck – most of them have been doing it far too long for that – and they know if a presenter has done his homework and is taking it seriously or not. They will have known that, back in the day, I was coming on and winging it, running on instinct rather than reading the packs they give you beforehand.

Now, through what I was doing on *606*, they would know that I'm studious these days, I'm paying attention, I'm analysing and I'm watching and seeing now. I've never lost my passion for the game: I'm simply better prepared. I read more now, I listen to more podcasts, I listen to more opinions . . . I know more now.

And that was what has made them think, 'Let's get him on'.

I so love being back on *Match of the Day*. I love the way I'm doing it now, and what with BT Sport and doing the internationals, I'm right back in the rhythm of football again.

Somebody said to me that, with the amount I'm doing, it must be like having a proper job, but I've had proper jobs and, believe me, this is nothing like that! This is like when I was playing football for a living and having to pinch myself on a weekly basis; now I'm *talking* about football – which I'd be doing anyway – for a living. It's like being part of football but without having to do training. All I have to do is read, watch DVDs and listen to stuff.

I have to say I've been very fortunate, which is why I will not let it get taken away from me again by stupidity, ego or anything other than the fact that my time is up. I'll work as hard as it takes to stay on top of being the best pundit out there.

I also know there's space for banter and having a laugh, as I do with Gary and Shearer and anybody else who's on. But that's not the first reason you're there – you're there to talk about football and you're trying to impart what you know to the viewers to help them get more out of the game they love. Without meaning to patronize anybody, I always try and explain the technical side of things like I'm talking to a twelve-year-old. Obviously not stuff like the offside rule, but when I'm trying to explain why, as a striker, the player has to do this, and why, as a defender, another player ought to do that, I break it down to such a degree that *all* viewers can get into it. It helps to let the viewers into the world that us guys sitting there know inside out, and it's so important to the success of the show.

It's as if I'm constantly trying to teach somebody something, but doing it in an easy-going way, rather than like they're in a schoolroom. When you give people this serious sort of knowledge, that's when they start taking you seriously because you're telling them something they didn't know in a way they can understand. That's how I approach punditry this time around, and I believe that if I'd had that attitude right from the start, it wouldn't have ended how it did.

To a large degree this was a matter of confidence, and I think I knew at the back of my mind that first time around I hadn't been doing enough homework. The reason people couldn't touch me on the football pitch in respect of knocking my confidence was because I knew not only did I have the ability, I'd also put the work in.

When I was on *Match of the Day* first time and people were saying he can't put more than three words together, he never finishes his sentences, he can't pronounce his aitches, it used to make me very insecure. I was fourteen when I left school and my self-doubts are always rooted in my schooling, which was something I could have overcome by putting in more hard work to be a pundit.

It was what Sir Trevor McDonald said that provided the key for me, and I applied it to punditry: get more knowledge, as much as you can, but don't change who you are or how you speak because that's what people like to hear and they like to hear you speak with passion. I had to learn how to become a television-friendly version of myself, still Wrighty, but making sure I did the job I was there to do first and foremost.

Even now, when people come on Twitter and all they say are things like, 'He can't string three words together' – which is their go-to line! – or they talk about my glasses or my shirts, it's because they can't say anything else. They can't talk about my content because I've worked on it.

First time around, it was a case of I *didn't* do enough work, now it's like I *can't* do enough.

One of the most brilliant things I've found is how enjoyable it is to go to the grounds as part of *Match of the Day* or BT Sport or whatever because you can go all over the place, into the manager's office, into the dressing-room area, and talk to people. It's more homework, but it gives you so much insight you can pass along to the viewers.

You can go in and pick people's brains about pretty much anything you like. For example, I could go into Mark Hughes's office at Stoke and ask him, 'What's so-and-so like as a player? How do they work in training?' Then I can go on air, saying something like, 'I was speaking to the manager and he says there's a definite improvement there, and we should be able to see the results of his hard work.' Or 'Steve Bould told me this player has been working on his positional play and he's surprised people . . .' Those are the sorts of insights you need to be able to give the viewers when you're on the touchline doing punditry live, or just use to inform what you're saying about the game in general.

It's great to meet up with other football people under these circumstances and it can do a lot to patch up things that might have happened in the past. I had a massive bust-up with Steve Bruce when we were playing, but I see him now as a manager and we talk and it's all cool. Me and Roy Keane are really good mates now, and it's good to have these chances to put any friction behind us.

The only downside of punditry is exactly the same as it is for players: if you get good at it, with the amount of competitions there are in the summer now, you get so little time off to chill out and be with the family. It's like the best footballers end up with much less recovery time because they get to the latter stages of the World Cup or the Euros or the Copa America. But that's just part of the game – I used to say to Shaun, Jermain Defoe and a few other players I used to speak to regularly, 'You've got to take your rest whenever you can get it and relish the time that you are at that elite level.'

I was in Paris for a month in 2016 doing the Euros, and being wanted for that length of time tells me that ITV rate me as a top pundit. While it was horrible being away from Nancy and the girls, I have to be there and the family understands. There were sixteen million people watching one of the games I was doing. For the last couple of weeks, I moved out of the hotel where the whole ITV team was staying and rented an apartment so the family could come out and that became their holiday. It made such a difference to me. The girls had schoolwork with them, as a condition of their coming out, so I'd do that with them in the morning, then go to work and they'd go all over the place in Paris. It was brilliant, and that mix of work and home life is something I can do as a pundit but couldn't have done as a player.

That first year I returned to *Match of the Day*, in 2015–16, the programme won awards and a massive amount of plaudits. While I'm not saying that's down to me, I know I contributed to it being such a good watch. I'm not going to deny that, because a lot of people have told me so and because I worked so hard to get back on it. I had to eat a huge helping of humble pie, too, which I didn't mind because I've always held my hands up when I've been wrong, and in that situation at that particular time I was wrong.

I might have had a couple of false starts, and I've had to deal with a few problems along the way, but, as with football, I always knew I could perform if I just had the chance, learned from those around me and worked as hard as I could.

Chapter Twenty-four

So What Have I Got?

The only time in my entire life I can remember not wanting to play football was that Auld Firm derby during the brief period I spent up at Celtic, as I felt that was not a football environment. Apart from that, I've always wanted to play football – from when I was a very little kid up until now.

My ankle is fused and my knee's shot so I can't run around like I used to and I can't play in the games I get invited to around the world, but that doesn't mean I won't have a game if I get the chance. A bit of five-a-side, or if my mate's Sunday morning team needs an extra man I'll jump on and play holding midfield. I enjoy that so much, I realize I don't need to play at Old Trafford or at the Emirates or wherever to get my juices flowing. Those low-key or spontaneous games are fine for me because it's all about *playing football* and it doesn't matter what stage I'm on. It's a gift, a total privilege to have earned a living from playing football and now to still be able to enjoy it to that degree.

Sometimes I think I've led a charmed life, and when anybody considers the near misses I've had it must appear that way – the time I had to run because those guys had stolen the rings . . . going to prison . . . more or less giving up on playing football professionally . . . getting back on *Match of the Day* after mouthing off like that.

When I look back at the times I've fallen on my feet, it's easy to believe that if there is a higher force out there then some-body is definitely looking out for me – there have been too many coincidences and things that just seem to have been put in my path. But, at the same time, I had to take advantage of them, so another way to look at it is that I'm a regular bloke who had some very good opportunities and made sure he took them, even if sometimes he took the long way around.

People talk about luck, but there's a Caribbean saying that luck is what happens when opportunity meets preparation, which is how I like to think I made my own luck. When I was playing I prepared as well as I knew how for whatever level I was at; when I was a chat-show host I learned everything I could about my guests; now, as a football pundit I'll study the games and the players to make sure I have the most detailed insight possible.

Yes, it involves hard work, which I believe is something that has defined pretty much every stage of my life, especially when what I've been doing involves the public – the fans. It could be Palace fans . . . Arsenal fans . . . Ian Wright fans . . . *Match of the Day* fans . . . England fans . . . I always owe it to them to be the very best I can be. Anybody in my position ought to feel the same.

Bill Shankly, the great Liverpool manager and a hero of mine, put it better than anybody else: 'If a man is playing in front of the public and he's being well paid and he doesn't dedicate himself to the job, he doesn't play with his heart and soul, for the fans, I wouldn't pay him. If I could I'd put him in jail . . . out of society, because he's a menace.'

I've got a clip of him saying that on my phone and I'll play it to anybody who doesn't understand what's required of us.

After one of Liverpool's many victory parades, Bill Shankly stood on the balcony at the reception and said, 'I cannot get it through to my players enough what it means to play for you.'

That's the same thing David Rocastle understood and used to try and drum into me: 'The game is about the fans, the fans are what make the game, it's the fans that love you. If you can't do it for them, you don't deserve to be here. You're literally in the wrong game.'

That is something that I've always tried to do – give my all for the fans on and off the pitch, to work hard and be nice. Being famous beyond the fans that you and your own team might have, however, is a very different matter.

I've been famous longer than I haven't been. It's never been something I've been particularly comfortable with and although I think I've dealt with it pretty well, as time has gone by it's got to the point where I find myself thinking if I could have done everything without the fame I wouldn't have missed it at all. Of course, I know that couldn't be possible and I love the fans – I've lived my whole career on the basis of what Rocky said to me – but in the last ten years I think every famous person's relationship with fame has changed.

Camera phones mean that just about anybody thinks they have the right to stop you at any time and take your picture, regardless of what you might be doing or who you might be with. And so many people are just blasted rude about it. These aren't the Arsenal fans or the football fans who usually have some respect because I mean something to them: these are people who might just have seen me on the television or in the paper a couple of times.

Standard behaviour is for people to shout 'Oi, Wright! Wright!' at me, which sets me off because they can't even use my first name – maybe that's because commentators use players' last names, but on the street it just sounds rude. Then they'll follow up with, 'Come 'ere, come 'ere, can I have a picture?' And they've already got their phone out by then.

As I've got older, I've become less likely to put up with stuff I would have let slide a few years ago, so the chances are I'll say, 'Why are you speaking to me so rudely?'

At that point they might resort to saying 'Please', but by then I'm walking past them saying, 'I don't want my picture taken with you or by you because you've got no manners.'

It's very frustrating as I come off looking unreasonable, but too many people think just because they've got a phone and they're walking on the same street as you they can treat you like something they've found on the bottom of their shoe.

I've had people try to physically move my wife out of the way, or try to come in between me and the kids when we're holding hands with no consciousness of my space or my family's space, just because they think I'm famous. The older I've got, the more intrusive this has become and I'm getting very, very prickly about it.

Then there's Twitter. If I was still playing the last thing I'd do is be on Twitter because all you're doing is opening yourself up to criticism, most of which is unreasonable and a fair amount is just abusive. When I was playing I knew that 50 per cent of the people liked me and 50 per cent hated me – it could have been more – but the fact was I didn't have to deal with them. Nowadays, any famous person who turns their phone on and goes to their Twitter feed will read people saying some really horrible stuff about them. So much of it is just nasty.

People are always telling me that I have to be on Twitter, that I need a bigger footprint, and that it's good fun and can be useful. That's true most of the time. For instance, Twitter and Vauxhall helped me to get Wembley for a one-off game for some of my million followers; I just picked some names off my phone and gave them a day out at Wembley.

But Twitter is also something that manages to upset me almost every day of the week. These total strangers are deliberately trying to impact on your life negatively because they are able to reach you on your Twitter feed. These are people who you would never, in ten lifetimes, have anything to do with, but now it's like they have access to you on a minute-by-minute basis.

My wife always says, 'Why are you bringing those people into your life? Do you really need to have their opinion to know if you're good or bad?'

I often wish I could just leave Twitter, that I could take it off my handset and not even think about it, but I guess I'm hooked because I know as soon as I do that, I'll have something good to write on there. That's why I stay on it, to tweet positive, useful things, catering to the decent people – I tweeted that Bill Shankly clip.

Like with Facebook: it too has its negative side, but if I wasn't on it I wouldn't have had this guy's family get in touch with me to say what a huge Arsenal fan he is, he's dying and he would so love to see me. I heard about it on the Monday and went down to Margate on the Tuesday. I don't see why I should be forced out of the good things about social media by a bunch of idiots.

As a kid it was a dream to be famous – Morris and I used to practise autographs and, of course, he'd always say his was better than mine – but now, at the age of fifty-two, if I could change one thing, have one wish granted, it would be to do everything I've done but without being famous.

Financially I'm doing OK but I've still got to work hard at it. I live far more modestly than some people might expect. I'm constantly getting cab drivers coming to pick me up, seeing I live in a normal terraced house and saying, 'Blimey, is this where you live? I expected something bigger.'

I've got no problems with that, because I am where I am – I'm not proud at all. I've had the 12,000-square-foot house with all the cars outside, like on *MTV Cribs*. I lost most of it in the divorce from my first wife, but that's all right – considering where I come from, at least I was privileged enough to have had it.

After a while, a different perspective takes hold and those sorts of things are no longer important – all I'm worried about now is that my kids get the right education, which comes back to me not paying enough attention at school so I want to make sure that they do.

The only serious cloud in those skies is the income tax issues that have been with me for a while now. It's not just me, either: there's a whole generation of footballers out there who are in the same boat and were wrongly advised and badly treated. It's not just footballers, it's musicians, actors, bankers . . . people from all walks of life who did what was recommended by independent financial advisers at that time. The wave of financial advisers that appeared around the 1990s took our money to carry out the advice we paid them to give us, but never paid the tax. They are long gone and have left us holding the baby.

I'm not a tax fraud, I'm not a tax cheat, but at the moment I'm at the complete mercy of HM Revenue & Customs because of things that happened back then. The fact that it was bad advice and probably some financial skulduggery is not their concern: they want to get paid and it's my name on the bill.

I thought the tax was being taken care of by my old management and the finance guys so I could just worry about football, but they were the worst people to look after the money. I'm not bitter about it because I'm not motivated by money, but I believe that the people I put my trust in let me down royally. And they know that too, which is what's quite sad about it.

At one point I had eight or nine properties but all I was left with was the first one I bought, which was my mum's house because I wanted to make sure she was all right. One after the other, the taxmen were coming for me over my former properties because of something called 'deferred tax', which, essentially, means it hasn't been paid. I put my trust in people who for twenty-odd years didn't give me the advice I should have got, and I'll be paying for that for a long time.

I'm one of the lucky ones because at least I can work to try and pay it off, which I am doing, but there are many big-name former footballers of my age out there who can't. It's a bit like the depression thing inasmuch as we all kept our problem to ourselves – when I was right under it, at no point did I realize there was a load of players I knew going through the same thing. Everybody was worried about their own particular predicament, which they thought was unique to them and therefore somehow more shameful. It was a very dark place and that made it even worse.

I've had a couple of accountants that have simply advised me to go bankrupt. I refuse to do that because it would take me decades to get out from under that – I would be about eighty-five! If I declared bankrupt my punditry career would be over and the papers would have a field day. I'd be on the front page of all of the tabloids in this country because of who I am. I'd be a prominent black man who had a successful career and ended up bankrupt . . . they'd probably say I spent it all on weed, or that I lavished it all on cars, clothes and an extravagant lifestyle.

Really, though, Revenue & Customs have been magnificent to me – which probably isn't a word you hear around them too much. They've been really patient with me when they could have made me bankrupt just to make a point that they take this sort of thing seriously. I think they know I'm an honourable man, not trying to worm my way out of anything – yes, I was advised badly but I will get myself out of it by hard work. The only thing I can do is to keep paddling, well aware that a wave could come along at any time and tip my boat over.

When I think back, what I would have done differently is given more money to my family instead of those financial advisers. I've looked after everybody I've had to look after: I've looked after aunts and uncles and cousins, I've looked after my mum . . . everybody. When I was doing all right they were all doing all right. But now I wish I'd given them a bit more. I still wouldn't have any money but I doubt if I'd have this tax bill.

In my home life I couldn't be happier. The relationship I have with Nancy and Lola and Roxanne couldn't be better. I missed out on so much of my other children growing up and I won't miss out on this.

It's taken me until the age of fifty-two to properly learn what love is. I didn't experience an enormous amount of love from my mum when I was a child, so I've had to learn what it is, and learn how to be happy and at peace. I've put other people through horrible experiences along the way. If people think that's selfish, then I'm really sorry. I mean no disrespect to the women that have been in my life, but only now do I really know what love is and respect the institution of marriage.

All the other times, I married or settled down because I thought it was the best thing to do, but the women deserved more than that – I wasn't ready, and when you're not ready and you try to do something simply to make people happy, you're actually making things worse for your partner.

I met Nancy earlier, but I was at the wrong stage of my life. She was seventeen and working on the shoot for my Nike Evil advert – it was her first job – then years later I used to see her because she shared a house with a guy who used to get the clothes for my TV show, but I was with Deborah and she was seeing somebody so nothing ever happened.

Then about five years after that, soon after I'd split from my wife, Nancy and I used to bump into each other and I remember saying to my good mate, Tony, 'You know what, I've met somebody and I *know* she's the one.'

He just said to me, straight out, 'Woah, man. You've literally just come out of one thing. Slow down.'

I was so sure, I said, 'Nah, she's the one. Where I am in my head now, I know it.'

Nancy is everything: she's intelligent, she's a good woman, she comes from a great family, she doesn't see colour, she didn't really follow football, and she was willing to take me on with all the baggage and angst I came with. I'm very fortunate to have her. It was hard work trying to court her, initially. I asked her to marry me as soon as I could, in 2011. When she said 'Yes', that was the happiest day of my life. She will leave me before I ever leave her.

When we got together, she learned to cook and now she's fantastic in the kitchen. When we had our daughters she was just instantly a fantastic mother. When we started to live together she was an unbelievable home builder – I'm one of those blokes who is no good at that. She's the perfect woman and I can't stand to be apart from her and our daughters, so you can imagine what it was like when I was away in Brazil working on the World Cup in 2014 and I got the call about the robbery at our house.

Being out there without Nancy and the girls was like torture in itself. Then she phoned up and told me they'd just been robbed at knifepoint by four kids – and they were kids – who had invaded our home . . . how one of them was standing in Lola's bedroom, one in Roxanne's bedroom, threatening to cut their fingers off if Nancy didn't tell them where the safe was.

It's hard to describe how it hit me. It was like I was out of it but still functioning – if anybody had asked me where I was or what I was wearing I wouldn't have been able to answer because, mentally and physically, I was completely overwhelmed thinking about what had happened at home. I could sit or stand or walk, but that was more down to reflexes than anything else.

I got the call at twenty-past-five in the afternoon and by seven o'clock I was on a plane flying home. That time between hearing about the robbery and getting through my front door were easily the worst fifteen or twenty hours of my life.

I wouldn't wish for anybody to go through that, but what I've learned from it is a lot of people do in this country. In the wake of it I got so many letters from people saying that they've been through it, expressing their sympathy and giving us words of encouragement.

That was lovely, as were ITV, who I was working for, and it must be said they pulled out all the stops for me. Niall Sloane and the production staff couldn't have done better by me; Glenn Hoddle was immense – that's why I have such a bond with Glenn; Lee Dixon, Adrian Chiles and the team from behind the scenes were fantastic.

They sorted the plane and everything else out and I can never repay ITV for what they did for me that day. The BBC were constantly trying to get me to do the 2016 Euros as part of the *Match of the Day* team, but after that I can't ever turn my back on ITV. What they did for us was above and beyond the call of duty, so for me to stop working for them they'd have to say to me, 'We don't want you any more.' I owe them that.

When I got home everybody was around – my mates Tony and Paul sorted out a car for me and they had already organized bodyguards. Mitchell was there too, along with many others wanting to do what they could for us.

I was so relieved that, with all the pulling and pushing about Nancy had been through, she wasn't hurt. She'd had the presence of mind to just give them what they wanted. Her biggest concern was that they didn't wake the girls. And it was a miracle neither of them stirred when these guys were in their rooms – there was so much shouting and screaming going on. Usually if you so much as turn on a light switch anywhere in the house they wake up, especially Roxanne. Yet they both slept through it. They weren't frightened and have no memory of it.

Obviously Nancy was shaken up, but I could see that essentially everybody was all right. The way Nancy was dealing with it was unbelievable. She said it didn't make any sense me staying there, that they were fine, Tony and Mitchell were taking care of things, and with all the press interest this was now the safest house in England. She said it was important that I kept on doing my stuff, because we couldn't let them see they'd got to us.

So I went back to Brazil. I know some people couldn't understand that, but it was like I said to Adrian in the piece I did on air about it – these things are speed bumps in your life, they might slow you down a bit when you go over them but you just keep going.

What made me so sad was thinking about the guys who did it. I feel they were not unlike some of the guys back in Brockley, and they were the same kind of guys that I was dealing with when I made *Football Behind Bars*: they were the same age, and had no respect for anybody or anything. They're the ones that are stabbing, killing and shooting people; they're the ones that will go into your house, hold a knife to your missus's throat, will go in your daughters' rooms while they're sleeping, saying they're going to cut their fingers off.

That's what we're dealing with, and it makes me sad to think that while we were doing that programme we proved that you can help those sorts of young people, but it wasn't followed through. After something like that happened to me, it would be easy to say, 'Fuck 'em, I don't want to do anything to help anybody', but that's not the way forward.

The police were embarrassingly poor. We must have had fifty police officers at our house, and they were terrible. Nancy had to go to the police station where they did a line-up of kids, but they'd had hoods on, and although she could have said how tall the robbers were, the line-up was sat down and she couldn't make out their heights. She told them this was pointless.

Maybe their hands are tied by the justice system, but it's as if the police are powerless at the moment. It seems the whole way they operate is so much in favour of the criminal – and the criminals know this and have got particularly bold because there's so little likelihood of them getting caught.

We've got people everywhere looking for the stuff that was taken because so much of it was really specialized, unique pieces – my Dennis Bergkamp watch, my Arsenal Double Winners watch, and a couple of other specially inscribed watches. Nothing has surfaced, though. I don't know how they're going to get rid of that stuff, unless they're going to do some serious defacing. Otherwise, once they turn up we'll know about it. It doesn't matter how long it takes. Those are the steps we've taken because we've got no faith in the police investigation, but, worryingly, other people are taking things further.

Very late one night I got a phone call from a voice I didn't recognize who told me it was no longer my problem.

When I asked, 'Who is this?', he said, 'You don't need to worry about who this is.'

The guy on the phone said it could be a month, it could be a year, it could be ten years, but if the thieves were saying they were going to cut my daughters' fingers off, they're going to pay for that.

There was going to be no retribution from my side – we just wanted to get on with our lives – and the last thing I wanted was anything to come back on my family, but this guy is telling me: 'Then you let people know that, make sure it gets out there that if anything happens to anybody it's got nothing to do with you.'

I said, 'I don't want . . .'

He cut me off saying it had nothing to do with me anymore. Then he hung up the phone and I never heard from that voice again.

And I had to do that. I went to Birmingham, I went to Harlesden, south London, Brixton, Manchester, all the people who I know, and let them know this was not of my doing. Those guys that robbed our house are a frightening generation of people and I didn't want any repercussions for my family.

It was like something out of a film: you get a phone call at two or three in the morning, you jump out of sleep simply because you assume something's wrong somewhere, and it's chilling.

I don't know what's going to happen there, but I am sure that at some stage we will hear something. Which is unfortunate for whoever it was robbed our house, and not the way I would go about things.

There was an incident after that, when I was driving down Finchley Road on my way to get my glasses done, and a Mercedes stopped me, pulled over and gave me a name.

I said, 'What am I supposed to do with that?'

The driver told me he didn't care what I did with it, but that was the name I needed. I said I didn't know what he was talking about and let him carry on about his business.

It's horrible to be in and around that world. I don't like it, especially for Nancy and the girls, but, sometimes, no matter how you conduct yourself, these things find you.

The tax thing hanging over me is the only thing that is keeping me from being exuberantly happy, but in respect of going along with my life I'm totally happy. I would love to have a better relationship with my seventeen-year-old daughter Bobbi, and I'm sure she'll blame me for that, but I saw how her brother Stacey worked things out so I know it's not permanent and it will come good in the end.

With the punditry now, I'm doing it for so many different companies I've got no excuse not to be busy doing something. Which is good because if I wasn't doing so much it would be easy to slip off into laziness or stupidity – idle hands and all that.

Even though I've got so much to focus on, I'm not getting ahead of myself and looking too far beyond my current contracts – BT have given me a year and the BBC have given me a two-year deal. With social media the way it is and everything being so scrutinized, if you say anything somebody considers homophobic or ageist or racist or misogynist or whatever, you can lose your job and you won't get another one, so I can't look past the next two years. All I can do is make sure that while I'm here I'm going to be the *best* pundit there is.

I've never been somebody who wants to be the crusader, who wants to change the world. I've got an opinion on things and I'm so glad I've had the chance to express some of them and have people listen.

I'd like to think that I'm a good man, now. I don't rob or cheat. No one's going to knock on my door and punch me in the face because I've done something to them or I'm sleeping with their wife. I'm at a place where I've levelled out. I can't apologize for all the mistakes I've made because, at the end of the day, I needed to make some of those mistakes to get me to where I am now.

I'm continually aware of how fortunate I've been, but I also think that I must be doing something right to have ended up where I am. With my wife and my family and in my work life, I'm happier than I was when I was at the height, scoring goals for Arsenal, driving Ferraris, going to clubs, people stopping their cars to ask for an autograph, and I was on cloud nine then.

To be as happy as I am, having lived through everything else, I know I'm blessed. I feel like I've gone full circle with the mistakes I've made and what I've learned from them. Right now I'm with my two little girls and I'm with my wife; we're never away from each other, and I'm going to give them as much support I can.

A Final Word: Oh, Rocky Rocky . . .

My favourite football photograph was taken at Southampton, in 1991, on my league debut for Arsenal. I'm on the floor with my arms up and David Rocastle's running towards me after he's scored – I'd hit the shot, the keeper had pushed it away, and he got the rebound.

His was the first goal in a four-nil win, I got the other three and it was my greatest ninety minutes of football – I was floating on air when I put an England shirt on for the first time, but to be there with Rocky, two boys from Brockley and both of us scoring, it was the perfect day. My hat-trick even stopped the Southampton fans singing 'What a waste of money!' at me!

I can remember knowing David well from the time I was about twelve. His family lived in a block of flats just down the road from where we lived. He was in the same class at primary school as my ex-wife Deborah, I was a couple of years above, which means we'd been around each other since I was about eight.

We'd been friends for so long, and had this unbreakable bond of coming up from exactly the same area and knowing how tough things could be, that when I was still at Palace I said in an interview that I wanted to come to Arsenal to play with David Rocastle, and I didn't care whose place I took. He had to phone me up about that, because it didn't go down too well with a few of the Arsenal players!

On 31 March 2001, when I was told he was gone I was devastated. He was just thirty-three years old. I knew he was very ill, so it wasn't as if it was unexpected, but I was inconsolable – I was like a little kid that cries so hard there's nothing anybody can do to stop them. I was like that for three or four days.

Such was the sense of loss that even now I don't like thinking about those days, and there is no other way I could end this book than with a tribute to my dear friend Rocky.

Before that dream debut in the league for Arsenal, the last time I can remember playing in a proper match with Rocky was back in south London when I was about fourteen, so he would have been eleven or twelve.

I was playing football around the flats with Conrad and this other guy Clive and his little brother Trevor. Rocky rushed up and asked us if we wanted to come and play for a team called Vista, in this big five-a-side competition over at Stillness School in Brockley Rise. I think some kids hadn't turned up and the manager had sent Rocky out to round up some more players. Of course we said yes.

We put Clive, who was a rugby player, in goal, Conrad went in midfield, Rocky went midfield and forward, and I played up front, with Trevor making up the numbers. And we only won the competition! It was brilliant. It was a serious competition, with all these teams with their mums and dads and sandwiches and Thermos flasks, and we just turned up, because we had nothing else to do, and we won it.

That afternoon said a great deal about Rocky, because he was always so enthusiastic about things that he had no problem going to round up players; he threw himself into it like it was the FA Cup final, never mind how cobbled together his team was. And he was so good the other, better prepared teams never stood a chance.

When he was a young kid playing football around the flats or at school, *everybody* used to watch him, because even at that age his ball control was fantastic. He could dribble past entire teams, no problem. Then as he got older, it wasn't just about him taking people on but his one touch with the outside of his right foot was perfect, his passing was spot-on – although he loved dribbling, he always knew when to pass – and he had a fair bit of pace. The Rock could move.

He made it through the district trials when he was very young and then went on to play for London, which is where he got scouted for Arsenal. It was May 1982 and he had just turned fifteen. When they took him on people in the area were so excited, because that just didn't happen to us – the most we used to think about was the Supermalt – so the whole area was 'David is at Arsenal?' . . . 'Yes, David from Turnham!'

It was once he got into the Arsenal youth team that I really started seeing him for the strong, inspirational character that he was. I was just working, still running round doing foolishness, and talking about not trying to push on with football any more. We used to meet on the Honor Oak bridge, which links Turnham to Crofton Park, where he would go to get the 171 bus up to Stoke Newington to train with Arsenal, and we'd speak for ages.

He would always tell me not to give up, that I was too good not to be a footballer, how I was much better than people he played and trained with – the sort of encouragement that made me stick at it.

When I got in at Crystal Palace he couldn't have been more proud; Rocky was a massive Palace fan and used to come and watch me every time he could.

He was the first person I told I'd signed for Arsenal, and I stayed at his house in Mill Hill, up near their training ground, the night before I reported in for the first time. I'm sure David was as excited as I was about it, and we stayed up until about four or five in the morning, just talking about Arsenal. I was like a kid going to a new school. nervous and full of questions. 'What's Tony Adams like? . . . How does George Graham talk to the players? . . . Will I fit in with them? . . .'

Rocky told me everything about Arsenal and what it would be like to play for the club, stressing the fact that it was a real step up for me, the attention I was about to start getting would be massive and how I would be expected to behave.

His mantra was, 'Remember who you are, what you are and what you represent', and he was the first person to tell me, 'Ian, what we do is all about the fans. If they stop you, you give them fifteen or twenty seconds because they'll remember that forever.'

He would sign a hundred autographs with a big smile on his face and give everybody the same amount of time. It wasn't that he craved the attention he genuinely loved the fans, so he was always generous with them – however, I do sometimes wonder how he would have coped these days when so many people are so rude when they approach you. I think even he would have struggled, and he was a saint.

On the field, Rocky was one of the hardest blokes I've ever come across. When we were playing, Stuart Pearce used to intimidate everybody – everybody except Rocky, who would have it with him at any time, because I don't think I've met a person who could fight like David Rocastle. He could tackle, too, and if you were there to be tackled he'd blast right through you, then make sure he picked you up and got on with it. A total professional.

When he went to Leeds in 1992 and I played against him – which was a weird experience in itself – there were a couple of times when I wasn't ready for it and it felt like he'd broken me in two! But that's how he played, no quarter given and no qualms about it.

When he was younger he could get into it off the pitch as well, if someone tried to put it on him. If he got angry his eyes would look like he was going crazy, which would often be enough to put anybody off. When Tony Adams got locked up for drink-driving, the boys were out socializing and some people in the place were taking the piss out of Tony. Rocky, who was unbelievably loyal to his friends, totally lost it with them and wanted to fight four or five people. The way he looked, they didn't want to know.

Hanging out with him, when we were at Arsenal, was always brilliant. He was the original reggae man, loved his reggae music and a bit of rare groove. Rocky loved to dance and I'd go out with him, Kevin Campbell and Michael Thomas to places like Night Moves, Phoebe's and Oasis over in east London and this spot in Peckham, Kings on the Rye. Those were some great times. Rocky loved his whisky and ginger, and used to pour so much of it down my throat that when I go to visit his grave I always take a whisky and ginger with me for him.

As well-known black footballers in black nightclubs like that, they used to make a helluva fuss of us but, everywhere Rocky went he'd attract a crowd, regardless. He had this magnetism so people would just flock around him, women adored him, men just loved him as a bloke, children were fascinated by him ... people just wanted to be in his company.

He was really generous to his friends – you couldn't spend money when you were out with him – and an unbelievable family man with three beautiful kids, Melissa, Ryan and Monique.

When he first got diagnosed with lymphoma, he phoned up and told us. To be honest, because he sounded almost casual about it, I didn't think too much of it – he was The Rock, he'd be fine. He'll get himself going he'll get the best medical attention he can and he'll sort himself out.

I never envisaged he was going to die, it wasn't a possibility. He was a young, fit footballer. Always so full of life. He stayed totally upbeat about everything, right up to the end.

He lived over in Windsor so I used to go over and see him all the time, and in spite of what he'd tell us we realized it was serious when his voice started going – he sounded like the huskiest Barry White voice you could imagine. Towards the end he was too weak for us to go and see him, which to me was a relief because it was too hard for me to see Rocky Rocastle like that.

We used to speak on the phone, and that was really horrible, because what do you say to a man like that on the phone? I'd listen to this kind of croaking on the other end of the phone and it was devastating. I'd come off the phone in tears, because the real heart-breaking thing was he refused to give up, he never succumbed and right up until the end it was, 'Yeah, I'll get more treatment then I'll be fine . . .'

But that was Rocky, he never gave up at anything, right to the very end. And it was those talks we had on Honor Oak bridge that taught me not to, either.

Acknowledgements

Thanks to my wonderful wife Nancy for the most amazing amount of patience and support over the last eleven years.

My brother Maurice for inspiring me to work hard on every aspect of myself.

Steve Coppell, Ron Noades, Mark Bright, Tony Finnigan, John Hollins, Stan Ternant.

My cousin Chris Lue for the wisdom.

Errol Palmer and Tony Davis from Ten-em-Bee football club for always believing in me even when I didn't believe in myself.

Peter Prentice, may he rest in peace.

George Graham for pushing me to the limits so I could achieve my dreams in football.

David Dein and Arsène Wenger.

Andreas Campomar for the idea and everyone at Little, Brown for their help.

My main man Lloyd Bradley for being that well educated brother that you could only wish was your big brother.

Steve Kutner and Minty Reeves for the kind of management that I wished I had twenty years ago!

And any football fan that I've made smile throughout my

career; like my dear departed friend David Rocastle said, 'E, it's all about the fans'.

Worldwide representation: SKM Ltd.
office@stevekutner.com

Index